Practicing Renaissance Scholarship

Medieval & Renaissance Literary Studies

Practicing Renaissance Scholarship

Plays and Pageants, Patrons and Politics

David M. Bergeron

DUQUESNE UNIVERSITY PRESS
Pittsburgh, Pennsylvania

Library of Congress Cataloging in Publication Data

Bergeron, David Moore.
    Practicing Renaissance scholarship: plays and pageants, patrons and
politics / by David M. Bergeron.
        p. cm. — (Medieval & Renaissance literary studies)
Includes bibliographical references and index.
        ISBN 0-8207-0313-3 (alk. paper)
    1. English drama—Early modern and Elizabethan, 1500-1600—History
and criticism.   2. Politics and literature—Great Britain—History—16th
century.   3. Politics and literature—Great Britain—History—17th
century.   4. Authors and patrons—England—History—16th century.
5. Authors and patrons—England—History—17th century.   6. English
drama—17th century—History and criticism.   7. Political plays,
English—History and criticism.   8. Pageants—England—History.
I. Title.   II. Medieval and Renaissance literary studies.
    PR653 .B47 2000
        822'.309358—dc21
                                                                99-050701

Printed on acid-free paper.
Printed in the United States of America.

CONTENTS

ACKNOWLEDGMENTS

A few years ago I asked my friend (and former student) Daryl Palmer of the University of Akron to read over something that I had written. In responding, Daryl observed that I obviously was writing a book on the subject of scholarship. I had not until then recognized that indeed I had been pursuing this subject in many different ways for many years, and that perhaps a group of essays could be brought together on the matter of practicing Renaissance scholarship. So, I owe a great debt to Daryl for raising the prospect of this book. I have benefitted from his interest and encouragement all along the way — as in many other projects.

I pursue the common theme of the scholar's relatedness to all that has gone before. In my own scholarship I have been the beneficiary of countless numbers of people. In the immediate past of putting together this book, I single out with profound thanks the help of Richard Hardin, Geraldo de Sousa, Daniel Kulmala, and J. Clinton Crumley. They asked questions, read essays, and stimulated my thinking about how I practice scholarship. I am also happy to have them as friends.

Because some of these essays have been published elsewhere, I record the kind permission granted me by the journals and publishers. The essay on *Richard II* is a bringing together and rewriting of two different pieces: "The Deposition Scene in *Richard II*," *Renaissance Papers 1974* (1975): 31–37; and "The Hoby Letter and *Richard II*: A Parable of Criticism," *Shakespeare Quarterly* 26 (1975): 477–80. Two essays come from *English Literary Renaissance*: "Elizabeth's Coronation Entry (1559): New Manuscript Evidence," *ELR* 8 (1978): 3–8; "Patronage of Dramatists: The Case of Thomas Heywood," *ELR* 18 (1988): 294-304. "Women as Patrons of English Renaissance Drama," appeared in a collection of essays, *Patronage in the Renaissance*, ed. Stephen Orgel and Guy Lytle (Princeton University Press, 1981), 274–90. I published "Francis Bacon's *Henry VII*: Commentary on King James I," in *Albion* 24 (1992): 17–26; and an earlier version of "Masculine Interpretation of Queen Anne, Wife of James I," in *Biography: An Interdisciplinary Quarterly* 18.1 (Winter 1995): 42–54, Copyright 1995 by the Biographical Research Center. "Thomas Middleton and Anthony Munday: Artistic Rivalry?" appeared in *Studies in English Literature* 36 (1996): 461–79, Copyright 1996, *Studies in English Literature*, reprinted by permission of the Johns Hopkins University Press. "Gilbert Dugdale and the Royal Entry of James I (1604)," was published in *Journal of Medieval and Renaissance Studies* 13 (1983): 111–25. To all of the editors and copyright holders I express my appreciation for being able to use this published material. I have revised all of these essays to greater and lesser degrees.

Bringing this project to a successful conclusion would not have been possible without the cheerful and skillful help — yet once again — of the staff of the Wescoe Word Processing Center of the University of Kansas: Paula Courtney, Pam LeRow, and Lynn Porter. They remained undaunted no matter what. I thank the College of Liberal Arts and Sciences at the University of Kansas for its financial support to reproduce the Stephen Harrison engravings in the final essay, and I thank the Folger Shakespeare Library for permission to use these illustrations.

I hope that this collection of essays will adequately reflect my love of research and scholarly activity. I thank colleagues, students, and friends who across the decades have challenged my thinking and encouraged my efforts. I am grateful to a number of libraries who through their collections have become research centers and havens for those on a quest for knowledge and insight. Excursions into such sacred places also produce pleasure.

Interrogative Metonymy

"Humanists who only gather 'bricks' of information no longer compete effectively with colleagues who can put their knowledge into larger contexts."[1] So writes Gerald Graff in the essay "The Scholar in Society," part of a Modern Language Association-sanctioned book. Graff adds: "the highest professional rewards have gone to work that advanced ambitious theories and broad cultural and interdisciplinary generalizations" (344). This bleak if accurate portrait of the scholar and the competitive climate raises disturbing questions about the plight of the humanist scholar at the end of the century. Few serious scholars see themselves as merely gathering bits of information, but gather "bricks" they must if they hope to reach any worthwhile generalizations. Graff's word choice of "compete" and "rewards" underscores a seismic shift in how we understand scholars. Up against "ambitious theories" the scholar engaged in archival research may always seem a bit dull. I worry that such ambitious theories and interdisciplinary generalizations risk taking the place of the hard, disciplined work that scholars must do. Graff does not explain how

one arrives at the mystical moment of being able to propound
theories that will earn the scholar professional rewards.

Even an official gathering sponsored by the MLA in 1987
could not successfully define the situation of literary studies.
Under the auspices of the MLA's Commission on the Future
of the Profession, representatives from 80 PhD-granting institutions met in Wayzata, Minnesota in April 1987 to consider
graduate programs in particular and the status of the profession in general. The results of this conference, published
as *The Future of Doctoral Studies in English*, suggest a fair
amount of disarray in literary studies. The editors of the collected papers of this conference admit that "no unanimity on
any significant issue emerged from the conference. . . . What
did become clear is that our subject has been destabilized and
that our methodologies are being radically questioned."[2]
The editors add: "As a consequence, there was little certainty
about what our graduate students should know both as developing scholars and as apprentice teachers" (vi). The towering
canonical figures have been displaced or at least challenged.
Competing ideologies and methodologies have appeared. The
center does not hold. In such an unstable world — and it
has not noticeably improved more than ten years later — the
scholars can rightly be confused about what they should be
doing. If the dominant professional organization cannot
define the tasks and sketch the future, then competition and
uncertainty increase.

In such a world fad and fashion threaten scholarship. I take
as another insight into the problem three books published by
Cambridge University Press: *A Companion to Shakespeare
Studies* (1934), *A New Companion to Shakespeare Studies*
(1971), and *The Cambridge Companion to Shakespeare Studies* (1986). These books can serve as a barometer, a snapshot
of Shakespeare studies at their respective moments. Studying
the contents of each volume provides glimpses into the shifting tides of scholarship: what's in, what's out. Topics fall out

of favor, and others emerge. For my purposes here I note that the 1934 volume contains an essay by J. Isaacs, entitled "Shakespearian Scholarship"; neither of the subsequent volumes includes such an essay. Shakespearean scholarship has, in this sense at least, disappeared.

No article in the 1934 *Companion* better epitomizes the paradox of romantic ideology wedded to scientific methodology than Isaacs's, which begins: "Shakespeare scholarship is of vast extent and complexity."[3] Isaacs then enumerates no fewer than 26 categories that make up the "major operations of such scholarship, all neatly arranged and delineated by the 26 letters of the alphabet. Most of these categories we would recognize and readily acknowledge as being the province of scholarship, such as source study, biography, chronology, linguistic background, and paleography. Isaacs spends much of his effort, not surprisingly, in writing about Shakespeare editors of earlier centuries. But he also writes about landmark publications of Revels documents, Registers of the Stationers' company, Henslowe's diary, and so forth. With scientific symmetry and synthesis Isaacs closes the essay by providing a list of things to be done. He envisions organized efforts from several countries to tackle the remaining problems. Synthesis, classification, evolution, systematic comparison — these terms expose the scientific methodology that Isaacs contemplates. But the goal remains romantic: "a satisfying and scholarly account of 'The Mind and Art of Shakespeare'" (324). Maybe Isaacs has hit upon one of those "ambitious theories" that Graff praises. In any event, subsequent editors of Cambridge *Companions* avoided the problem of saying anything explicit about Shakespearean scholarship, perhaps finding the topic too daunting. Isaacs's excesses aside, he has at least attempted to outline the territory for scholarly endeavor.

If a special MLA Commission cannot define what "developing scholars" should gain from their graduate studies, if editors of the Cambridge *Companions* of 1971 and 1986 decide not to confront the question of scholarship, and if we learn that professional rewards go to those with ambitious theories, then what should brick-gathering scholars do? We can perhaps take heart from recalling Ben Jonson's brick-laying background; this at least seems to have done him no harm when he came to write dazzling plays. Somewhere and somehow we have to lay a foundation on which scholarship rests.

In radical contrast to Graff, Wayne Booth had earlier written an essay entitled "The Scholar in Society" for a MLA publication. He writes: "Every scholar, good or bad, becomes a scholar by *associating*. . . ."[4] This process and condition of association and affiliation, what I refer to as the "metonymy" of scholarship, therefore become a major focus of this collection of essays, however we may choose to define the scholarly task. We scholars place ourselves in relationship to our contiguous past and local present. But even as we associate, we also question the scholarly past that has come to us. We remain appropriately skeptical and interrogative.

We may also long nostalgically for a past in which scholars seemed to have enjoyed enormous social and academic prestige — whatever the actual truth may have been. Fiction has provided many examples of scholars: from the bumbling, timid Tesman in Ibsen's *Hedda Gabler*, to the disturbed but fascinating George in Albee's *Who's Afraid of Virginia Woolf?* to the audacious scholar-on-the-make Morris Zapp in David Lodge's *Small World*. Often such people provide great sport for the writer and reader. I feel great sympathy for Godfrey St. Peter in Willa Cather's *The Professor's House*, a flawed novel that I nevertheless like.

When Wayne Booth writes about the necessary isolation of the scholar who must be able to sit alone and lonely for days on end, I recall the image of Godfrey St. Peter's splendid isolation in that cranky attic of his house. Cather writes:

> During the fifteen years he had been working on his *Spanish Adventurers in North America*, this room had been his centre

of operations. There had been delightful excursions and digressions; the two Sabbatical years when he was in Spain studying records, two summers in the Southwest on the trail of his adventurers, another in Old Mexico, dashes to France to see his foster-brothers. But the notes and the records and the ideas always came back to this room. It was here they were digested and sorted, and woven into their proper place in his history.[5]

This scholarly place provides St. Peter with "isolation, insulation from the engaging drama of domestic life" (16). It offers a place for him to work, to associate himself with the past, with the records and documents that he has collected — a place not only to write his history but also to create his own history. But he cannot remain hermit-like; he must also associate himself with his social world. Out of fuel for his kerosene lamp, he must journey down into the house: "On that perilous journey down through the human house he might lose his mood, his enthusiasm, even his temper" (18). Exactly. But scholars occupy the whole human house, even if it becomes on occasion distracting. We balance the demands of our research and intellectual life with human and social requirements. Danger lurks in such associations.

The professor's house and *The Professor's House* contain, embrace, and trigger many questions. Godfrey St. Peter cannot remain inviolate, immune to scholarly questions or to life's questions. He critically examines the scholars who have preceded him. When his grown daughters fight, he wonders if this is what the talented and romantic Tom Outland has given his life for. Certainly in the last section of the novel, St. Peter engages in profound and sometimes unstated questions about his own life. He survives a nearly deadly experience, but we readers have to wonder about his future. Our scholarly lives may be less dramatic but no less interrogative.

We can also talk about *associating* by using Booth's term *consideration*, from the essay cited above. This quality exists as one of the several scholarly virtues that Booth enumerates in ways that Graff would doubtless find too idealistic or even sentimental. Booth defines *consideration*: "Good scholarship requires . . . a steady habit of sustained attention to other people's reasoning. It is thus largely good listening and reporting" (137). Consideration affects not only how we read and respond to the scholars who have preceded us but also, according to Booth, how we write: "The inherent drive of scholarship itself is thus toward a considerate style that assists other people as much as possible in a joint endeavor" (138). The metonymy of scholarship puts us in a Janus-like position that looks to the past and faces the future. In both directions we express consideration by how we come to understand earlier scholars and how we write considerately so that present and future scholars will be able to comprehend us.

We must show proper consideration for what scholarship has achieved and acknowledge its contribution. At the same time, we cannot afford to let reverence supplant regular questioning of ideas and facts that may have arrived shrouded in the aura of authority. A common thread runs through the essays in this collection: an insistent questioning of earlier scholarship, an attempt to expose problems in logic, faulty or unreliable evidence, and ideological agendas that may blind the scholar to the truth. Scholarly activity demands a rigorous and systematic interrogative attitude and approach.

In its simplest terms scholarship has three tasks: to discover, uncover, and recover. *Discovery* means that the scholar may find new evidence or documents, previously unknown. We might find a new poem by Shakespeare or new evidence about his life that suggests a Catholic connection to Lancashire. We might discover previously unknown work by Ben Jonson or Thomas Middleton. Or, as in the case of one of the essays here, we take another look at documents from the Master of the Revels in Elizabeth's reign and see how this evidence reveals important information about the queen's involvement in the preparation for the coronation civic pageant given in her honor.

Perhaps we *uncover* errors in fact or interpretation. What if an earlier scholar has misread a manuscript or archival document? We expose that error and offer a correction. In the case of Shakespeare's *Richard II*, for example, some scholars have read Edward Hoby's letter as offering "proof" of an early performance of the play; this evidence therefore helps date the play. I argue to the contrary that the alleged evidence tells us nothing about a presumed performance of *Richard II* — or of anything else. Perhaps our task of uncovering includes exposing a certain documentable bias working among scholars. I find a particularly striking and disturbing example in the attitude of most male historians to Queen Anne, James's wife, who dismiss her as frivolous. These historians' assumptions have remained largely unquestioned.

We may find ourselves *recovering* important material previously neglected. Decades earlier a scholar may have presented evidence or ideas that then slipped, for whatever reason, into undeserved obscurity. I try to recover, for example, Glynne Wickham's scholarly position regarding the importance of Lord Mayor's Shows in the Jacobean and Caroline culture. Probably most scholarly enterprises embrace with varying degrees of emphasis all the activities of discovering, uncovering, and recovering. Certainly all three, as I argue, involve our skeptical consideration, our contiguous interrogative mood.

In English Renaissance studies the problem of what constitutes *evidence* looms quite large. Old documents may literally be harder to read than more recent ones. Even if we have sufficient paleographical skills, we face the daunting challenge of interpreting the early documents, in part because they exist in a cultural context that may be difficult if not impossible to know. I remember vividly my first research trip to England, full of doubts about my research skills and well-founded uncertainty about my ability to read manuscripts. But I needed to see the city records from the cathedral city of Wells to find information about the pageant entertainment presented to

Queen Anne in 1613. The small city of Wells had no archives, but the Town Clerk assured me that they did possess the records for 1613. But, he added in a letter to me, "they are impossible to read." The clerk's "interpretation" of the documents nearly stopped me in my tracks. What if I went to Wells and indeed found the records "impossible to read" — a very real possibility, I thought? Youthful energy, however, overcame scholarly doubt. I went to Wells, went to the Clerk's office where we entered a cool vault and retrieved the appropriate city records. To my everlasting relief, I found the handwriting to be beautiful and clear: I could readily read the document. But this evidence seemed impenetrable to one who had had no practice in reading early seventeenth century handwriting and who had no reason to do so. Not only was the handwriting blessedly clear, but also I understood the context for these archival records. I knew the basic outline of what had occurred in August 1613 in Wells. Metonymy worked in my favor. Evidence does not exist in a vacuum, although at times we may be unable to fathom its surroundings. Evidence has an independent existence, but it has little scholarly meaning without interpretation.

I do not know any easy, fail-proof "rules" about what constitutes reliable evidence. Indeed, such questions occupy scholarly endeavors. If such matters could always be readily ascertained, we presumably would not need scholars. The world of research and intellectual pursuit has placed on scholars the curse of determining the reliability and appropriateness of evidence. We may cozy up to, indeed associate with, evidence, but we must also relentlessly question it. We search, gather, sift, and analyze evidence so that we may establish a basis for interpretation. The essays in this volume in varying ways regularly confront questions about evidence.

Some studies that can be characterized as "new historicist" suffer from an excess of generalization compared to established facts. Evidentiary leaps can be found in several analyses of the theater's connection to the royal court. I call this the "Whitehall syndrome," which focuses exclusively on the court at the expense of understanding other sites of power. Some scholars see James's putting all the adult acting companies under royal patronage as a sign of his interest in theater and his desire to have the theater manifest royal concerns. For example, Stephen Orgel suggests: "King James wanted the theatrical companies under royal patronage because he believed in the efficacy of theater as an attribute of royal authority."[6] The actors therefore formed "part of the pageantry of Jacobean royal power, the outward and visible signs of James's sense of his office" (22). Leeds Barroll has called into question such an analysis and the attempts to link the theater to the court in terms of James's presumed interest in drama.[7] To put the matter simply: how do we know that James believed in the efficacy of the theater as an attribute of royal authority? I conclude that we do not know such in any definitive way, determined by evidence. Orgel's sacramental view of the actors as "outward and visible signs of James's sense of his office" transubstantiates the place of the theater: not merely a place of entertainment, social exchange, and politics, it has acquired a quasi-spiritual function with the king as its deity. Zeal for determining the importance of theater in culture has by now clearly outpaced established facts, a point reinforced in Malcolm Smuts's historical analysis.[8]

We also acknowledge that the rules of evidence may change. What may be acceptable in one century or generation may not be in the next. I think of the late nineteenth century fascination or obsession with "metrical tests" that "proved" all kinds of things about Shakespeare's texts, especially authorship and chronology. No one today would likely give much credence to this "evidence," although it had its believers 100 years ago. Since 1842 we have had the evidence provided by Ben Jonson, in his conversations with William Drummond in 1619, that he had taken John Marston's pistol from him and beaten him with it and written *Poetaster* about Marston. Nineteenth century scholars had little trouble accepting the veracity of this evidence. In my essay on the War of the Theaters, I question what this evidence proves and how reliable it might be for throwing light on the alleged dramatic war. Or, as I show in the essay on *Richard II*, what strikes some scholars as proof of early performance of the play has remained dubious for others. This results in part from different standards about evidence.

Nowhere do the "rules" about evidence seem more suspect, more fragile than in textual studies. In the case of Shakespeare, the understanding of the relationship among quarto editions and the first Folio undergoes radical transformation as we move from the eighteenth to the nineteenth to the twentieth century. This can seem disheartening since textual investigations contain hallmarks of "scientific" inquiry and should therefore be subject to easy substantiation, to objective proof. Ironically, such a perspective we now view as hopelessly romantic. Our most scientific dimension of the scholarly profession shares all the doubts and uncertainties of the other research areas. The rules of editing, whenever and wherever they have been articulated, have not enjoyed a long shelf life, even if the names associated with them are Pope, Malone, Gifford, Greg, or Bowers.

We can readily find evidence of textual variants, for example, as we compare copies of the same edition or subsequent editions of early texts. But scholarship requires that we move beyond this activity to question what such variants may mean. Collations of textual variants, appearing for example in Bowers's edition of Dekker, look for all the world like ironclad evidence. Someone has to tell us what this evidence means. Do x number of variants prove a separate edition? At certain points in our history textual editors have indeed embraced such rules. What if moral and aesthetic rules govern one's editorial practice, as regularly happened in the eighteenth century? Clearly, at the end of the twentieth century no such rules operate. The printed words on the pages of the texts remain the same, but the procedures and assumptions by which these marks can be understood change radically. "Rules" of evidence shift and become culturally bound in a metonymic relationship.

Knowledge stands as the essential prerequisite for grappling with problems of evidence. We cannot get very far in sorting out textual problems, for example, without understanding much about the early printing process and the probable manuscript copies that went to the print shop. We cannot begin to read early manuscripts without being aware of different handwriting styles. The structure and organization of the Elizabethan acting companies become essential in understanding the theatrical repertory system and production schedules. If we know about the talented actor Richard Burbage, we have an insight into Shakespeare's construction of tragic heroes. To write about civic pageants requires knowledge of city government and the guild system. To analyze court masques means understanding court and aristocratic culture. On and on one could multiply the examples. The scholar of English Renaissance studies bears a heavy responsibility for knowledge, ever aware of the difficulty of obtaining sufficient knowledge. The scholar remains considerate of the vast storehouse of knowledge, yet wants to know more and enjoys the pursuit.

Knowledge means research. I equate scholarship with research; I cannot imagine one without the other. This does not mean that we must rummage around in dusty archives in order to qualify as scholar; we may in fact work in clean, well-lighted rooms. But we must be engaged in some kind of research project that has a purpose, the results of which we intend to communicate in a considerate style. We associate with other scholars in research activities; we pick their brains, learn their techniques, and question their assumptions. If we traffic in Renaissance studies, we doubtless enjoy handling and reading old books. The joy of such activities overcomes the occasional and inescapable tedium and drudgery. In the research and in the acquisition of knowledge we equip ourselves to test evidence and inference.

The essays of this collection come together on matters of *evidence* and *interpretation*, involving research practices and the subsequent questions raised and answered. They show the interrogative metonymy of scholarship at work, as focused on Renaissance studies — literary and historical subjects. In these essays I demonstrate how some scholars have been tripped up by misinterpretation of evidence or by a failure to pursue the full implications of their work. I include myself among the guilty party — see especially the piece on Middleton and Munday's presumed rivalry. I seek to build up the activity of scholarship, to acknowledge its accomplishment, and to insist on the hard work and discipline that scholarship requires. Even as I show consideration for previous scholars, I question some of their conclusions. This means an active process of revision, not to be fashionable but to acknowledge that earlier ideas, conclusions, and even research may need to be revised. By the eclectic range of these essays I suggest something about the kinds of topics a scholar may work on over the span of decades.

The essays fall into four groups: *plays, patronage, politics,* and *pageants.* Each category in various ways impinges on the others, culminating in pageants that certainly evoke issues of the theater, patronage, and politics. All ask questions about how we do our scholarship. Politics constitutes the largest category, for I include here historical interpretations of Queen Anne and nineteenth century scholarship about Renaissance drama. The common denominator derives from the political concerns of the interpreters who have their own agendas.

I start with *Richard II* and the problem of external and internal evidence. As I have indicated above, scholars have offered the evidence of Hoby's letter in order to substantiate something about an early performance of the play. An objective examination of the letter leads me (and others) to doubt its contribution to dating the play. Part of the essay sketches the process of association by which scholars have latched on to authority without adequate skepticism and sometimes without paying attention to contrary views. The deposition scene raises questions of internal evidence. The early quarto editions do not include the lines that have become well-known to us, namely, Richard's appearance in act IV. Not until Quarto Four does the king appear. Where has he been? The prevailing answer has been that this section of the play fell victim to censorship. I seek to uncover a problem in logic and the lack of evidence. We simply have no evidence of such censorship; therefore, scholars have theorized about censorship in order to explain a vexing textual peculiarity. The absence of evidence captures my attention in this piece. I note how scholars have uncritically repeated the idea of censorship.

For some time I have been drawn to the difficult subject of patronage of drama. The first essay, on Queen Elizabeth's involvement with her own 1559 pageant, displays a scholarly discovery of manuscript material previously ignored. Here, therefore, I offer new evidence that scholars must interpret. I draw on materials from the Loseley manuscript collection in the Folger Library that show how Elizabeth ordered her Master of the Revels to provide costumes for her coronation pageant, to be presented by the City of London on 15 January 1559. This seemingly minor piece of evidence has large implications: it forces us to rethink the relationship of court and city in such entertainment; it offers inescapable documentation about this queen's active interest in how she will be entertained; it throws another light on patronage. Queen Elizabeth becomes a patron of drama in a way that we had not formerly known.

In the essay on Thomas Heywood, I respond to the common scholarly paradigm that insists that dramatists moved away from established systems of patronage because theater-going, paying audiences supplanted the need for such support. I argue the contrary, citing evidence from Heywood's career in the 1630s. Therefore, I recover an earlier concept of patronage, which includes various social groups and institutions as supporting dramatists. My evidence focuses on Heywood's dedication of dramatic texts to ordinary citizens and noblemen. Despite theater audiences, dramatists continued to need or desire aristocratic patronage. They no longer lived in the great houses of noblemen, but they still depended on support from various groups. The case of Thomas Heywood in the 1630s makes clear that systems of patronage, familiar in the Renaissance, remained intact.

Further signs of this pattern of patronage come from the active dedication of dramatic texts to noble women. The 14 whom I identify in the essay on women patrons range from the well known to the relatively obscure. Formal dedications constitute the principal evidence for an examination of this form of patronage. I try to answer the question of why dramatists thought it appropriate or potentially beneficial to single out these women for their patronage. Many dramatists simply sought recognition, hoping that the patroness's name would lend a kind of luster to their effort. Such an investigation into neglected material revises and enlarges the place of women in the theater culture, as their patronage becomes crucial for some dramatists.

As I turn to politics, I include two essays that focus on Queen Anne, James's wife. They underscore my ongoing interest in cultural history, which has led me to take my literary critical and scholarly skills and interpret historical figures. Methods of research, gathering of evidence, and interpretation constitute a vast common ground between historians and literary scholars. Increasingly at the end of the twentieth century, we each poach on the other's presumed territory — often with salutary effects. Francis Bacon seems a ripe terrain for almost any kind of investigation, so wide-ranging were his political and literary careers. In the essay on his *Henry VII*, I see the political and literary worlds intersecting in surprising ways. The discredited and banished Bacon clearly wrote this history to curry favor with King James. But I expose how little Bacon could have known about Henry VII and especially about his relationship to his queen, Elizabeth. Bacon overcame this vacuum of evidence by simply inventing a fiction about the husband-wife relationship. I show that he ascribes to Elizabeth qualities that he had observed about Queen Anne and her relationship with James. Bacon projects a current reality back into the past without acknowledging it — perhaps without even being aware of this tactic. Building on evidence about Anne, I can argue for what Bacon has done and thereby solve some puzzles about his *Henry VII*. I do not see this procedure as radically different from, say, interpreting Shakespeare's history plays in light of the historical sources available to him.

This concern about an understanding of Queen Anne led me to investigate how historians have viewed her. In the process I uncovered a distinct bias against her among male historians, a bias that may grow out of a certain political understanding. I track a pattern of association among scholars who largely repeated what they had picked up from earlier historians, although sometimes resorting to embellishing the account: metonymy without interrogation. Word-choice and the events or characteristics historians choose to focus on determine the portraits of Anne, portraits that become quite unfavorable. I trace the trajectory of such male bias, believing that we must know where our views come from and constantly question them. Gender differences in how historians view Anne stare us starkly in the face. Patriarchal ideology seems to have taken root among historians in the nineteenth century, at least among those writing about Anne. An increasingly feminist perspective about Anne now offers a corrective to the dominant view, breaking the mold of ideological blindness.

Politics of the nineteenth century scholarly world forms
the basis of the next two essays, in which I examine how
scholars understood the "rivalry" between Thomas Middleton
and Anthony Munday and also the "War of the Theaters."
One marvels at the activity, achievement, acerbic and political nature of much nineteenth century scholarship. But
serious questions about evidence emerge in the pattern of
associating scholars. In both cases we encounter uncritical
transmission of presumed information. The evidence of a
Middleton-Munday rivalry does not exist; instead, the idea
becomes a fiction of nineteenth century creation. I date the
beginning from William Gifford's 1816 edition of Ben Jonson
and trace the largely unwavering pattern of scholarly acquies-
cence across the nineteenth and into the twentieth century.
One would not look here for a model of how to conduct scholarship. I argue that the fiction of the rivalry grows out of a
romantic cult of the proprietary single author; I try to shift
the emphasis to acts of "collaboration," for which many examples exist between Middleton and Munday. Something
about the politically charged atmosphere of nineteenth century scholarship enjoys the sense of rivalry, contest, and fights.

Certainly such an attitude governs the scholarly battles over
the "War of the Theaters." If not entirely a fictional creation
of the nineteenth century imagination, it comes close. The
War of the Theaters seems to belong to the nineteenth century from which it received new and vigorous life. I examine
the evidence of such a war, presumably among Jonson, Dekker,
and Marston, suggesting that the evidence from the period
remains suspect or problematical. But in the give and take of
scholarly life, nineteenth century writers were inclined to add
to the concept of a war, raising the struggle to new heights
of fantasy. I observe that these scholars also create their
own personal war in attempting to write about the War. The
ingredients of the Elizabethan War often hinge on chronology
and character identification, two scholarly areas of suspect

reliability. Skepticism must govern any approach to how earlier scholars understood the evidence of a War and how they constructed a narrative to fit it.

For my entire professional life I have devoted much effort to research and writing about civic pageants. While not alone, I have not enjoyed a large association — many questions but not much metonymy. In contrast, I look across the scholarly landscape in the twentieth century and find a relatively intense involvement with studying and publishing about court masques. I am not only envious but slightly puzzled. I see these somewhat neglected pageants as bringing together scholarly concerns about plays, patronage, and politics. The royal entry of King James into London in March 1604 stands out as one of the most spectacular, costly, and important English civic pageants of the Renaissance period. Therefore, I begin with an essay that examines Gilbert Dugdale's *The Time Triumphant* (1604) as an eyewitness account from one who moved through London's streets and then commented on this glorious pageant. I argue that to have a complete understanding of this theatrical event, under the patronage of the City of London and full of symbolic and political import, we must include Dugdale's text and place it alongside those by Jonson, Thomas Dekker, and Stephen Harrison. The scholarly recovery of Dugdale's text highlights the process of accumulating evidence about an actual event, one that contains a dramatic fiction and a real king and royal family.

In the final essay on pageants vs. masques I try to sort out my views on the subject of the politics of scholarship. We do not lack evidence about the importance of pageants; we lack the scholarly will to explore them. The allure of the royal court — the Whitehall syndrome — offers its tantalizing siren call to scholars, leading some to offer ambitious theories about theater and its participation in royal power and politics. The benign neglect of pageants in studies of English Renaissance theater marks a failure of scholarship. Therefore, in this final essay I set up an opposition between Inigo Jones, the architect and designer of court masques, and Stephen Harrison, the architect for the triumphal arches of James's 1604 royal entry pageant. I discuss Harrison's indebtedness to one of the earliest English books on architecture, one that helped usher in Vitruvian principles. Harrison's completion of his task by publishing a book of engravings of the arches — the most important pictorial record of a pageant — sets him apart even from Jones. The investigation of Harrison leads to a consideration of why so many scholars have placed an emphasis on masques to the exclusion of pageants. I therefore attempt to redress an imbalance brought about by scholarly neglect and prejudice.

Through this final essay I mean for us to think anew about the hard work of brick-gathering scholars, engaged simultaneously in archeological excavations and in constructing edifices of thought and meaning: evidence and interpretation. For me civic pageants offer a particularly rich area of exploration, in part because of their relative scholarly neglect and in part because they offer a treasure of possibilities at the vortex of plays, patronage, and politics. As scholars we incur an obligation to look where others have not looked or have looked incompletely, whatever the subject matter. In our considerate and considered investigations we ask searching questions even as we associate with a scholarly legacy.

If we cannot always easily define or recognize scholars, we nevertheless know what they are not. Scholars do not engage in niggling antiquarianism or arcane pedantry. Shakespeare has shown us this most compellingly in *Love's Labour's Lost*. Here learning runs amok in the guise of the play's two official scholars, Nathaniel and Holofernes, who have carried to an extreme the treacherous course of the King and his fellow bookmen of Navarre. In the midst of Nathaniel and Holofernes's "three-piled hyperboles" and "figures pedantical," we hear the sensible voices of Moth and Costard. Moth observes: "They have been at a great feast of languages and stolen the scraps" (V.i.35–36); and Costard responds: "O, they have lived long on the alms-basket of words" (37–38). The play's pedants do not embody a considerate style. Good scholars celebrate the feast of languages for its sustenance. In the essays that follow I hope that readers will find scholarly substance — indeed, food for thought.

Whatever the twenty first century may offer in scholarship, I trust that it will embrace a relentless but benign questioning of evidence, assumptions, and ideology. In the midst of this interrogative mood we must recall our metonymy. Not driven by nostalgia or sentimentality, scholars remain aware that we exist in a vast continuum of scholarship, that we regularly and beneficially drink from wells that we did not dig, warm ourselves beside fires that we did not build, and dwell in buildings made of bricks that we did not gather or fashion.

ONE

Richard II

ﻪ

External and Internal Evidence

In a wide-ranging study of the uses of external and internal evidence, Samuel Schoenbaum writes: "External evidence may and often does provide incontestable proof; internal evidence can only support hypotheses or corroborate external evidence."[1] I want to adjust this statement somewhat by focusing on *Richard II*, its problems of evidence, and the necessity of interpreting any evidence. Although investigations of such evidence have typically centered on problems of attribution or authorship, as in the case of sorting out the Beaumont and Fletcher canon, I want instead to look at external evidence that has been used to date the composition of *Richard II* and internal textual evidence that has prompted questions about possible censorship of the printed play. No disputes about Shakespeare's authorship of *Richard II* occur, but struggles over interpretation of some external and internal evidence continue. These disputes call into question what constitutes evidence. I will argue that Sir Edward Hoby's letter, often purported to constitute external evidence about dating the play has no validity for this purpose, and I will examine how scholars have nevertheless hung onto this "evidence," occasionally even embellishing it. I will further analyze the internal problem of the deposition scene that does not appear in the text of *Richard II* until Quarto 4 (hereafter Q4) in 1608; I will argue that the evidence does not lead to the conclusion of censorship, as many have claimed. Additionally, we will gain insight into how scholars have understood and interpreted the evidence, and how some scholarly positions get established and entrenched, resistant to modification or challenge.

In trying to pin down the likely date of composition of *Richard II*, I have uncovered a blatant example of how some external "facts," questionable at best, have had a long and happy life despite the efforts of scholars to lay them to rest. I refer specifically to the letter from Sir Edward Hoby to Sir Robert Cecil, dated 7 December 1595, allegedly referring to a private performance of *Richard II*. E. K. Chambers was the first to cite this letter and to make its existence known to the literary world in a note in *The Elizabethan Stage*,[2] although the letter had been available in published form as early as 1894.[3] Chambers first reproduced the item in *Review of English Studies* and then again in his *William Shakespeare*,[4] from which I quote the brief letter:

> Sir, findinge that you wer not convenientlie to be at London to morrow night I am bold to send to knowe whether Teusdaie may be anie more in your grace to visit poore Channon rowe where as late as it shal please you a gate for your supper shal be open: & K. Richard present him selfe to your vewe. Pardon my boldnes that ever love to be honored with your presence nether do I importune more then your occasions may willingly assent unto, in the meanetime & ever restinge At your command Edw. Hoby *[Endorsed]* 7 Dec. 1595 *[and]* readile.

Possibly because of the authority of Chambers, many were ready to believe with him something that the document simply does not say: on its face it scarcely "proves" a performance in 1595 of Shakespeare's *Richard II.*

Tracing briefly the reaction to this letter reveals something of the mysteries of criticism and scholarly interpretation. We can begin with I. A. Shapiro in *Shakespeare Quarterly* who reviews the supposed evidence and concludes that Hoby does not refer to any play at all.[5] He suggests that Hoby could just as easily be implying a portrait and asserts: "It is already apparent, I hope, that we cannot use Hoby's letter as evidence for the date of *Richard II*" (205).

A selective survey of editions shows that the validity of what Hoby's letter purportedly proves has been accepted in many quarters. In 1958, the same year of Shapiro's article, Peter Alexander reports Chambers's discovery of the document and concludes that Robert Cecil "was among the guests at supper and entertainment. . . ."[6] But Peter Ure, in the 1961 Arden edition, explicitly refers to Shapiro's essay and doubts the claim of the Hoby letter,[7] which he had completely accepted in the 1956 fourth edition. The editors of the *Folger Library General Reader's Shakespeare*, offering no additional evidence, say that the play "appears to have been first performed in the season of 1595–96," an apparent acceptance of Hoby.[8] Under the heading *Richard II*, F. E. Halliday cites the Hoby letter as the earliest evidence of a performance, though under "Hoby" Halliday says that the play was "probably" *Richard II.*[9] The editors of *The Reader's Encyclopedia* (1966) skeptically suggest that the evidence is uncertain and could refer to *Richard III.*[10] Similarly, Matthew Black regards the reference as equivocal,[11] but Ribner in his revision of the Kittredge text seems at least partly to accept the evidence, admitting that it is "impossible to be entirely certain of this."[12] Kenneth Muir cites the date 9 December, "when there was a private performance before Sir Edward Hoby and his friends."[13] In his first revision of

Hardin Craig's edition, David Bevington alters Craig's view in favor of doubting that the letter proves a performance; and in the fourth edition Bevington reproduces the letter in an appendix and says that "it is by no means certain that this passage refers to a private performance of Shakespeare's play," which does not completely rule out what this evidence purports to show.[14] But Herschel Baker, writing in *The Riverside Shakespeare* edition, suggests that the Hoby letter implies "what sounds like a private showing of the play," a statement carried over into the 1997 Riverside edition, although a comment in the appendix calls the evidence not clear.[15] Andrew Gurr in the Cambridge edition writes "That *Richard II* was on stage in 1595 is suggested most clearly in a letter written by Sir Edward Hoby on 7 December of that year."[16] Gurr adds that Hoby "was offering his guest a specially commissioned evening performance by Shakespeare's company of one of their newest plays" (3). The contributors to *William Shakespeare: A Textual Companion* say that the Hoby letter "has usually been assumed" to refer to a performance of *Richard II*, although they admit that this view has been challenged.[17]

Since 1958 and beyond, a significant number of editions or reference books surveyed still held with varying degrees of fidelity to the presumed evidence of the Hoby letter, suggesting that they either paid no heed to Shapiro's argument or simply echoed earlier editions. We can notice in more recent editions a tendency to pay no attention to the Hoby material, as in, for example, the Norton Shakespeare edition.[18] Many recent editions have apparently found the Hoby letter sufficiently resolved; as they have abandoned traditional discussions of such matters as date of the play, sources, and early performances, concern about external evidence has receded.

Before all credit devolve upon Shapiro for exposing the "Hoby myth," I should point out what he failed to observe, namely, that eight years earlier in 1950, C. A. Greer had raised essentially the same argument in an essay specifically on the date of *Richard II*.[19] To date the play in 1595 on the basis of the letter, Greer says, "simply will not hold up." And he adds: "Hoby's letter does not even designate Shakespeare's play. As a matter of fact, it does not even identify a Richard II play, as Hoby might well have had a Richard III play in mind" (403). Shapiro improves on Greer, to whom he makes no reference, by arguing that the evidence implies no theatrical perform- ance. The editions appearing between Greer and Shapiro (1950– 58) perpetuate the validity of Chambers's claim for the letter, except for the Variorum, which views the letter skeptically, though it does not cite Greer specifically on this point.[20] Writ- ing in 1951, Hardin Craig observes that Chambers "has re- cently found a piece of evidence which may confirm the date 1595, or at least show that *Richard II* was possibly a novelty in that year."[21] Curiously, Harrison's edition of 1952 makes no mention of the letter whatsoever, either to accept or to discount it.[22] Charles Sisson claims that there was a private performance in 1595 "on the evidence of an extant letter from Hoby himself to Cecil."[23]

As noted above, Ure, in his fourth edition of the Arden text (1956), accepts the evidence and adds that the quickness with which the play could be prepared for this private performance suggests that it was "being performed publicly elsewhere" (xxx). The editor of *Richard II* for the Yale Shakespeare refers to "a contemporary letter from Sir Edward Hoby to Sir Robert Cecil which mentions a performance of a play called *Richard II* in 1595"[24] — a misleading statement since the letter does not specifically mention a title.

Like Shapiro, Greer also commits a sin of omission, for he fails to give full credit to the first person in print to challenge Chambers's assumption, G. L. Kittredge. In his influential 1936 edition Kittredge reproduces the letter and adds: "If Hoby was referring to a dramatic entertainment (as may or may not be the case), nothing proves that he had Shakespeare's play in mind, for there were other dramas in existence dealing with the same reign; nor is it certain that some Richard the Third

was not the piece in question."[25] Here in 1936 lies the heart of
the argument seemingly advanced as new by Greer in 1950
and by Shapiro in 1958. But Kittredge did not have to wait 14
years to be ignored, for John Dover Wilson (1939) accepts the
Hoby evidence enthusiastically and adds a couple of extra
observations: "the picture which Hoby calls up, of cooks and
players (including no doubt Shakespeare) all agog for the great
man's entertainment, waiting into the night for the porter's
word of his arrival at the gate"; "the terms of Hoby's letter
suggest . . . that Cecil had himself heard of the play, and may
have even perhaps expressed a desire to see it."[26] Shapiro rightly
calls this a flight of fancy; one begins to wonder how many
conclusions can be squeezed out of one simple document. More
sensibly, the editors of the New Cambridge Edition in 1942
suggest that "it is by no means certain that the reference is to
a play at all, or that, if it is, that it was Shakespeare's or that
the Richard was Richard the second."[27] Although O. J. Campbell expresses some uncertainty, he concludes that the reference "is most likely to be Shakespeare's *Richard II*."[28]

I think that if we return to look at the Hoby letter carefully,
we cannot reasonably conclude that this external evidence
establishes anything about the possible date for the composition of *Richard II*. Squeeze this evidence as hard as we might,
or "crush" it, as Malvolio would say, and we still come up
empty handed. Scholars have to be careful not to will into
existence meaning that the evidence clearly does not support.
Investigating how scholars have interpreted the letter provides
a sober parable about scholarship occasionally gone awry.
In the case of this play, external evidence does not provide
"incontestable proof."

As we turn to internal evidence, we encounter a textual
problem that reaches outside the play for an explanation. Missing from the earliest quarto editions of *Richard II* is a large
segment of the deposition scene, act IV, lines 154–318 (or 2074–
2243, Folio text), roughly half the scene, including Richard's
appearance at his formal abdication. Editors have had to come

to terms with this problem, a problem of some concern to all who study the play. I should like to examine the issue again and suggest that this part of the scene did not exist until sometime after 1601, perhaps not until after the death of Elizabeth. I readily admit that my argument will be grounded on circumstantial evidence; nevertheless, since the present generally accepted theories rest on circumstantial evidence, I do not hesitate to suggest another plausible alternative.

The play text first appeared in 1597, although it may have been written a few years earlier, and in 1598 two more quarto editions, none containing the lines cited above. Evelyn Albright offers fairly typical explanations for this phenomenon: "this scene, so important to the purpose of the play, was cut from the earlier versions, and not added to a later one. For without the 'parliament scene,' the passage which should follow it (IV. i.321), 'A woeful pageant have we here beheld,' is meaningless. This fact, together with the first appearance of the scene in one of the two quartos of 1608, makes it very likely that the absence of the scene from quartos issued in the lifetime of Elizabeth is due to the fact that it was cut out by the official censor because the queen traced a likeness to herself in Richard II."[29] We know that Elizabeth viewed herself in some kind of relationship to Richard II, but to assert that this fantasy led to censorship of this scene in the play remains another matter. Political censorship becomes the most commonly echoed reason offered for the missing lines.

But, one may rightly ask, where does the evidence exist? Nowhere, I answer. Many of the same scholars who posit the theory of censorship nevertheless insist that the scene had regular performances on the stage. If, however, the ritualistic deposing of Richard seemed too scandalous for the printed page, how could it then be allowed on stage where many thousands of people had the chance to be corrupted by it? While one would not attempt to explain the motivations of the proposed censorship, what about the missing part of the deposition makes it so dangerous? After all, Richard has already been thoroughly humiliated in act III and has in fact abdicated the throne; the action of the ceremonial deposition only makes *de jure* what is certainly *de facto*. Obviously a comparable scene in Marlowe's *Edward II* remained intact. Further, if one has concerns about Richard's portrait, then all the more reason to include the whole scene since the missing part generally evokes a sympathetic response for Richard from audiences. For lack of concrete evidence, the explanation of political censorship remains at best a theory and not an inescapable one.

For whatever reason, Quarto 1 (hereafter Q1) appeared in 1597 without the formal deposition. Despite the missing lines, I believe that the text retains its integrity — but more of that later. Indeed the text seems to be based on Shakespeare's manuscript or a fair copy, and because of its reliability editors generally use it as the copy text.[30] Clearly textual corruption does not account for the missing lines. The two quartos of 1598, both based on Q1, carry no additional authority. Understandably, these quartos do not contain the deposition either. If Q1 had been censored for political reasons and thereby somewhat crippled, why then issue two more separate editions in the following year? Logic may suggest that printer and publisher would not wish to continue to publish incomplete texts — not that one can always expect logic to prevail in such matters.

In any event, not until Q4 in 1608 do we get the complete text. I can observe that Albright incorrectly refers to *two* quartos in 1608 when only one exists, though with two slightly differing states of the title page. One title calls attention to the new material: "The / Tragedie of King / Richard the Second: / With new additions of the Parlia- / ment Sceane, and the deposing / of King Richard, / As it hath been lately acted by the Kinges / Maiesties seruantes, at the Globe." This sufficiently ambiguous title teases one with the possibility that the printer refers to wholly new material in the play, not just newly printed material. Further, does the phrase "As it hath been lately acted" modify specifically the "new additions"? If such an interpretation is possible, then the incident of Richard's deposition could be a recent addition to the stage presentation as well. Assuming the reliability of this title page, one might want to question Albright's assertion: "this scene . . . was cut from the earlier versions, and not added to a later one." Her statement surely misleads.

The new section of act IV as found in Q4 is not especially reliable, and most editors argue for some memorial reconstruction.[31] Therefore, editors usually follow the Folio text for this part of the deposition scene. But assuming memorial reconstruction in Q4, which obviously implies some stage presentation containing the lines in question, we can still argue for a date as late as 1608 for the first appearance of the complete deposition. In other words, the theory of memorial reconstruction does not prove that the lines have been present in stage performances from the beginning. One could safely conclude that by 1608 productions of *Richard II* included the complete scene.

Why in 1608 should a complete text suddenly be printed? If the problem had been Elizabeth's political sensitivity, why not issue an edition shortly after her death? Interestingly, one observes that in 1603 the publisher Andrew Wise transferred his rights to *Richard II*, along with other items, to Matthew Law, according to an entry in the Stationers' Register on 25 June 1603.[32] Yet some five years pass before a full edition appears. Was James I less sensitive to a stage representation of the deposing of a duly constituted monarch? Possibly. I know of no evidence that suggests he likened himself to Richard, but we surely know that he remained sensitive to satirical criticism: witness his response to *Eastward Ho* which sent the three dramatists to jail. If one starts with the assumption of political censorship because of Elizabeth, then one can argue that the full deposition scene could not be published until after her death. But if, on the other hand, one finds no evidence for such censorship, except as an *ex post facto* explanation, then one looks elsewhere for an alternative reason.

Another issue intrudes into this murky matter: the presumed performance of *Richard II* on 7 February 1601, the eve of the Essex rebellion, on behalf of the rebellious forces. Albright and Matthew Black have already covered this ground quite well, and I do intend to rehearse all of it. But C. A. Greer several years ago questioned whether indeed the actors performed Shakespeare's *Richard II* on this occasion; and although Greer's arguments have not gained general currency, he raises some thought-provoking issues.[33] While admitting some uneasiness, I accept the probability that the actors performed *Richard II* for that event, and I believe that some of Greer's points can be used to support my argument about the deposition.

For example, he states: "Certainly a scene cut for political reasons in 1597 and 1598 . . . would not have been played on this occasion. If the scene was dangerous in 1597 and 1598, it was dangerous, only more so, in 1601" (270). I concur and add that this argues against the scene's being performed at all during this period, if political reasons had anything to do with its alleged excision. If the scene is not performed and does not appear in any printed text, one can theoretically argue that it does not exist. But when Greer says, "a play without a deposition scene would not have served the ends of the conspirators," I demur. The defeat of Richard has already occurred before we reach act IV; the rebel Bolingbroke has clearly been victorious, a point not lost on the Essex followers. We do have, in the truncated Q1, York's statement to Bolingbroke that Richard has abdicated and names him heir, as we also have Bolingbroke's stated determination to ascend the throne and his announcement of coronation plans.

Could not one argue that the abbreviated act IV would serve the Essex rebels quite nicely? After all, the play, even without lines 154–318, demonstrates forcefully the overthrow of a legitimate sovereign. As Q1 stands, we do not see Richard from III.iii, until he appears on the way to prison in act V. Would it not suit the rebel cause to glimpse the weak Richard coming down like glistering Phaeton and then next see him ignominiously on his way to prison and certain death? Indeed, would renegades intent on rebellion have asked for a play containing Richard in act IV at his histrionic and poetic best? The likely sympathy stirred by his presence there would conflict with their purposes. For me, then, the absence of Richard in act IV would serve the "ends of the conspirators," contrary to Greer's argument. The Shakespearean version of *Richard II* available to them would have been the abbreviated one.

In the trial that quickly followed the abortive Essex uprising, two pieces of testimony impinge directly on the question of what play had been performed. When the Lord Chief Justice on 17 February examined Sir Gelly Merrick, one of the conspirators, he offered this information: "On Saturday last . . . dined at Gunter's in company with Lord Monteagle, Sir Christ. Blount, Sir Chas. Percy, they went all together to the Globe . . . where the Lord Chamberlain's men used to play, and were there somewhat before the play began, Sir Charles telling them that the play would be of Harry the Fourth . . . thinks it was Sir Chas. Percy who procured that play. . . . The play was of King Henry the Fourth, and of the killing of Richard the Second, and played by the Lord Chamberlain's players."[34] While no one thinks of Merrick as a drama critic, clearly he does not refer to Shakespeare's *Henry IV*, which has no killing of Richard. If, on the other hand, the actors performed *Richard II* without part of the deposition scene, then Merrick might well have concluded that the play was "of Henry the Fourth, and of the killing of Richard the Second" — the parts of the action no doubt most impressive for a would-be rebel. Thus I disagree with Greer, who infers on the basis of Merrick's testimony that the play was other than *Richard II* (270).

Though the members of Shakespeare's acting company es-
caped prosecution, at least one, Augustine Phillips, testified
at the trial. His comments on 18 February offer additional information about the play: "several [of the conspirators] . . .
spoke to some of the players to play the deposing and killing
of King Richard II, and promised to give them 40s. more than
their ordinary, to do so."[35] Although an attractive offer, Phillips
adds: "Examinate and his fellows had determined to play some
other play, holding that of King Richard as being so old and so
long out of use that they should have a small company at it,
but at this request they were content to play it." The phrase,
"so old and so long out of use," is troubling, and Greer again
concludes that the play could not have been Shakespeare's
Richard II. But, of course, Phillips's use of the phrase could
have been relative and inexact and a means of making the
company look better by its seeming reluctance to undertake
this project. At any rate, Phillips's testimony emphasizes that
the play contained the "deposing and killing of King Richard
II," an analysis perfectly plausible for a production of *Richard
II* minus the complete deposition scene.

I return to the matter of the integrity of the presumed incomplete Q1, and I refer to dramatic, not textual, integrity.
Commenting on the missing lines, Greg writes: "This appears
to have formed part of the original text, and in spite of some
tinkering its excision leaves an obvious scar on H2. The de-
fect was made good in 1608. . . ."[36] But how obvious is that
"scar"? Part of the difficulty derives from our knowledge of
the lines that appeared in Q4 and that all modern editions
include, and therefore we cannot conceive of *Richard II* without this incident of the deposition. How many of us gained
our first knowledge of the play by reading Q1? Suppose we
took mature, intelligent readers and had them read *Richard II*
for the first time in the Q1 version — would they note an obvious scar? More interesting, stage the Q1 version — would a

new audience suspect something was missing? Probably not.

However brilliant Richard may be in his appearance in act IV, nothing that he says or does advances the narrative development of the play. Bolingbroke in line 316 does sentence him to the Tower; but we can perhaps infer such a development earlier from III.iii.208, where Richard says, "Set on towards London, cousin, is it so?"; or from III.iv.95–96, where the Queen says, "Come, ladies, go / To meet at London London's king in woe." Or if we missed those hints, the Queen, at the opening of act V.i, says that Richard is on his way "To Julius Caesar's ill-erected tower" (line 2).

After Carlisle's prophetic speech, Northumberland in Q1 arrests him on grounds of capital treason and bids Westminster "To keepe him safely till his day of triall" (line 153), omitting the line, "May it please you lords, to grant the commons' suit?" Bolingbroke responds, "Let it be so, and loe on wednesday next, / We solemnly proclaime our Coronation, / Lords be ready all," which in Q4 and subsequent texts comes at lines 319–20, slightly altered. After York, Bolingbroke, and Northumberland exit, the Abbot comments, "A wofull Pageant haue we here beheld." Albright and many critics believe that this line makes no sense unless we have witnessed Richard's abdication in this scene. But could not the Abbot's statement in the Q1 version simply refer to all that has preceded in the scene which includes the arrest of Carlisle, the announcement of Richard's abdication, Bolingbroke's ascent to the throne, and his plans for coronation? Those events seem sufficient to lead one like the Abbot to complain of a "wofull Pageant." Indeed the Abbot makes no explicit reference to Richard at all, but joins Carlisle and Aumerle in devising a plot to overthrow Bolingbroke. The emphasis, in other words, falls on getting rid of the new Henry IV, not necessarily a sympathetic response to Richard's paroxysm of grief. In short, the Abbot's statement can make sense in the Q1 version.

The debate about the missing part of the deposition scene

continues. In their *Textual Companion*, Gary Taylor and Stanley Wells in discussing textual matters assert: "It is widely accepted that the episode [deposition] was censored . . ." (307). This gets a somewhat different twist from the editors of the Norton Shakespeare, themselves indebted to the Oxford Shakespeare: "Some scholars have argued that Elizabeth's censors considered the passage [deposition] too provocative to stage and insisted that it be deleted; after Elizabeth's death, it was possible to reinstate the offending material. Others argue that Shakespeare revised the play during the first decade of the seventeenth century and wrote the deposition scene at that time" (950). But these editors take no final position, nor do they cite the scholars who have taken these contrasting views. Gurr, in the 1984 Cambridge edition, accounts for the deposition scene as "evidently deleted from the early printed quartos as an act of censorship" (9). Bevington in his 1997 edition of Shakespeare writes, repeating what he had earlier stated: "The scene of Richard's deposition (4.1) was considered so provocative by Elizabeth's government that it was censored in the printed quartos of Shakespeare's play during the Queen's lifetime" (721). This statement leaves open the possibility that early stage performances may have included the censored material. Margaret Shewring refers to the "politically sensitive" nature of the play, but early performances "may well have included the deposition scene that was not permitted to appear in print in the first Quarto in 1597."[37] Another recent book takes a similar tack. Russ McDonald says: "*Richard II*, for example, was originally printed, almost certainly for political reasons, without the section in act 4, scene 1, in which the king is actually deposed."[38] "Almost certainly" provides a way out of the daunting problem of internal evidence that seems to require some external evidence to provide "incontestable proof."

In more extended treatments of the deposition scene, Leeds Barroll, Janet Clare, and Cyndia Clegg have offered varying ways to explain or at least situate this scene in terms of topical political events. Barroll frames the discussion in light of new historicism's narrative about the play and the Essex rebellion, and he reaches some conclusions similar to mine. He writes: "But considering what we can know only from the texts of Shakespeare's quartos of *Richard II* themselves, the concept of a deposition scene as 'suppressed' is a curious and distressing intellectual position for critics who are interested in new approaches to and apprehensions of the history of Shakespeare's time. For the traditional view of a suppressed deposition scene is based on a limited concept of textual transmission in Shakespeare's quartos as well as on formalist assumptions about *Richard II* itself."[39] Barroll focuses on John Hayward's *Life of Henry IV* (1601) as the object of the Privy Council's concern. By contrast, Clare readily accepts the government's interest in this play and others, and she comes down on the side of a kind of self-censorship on Shakespeare's part. She writes: "From his treatment of the events leading to the deposition it seems that Shakespeare was indeed conscious that he was dealing with intractable political issues which demanded cautious representation."[40] Therefore, a kind of "circumspection" governs the playwright's narrative.

Clegg shifts the terms yet again, arguing that the "paradigm for investigating *Richard II*'s potential censorship during the reign of Elizabeth I be relocated in the local history of texts certainly censored and the practices that suppressed them."[41] Therefore Clegg concludes: "From this perspective one can argue that the so-called 'deposition scene' was perceived as dangerous and was thus absent from the Elizabethan quartos not because it represented usurpation or deposition but because, as the 'Parliament Sceane,' it corroborated late-sixteenth century resistance theory." Clegg thus opens the play to another narrative: the importance of Parliament, epitomized in Robert Parsons's *A conference about the next succession* (1595). "In *Richard II*'s Parliament/deposition scene's gross corroboration of Parsons's," Clegg writes, "we have a motive for censorship; in the persons and concerns of the ecclesiastical authorizers, we have a means" (447). Clegg's alternative narrative moves us away from narrowly construed ideas of a repressive government determined to ferret out and censor incidents within plays in order to contain subversion.

In a different way, I argue from the internal evidence of the play: if the idea of political censorship has no confirmed basis in fact, if three quartos appeared without any apparent violence to the text, if the Essex rebels would possibly have preferred a *Richard II* without all of act IV, and if the Q1 text makes dramatic sense without lines 154–318, then I submit that Shakespeare added the lines in the 1608 text, that they were indeed new and thus had not been excised in the early editions. Lest this approach be deemed entirely heretical, I should quickly add that no actor, director, spectator, or reader would truly want to be deprived of this new appearance of Richard at his formal abdication. His appearance in act IV enriches his portrait as we watch his fertile imagination stage manage this scene even with Bolingbroke ostensibly in control. I, like all others, delight in Shakespeare's wise decision to add these lines in act IV sometime between 1601 and 1608.

Scholars wrestling with external or internal evidence in *Richard II* confront a letter that does not specifically refer to a performance of the play, no matter what some scholars have willed into existence as proof. And we encounter missing internal textual evidence that many interpreters seek to explain by constructing a narrative of censorship. In an appropriately interrogative mood, I think that we must discount the Hoby letter as confirmation of performance, and we should accept that the full deposition scene represents Shakespeare's revision of the text rather than a censored text that provoked government authorities.

TWO

Elizabeth's Coronation Entry (1559)

‹›

New Manuscript Evidence

The 1559 royal entry of Queen Elizabeth through London was a grand dramatic event. But it was also important for its symbolic value, establishing a sense of release from the oppressive past and hope for the future under Elizabeth. New manuscript evidence about preparations for this civic pageant, not cited in previous discussions,[1] sheds additional light on the entertainment, revealing for example Elizabeth's keen interest in the quality of the costumes and the active involvement of the Revels Office. The implications are potentially far-reaching — namely, Elizabeth is sensitive to the political and spiritual significance of civic drama and will do what she can to enhance and enrich the experience, thereby reaping the benefits. She will be no mere passive spectator or grateful recipient of the event.

As I have demonstrated elsewhere, the records of the Corporation of London indicate the preparations made by the city and guilds for this pageant, plans first made in December 1558.[2] Obviously the financial burden rested with the City of London and the trade companies; the pageant was, after all, their offering, a gift to the new sovereign. The city assured the long-lasting effect of this triumphant occasion by having a commemorative pamphlet printed shortly after the event. The text, written (according to city records of 4 March 1559)[3] by Richard Mulcaster, describes the tableaux, records the speeches, and captures something of the vivid nature of this occasion.[4]

In the papers of Sir Thomas Cawarden, Master of the Revels when Elizabeth came to the throne, are two items that bear specifically on this pageant. These papers are part of the Loseley Manuscripts housed at the Folger Shakespeare Library. The first item, Folger MS.L.b.33, I transcribe as follows:

> Elizabeth R By the Quene.
>
> Whereas yow haue in your custodie and charge certen apparrell as officer for *our* maskes and Revelles, Thies shalbe to will and commaunde yow imediatlie vpon the sight hereof that you deliuer or cause to be deliuered vnto John Gresham and John Elyot citizins of *our* Citie of London suche and so muche of the said apparrell as they shall require for the setting forthe of those pagentes *whi*ch be appoynted to stande for the shew of our Cytie at the tyme we are to passe thorough thesame towardes *our* Coronation wherein you shall vse your discretion to deliuer suche percelles as may most convenie*n*tlie serve their torne and therew*i*thall take lest hurte by vse Receaving also of thesaid Gresham and Elyot a bill subscribed by their handes whereby to charge them *wi*th the saulf Deliuery & restituton of the said apparrell And thies our *lettr*es shalbe your sufficie*n*t warrante and Discharge in that behaulf. Yeven vndre *our* Sygnet at *our* Pallace of Westm*inster* the third of January the first year of *our* Reigne.
>
> To *our* trustie and welbeloued
> S*ir* Thomas Cawarden.
> Knight.[5]

An incomplete and somewhat inaccurate transcription appears in the Appendix of the *Seventh Report* of the Historical Manuscripts Commission.[6] The John Gresham referred to in the document is the brother of the better-known Sir Thomas Gresham.

The second document reveals the fulfillment of the first when ten days later (January 13) Cawarden delivered to the two Mercers garments to be used in the pageant on the 14th. This manuscript, designated Folger MS.L.b.109, reads as follows:

> The note indented of suche garment*es* are this present xiij[th] of January 1558 deliu*e*red by Sir Thomas Carden Knight M*aster* of the quenes revell*es* vnto John Gressham & John Eliott M*e*rcers to be redeliu*e*red the xvj[th] of this p*re*snte moneth of January nexte comynge that is to say
>
> First a kirtell for a woman of yelowe cloth of gold vpperbodied
>   wi*th* tynsell and sleves of gold
> Item a red cloke lyned wi*th* whyte sarcenet & a cape of silu*e*r
> Item a womans garment of tynsell vpperbodied wi*th*
>   skalop'shell*es*
> Item a mans gowne of russett velvett
> Item iij garment*es* of blewe cloth of gold wi*th* sleves of flat silu*e*r
> Item ij longe garmnent*es* of cloth of gold wi*th* black tynsell
>   sleves and capes
> Item ij garment*es* longe of red saten striped wi*th* gold and sleves
>   of white cloth gold & red
> Item a cloke of yelowe cloth of gold turfed wi*th* white & a sword
> Item a coat of flat silu*e*r
> Item an irishe garment of yelowe gloth of gold and yelowe
>   sarcenet
> Item iiij pair of buskens ij pair of blew velvett & ij pair of red
>   botkyn and one other pair of red botkyn
> Item vijj cappes & hatt*es* of cloth of gold
> Item a white purse for a fawken*e*r
> Item a hobert
> Item ij white garment of silu*e*r lawne white wi*th* sleves of cloth
>   of silu*e*r

Item ij Ierkens of taffata chaungeable red & yelowe garded w*ith*
   cloth of gold

By me John Elyott M*ercer*

These manuscript materials affect our understanding of the
royal entry in several ways. They are innately interesting and
valuable because they provide new information. More important, they reveal Elizabeth's eager interest in such festivities.
She understands the political and social value of the display.
Her attitude seems to be that if the city needs assistance in
making the entertainment more colorful, more spectacular,
then let the citizens have what they need, even if the queen
must provide it. Such an attitude says much about Elizabeth's
sensitivity to public occasions, about her sense of drama. No
matter that the city is making the offering to her, she'll enhance it, make it it more brilliant. Elizabeth is thus not only
recipient of the pageant, spectator of and "actor" in it, but
also provider of costume. She is accordingly part patron of
this drama.

I have been unable to make any absolute correspondence
between the Cawarden list of garments and costumes required
by the printed text. Part of the difficulty is the general nature
of the descriptions in the pamphlet, though we see throughout the concern for costume, as when Mulcaster refers to the
"Poet" at the end who is "richely attyred" (58). I will venture
a few conjectures. The "ij garment*es* longe of red saten striped
w*ith* gold and sleves of white cloth gold & red" could be appropriate to the figures at the first tableau, "The vniting of
the two houses of Lancastre and York" (33). On the lowest of
the three "stages" sat representations of Henry VII and his
wife, Elizabeth, he "enclosed in a read rose" and she "with a
whyte rose, eche of them royallie crowned, and decently
apparailled as apperteineth to princes" (31–32). The mingling
of red, gold, and white offers the correct colors, and the garments would doubtless constitute "decent" apparel.

On the scaffold at the end of Soper's lane were children representing the Eight Beatitudes, and "Euerie of these children wer appointed & apparelled according vnto the blessing which he did represent" (41) — exactly what "Poor in spirit" or the "merciful" might have looked like is left to our imagination. Perhaps the Beatitudes are the ones for whom the "viij cappes & hatt*es* of cloth of gold" are intended. The device at the Little Conduit in Cheapside includes in addition to the two hills, one barren, the other flourishing, the appearance of Time and his daughter Truth. Time is "apparaylled as an olde man with a sythe in his hande, hauynge wynges artificallye made," while Truth "was fynely and well apparaylled, all cladde in whyte silke" (47). The "ij white garment of silu*er* lawne white w*ith* sleves of cloth of silu*er*" could have been used by Time and Truth. While "lawne" is fine linen, not silk, the term "silk" is a generic term, as in a different manuscript list of "silks" delivered to Cawarden for Elizabeth's masques and revels, which includes some five different materials among which "velvet seems far removed from "silk.""[7]

The final pageant tableau had a person representing Deborah, judge of Israel, "a semelie and mete personage richlie apparelled in parliament robes, with a sceptre in her hand" (53–54). The first item on the 13 January list might suit her: "a kirtell for a woman of yelowe cloth of gold vpperbodied w*ith* tynsell and sleves of gold." This seems an appropriate garment for Deborah, especially in light of what Elizabeth herself was wearing that day, as described by the Venetian ambassador: "a royal robe of very rich cloth of gold, with a double-raised stiff pile, and on her head over a coif of cloth of gold. . . ."[8] If the costume of the Deborah figure were similar to that of the actual queen, then symbol and reality would have fused. Even though uncertain of all details of their use, we now know much more about the costumes of the pageant, though I would still like to know where the "fawken*er*" and "a hobert" (hawk) fit in. So to wonder may simply remind us of the almost inevitable limitation of the printed description of such a colorful and lively entertainment.

A glance at the Revels Accounts, as presented by Feuillerat, indicates how that office would have had the necessary materials for the garments given to the two citizens of London. For example, items purchased on 1 January have some correspondence to the garments loaned the city:

> Henry bechere for viij peces of gowlde and and [sic] syluer sendalls [thin silken material] narrowe at xx^d the yarde . . . vij peces narrowe gowlde sarsenett at ij^s the yarde . . . three peces more of narrowe gowlde sarsenett at iij^s the yarde . . . vj peces of laune rewed with counterfete gowlde narrowe at iij^s the yarde . . . and for vij peces of fyne gowlde sarsenettes broode at vj^s the yarde . . . of him bowghte the fyrste daye of Ianuarye 1558. Anno primo reginae Elizabeth and spente in rowles and wrethes tufting tyringe of hedpeces and gyrdells vsed in dyuerse Maskes betwene christmas and shroftde that yere. . . .[9]

The "peces of laune" purchased from Henry Becher may have been used for the two garments of "lawne" in Cawarden's list. In any event, the Revels Office was well stocked for the season of festivities. Other accounts, included by Feuillerat, confirm the nature and extent of supplies gathered in late December and early January.

When, on 13 January, the two Mercers received the items for the pageant, they were required to return them to the Revels Office on the 16th. The Revels Accounts show why — namely, preparation for a masque:

> Iohn Holte for toe lb di. of blacke threede-v^s
> j lb of whate threede-xx^d j lb di. of threede
> in colour-iij^s and for viij lb of candells-ij^s xj^s viij^d
> by him bowghte and spente benethe in the Maske
> shewen the morowe after the Coronacion.[10]

The requirement that the garments be returned on the 16th not only satisfied the queen's stipulation for "the saulf

Deliuery & restituton of the said apparrell" (Folger MS.L.b.33),
but also meets the practical necessity of costumes for a masque
on that day, though we do not know which masque it may
have been.

However one may view these "new" manuscript documents, they do illustrate Elizabeth's explicit interest in and
support of drama from the earliest days of her reign — a good,
vital harbinger of things to come. She readily assumes the role
of patron of a dramatic form generally noted for its exclusive
support by guilds and city governments. Perhaps this should
alert us to her attitude toward drama and spectacle, as it points
the way, I believe, to the eventual active patronizing of acting
companies at court. This information affords us a glimpse at
the Revels Office, which, in addition to its usual and primary
functions, might be called upon to provide apparel for public
shows. Here the interrelationship of civic pageant and court
masque is unmistakable, suggesting that if costumes can
be exchanged, then the two kinds of drama are not alien or
mutually exclusive dramatic forms or experiences. With one
swift stroke Elizabeth was able not only to enrich the pageant
entertainment but also to solidify support in London, revealing, as she was to do many times, her understanding of the
political value of civic entertainments. Pageants are not insubstantial, especially when royal patronage joins with royal
presence to lift the art and exalt the triumph.[11]

THREE

Patronage of Dramatists

ప

The Case of Thomas Heywood

Werner Gundersheimer, writing on the subject of Renaissance patronage, asks whether Shakespeare's awareness of how the political and social order of European society was reflected in the system of patronage may have "led him to prefer the support of the London crowds to that of a single *patronus*[.] If so, we may view his career less as a product of, than as a departure from and perhaps a challenge to, the traditional relationships that define patronage in the Renaissance."[1] I do not think that Shakespeare's dramatic career represents any kind of challenge to the system of Renaissance patronage; instead, I think that the terms had changed through the natural process of the building of permanent theater buildings and the establishment of secure acting companies. After all, the group with which Shakespeare worked was first known as the Lord Chamberlain's Men and then triumphantly in 1603 as the King's Men, servants of the royal household. In many ways, one might argue, this situation reflects precisely the system of patronage well-established in Renaissance societies.

In what follows I want to touch on some of the major groups that served as patrons of English drama and then move to the case of Thomas Heywood in the 1630s, the last full decade of dramatic activity before the theaters were closed in 1642 by an Act of Parliament, led by Puritan forces. One should first acknowledge theater-going, paying audiences as major patrons of drama — the "London crowds" that Gundersheimer refers to. Numbers vary, depending on the time, but fairly reliable estimates suggest that 25,000 to 30,000 Londoners went to the theater in a given week at the peak of theatrical activity. Even allowing for slight exaggeration, we nevertheless know that the crowds had to go regularly in order to keep the several theaters operating. In a sense such audiences freed dramatists and actors from dependence on a single patron. That is certainly true — but not the whole story.

With the advent of theater buildings, dramatists became beneficiaries of the support of thousands of people; and for several decades that system worked well, making it possible for the first time in English history to be a professional theater person — that is, one who made a living in the theater. More difficult to ascertain is how much these audiences influenced what dramatists and acting companies served up to them; that is, how directly did such patronage affect the art produced? Did dramatists try to create taste among such a large group of patrons, or did they often follow the path of least resistance and offer sure-fire dramas destined to please the audience? We can probably answer both questions with "yes." Paying audiences may be the most obvious source of patronage of drama; but as we move along the list of possible patrons, matters get more complicated.

The court supported drama in various ways, from Elizabeth's royal patent to Leicester's Men in 1574 to James's placing all

acting companies under royal patronage in 1603. Such actions
by the sovereign offered one of the vital ingredients of patronage: protection. Such protection solidified the position of
acting companies against ongoing attacks by Puritans and
others. Only a vulnerable kingship under Charles I led to
Puritan triumph in Parliament. Glynne Wickham suggests
in one of his volumes of *Early English Stages* that the royal
protection of James was the ultimate form of censorship.[2] Perhaps, but I know of no evidence that truly bears out that assertion. Obviously any system of patronage could lead to the
abuse of censorship, but that does not mean that it in fact did.
James seems not to have interfered with or censured dramatic
productions more than Elizabeth did. It was, after all, the function of the Master of the Revels to keep a wary eye on all dramatic activities.

In addition to protection, the court offered something
equally valuable: money. Court performances added handsomely to the coffers of acting companies. The typical payment for a performance at court was £10, at least in the early
seventeenth century. Based on records in Chambers's *Elizabethan Stage*, I calculate that the King's Men between 1603
and 1613 earned slightly over £1277 from the court — that is,
nearly the amount of money that it took to rebuild the burned
Globe Theatre in 1614.[3] The Court not only paid for performances; it also paid the King's Men for not being able to per-
form in public because of the plague. At least three payments
made during the 1603–1613 period helped sustain the company when it could earn no income from public audiences, as
in the payment in February 1610 of £30 to John Heminges
"for himselfe and the reste of his companie being restrayned
from publique playinge w[th]in the citie of London in the tyme
of infeccon duringe the space of sixe weekes in which tyme
they practised pryvately for his ma[tes] service."[4] I can think
of no more compelling evidence of patronage than such a

payment: the court made up for lost income. The King's Men had much reason to be grateful that they were servants of the royal household: the Court protected and paid.

The 12 principal trade and craft guilds of London provided dramatists with employment and substantial pay for writing and producing Lord Mayor's Shows, one of the primary forms of civic pageants, designed to honor the new mayor on the occasion of his inauguration. Many other kinds of artists, such as painters, musicians, and even some well-known actors, also benefitted from the patronage of the guilds. Guild sponsorship of drama goes back at least to the fourteenth century and the beginnings of the great Corpus Christi drama, and extends unbroken through the seventeenth century. The guilds' financial support of drama remains a subject as yet inadequately treated. Because of records from places like York, Chester, and others, we know much about the financial arrangements between guild (patron) and dramatist (artist) in the period from the late fourteenth century through the sixteenth. London guild records offer a rather full account of payments and preparations for civic pageants, starting with the Midsummer Shows of the sixteenth century, eventually the annual Lord Mayor's Show in the middle of that century, and continuing until theater activities ceased in 1642. One could safely argue that patronage by the guilds reached a wider array of artists than did that of the court. In any case, dramatists and actors did not depend on a paying audience in theater buildings; they benefitted from the largesse of the court and the London guilds.

Typically, the dramatist appeared before a committee of the guild and presented a plan for the pageant. If accepted, the dramatist might then be in charge of a wide range of duties, sometimes including seeing that the text of the pageant got printed. On occasion the artist and the guild disagreed about the value of the services rendered. A few examples will suffice. The first Lord Mayor's Show of the Jacobean period occurred in 1604, the previous year's having been cancelled because of the plague. Although no text survives, details of expenditures from the Haberdashers's Guild accounts exist. Here we learn that Ben Jonson wrote the pageant and received £12 "for his device, and speech for the Children."[5] Anthony Munday received £2 "for his paines" — presumably a sketch for the pageant that lost out to Jonson in Jonson's only excursion into Lord Mayor's Shows. From this moment, Jonson moved into court entertainment, principally the masque, and Munday produced several civic pageants, starting with the 1605 Lord Mayor's Show. With the 1609 pageant Munday received payment of £20 (77). But the records also show considerable disagreement between Munday and the Ironmongers Guild over the quality of the pageant, the guild refusing his request for an additional £5 (77).

In the 1613 pageant, *The Triumphs of Truth*, the most costly of the mayoral shows, Thomas Middleton and Munday both received generous payments. Munday received £149 "for the devyse of the Pageant and other shewes, and for the appareling & fynding of all the personages in the sayd shewes (excepting the Pageant) and also for the Portage and Carryage both by land and by water" (87). Middleton got £40 "for the ordering overseeing and wryting of the whole Devyse & alsoe for the appareling the personage in the Pageant" (87). In 1617 the Grocers again chose Middleton to write the pageant; but both Munday and Thomas Dekker received payments for their "paines": Munday £5 and Dekker £4. Even if one lost in the competition, the pay from the guild was attractive. The records of Philip Henslowe show that dramatists received somewhere between £3 to £5 for their plays at the end of the sixteenth century. Thomas Dekker received a total of £8 for *Old Fortunatus* in 1599, the payments coming in four installments.[6] Thus in the 1617 pageant Munday and Dekker received as much as many of their counterparts in the regular theater for full-scale plays. If one asks why so many of the major dramatists of the period wrote Lord Mayor's Shows, a ready answer is the attraction of money. The examples cited here could be multiplied many times; but the point remains: the guilds served effectively as patrons of drama, offering lucrative employment to dramatists and others associated with mounting these increasingly complex theatrical spectacles in the streets of London.

A relatively large number of noblemen or wealthy citizens who in various ways supported drama forms the final major group of drama's patrons that I want to single out. In the Elizabethan period noblemen served as sponsors of the acting companies: the Earl of Leicester's company, for example, received the first royal patent in 1574. The precise relationship between noble patron and the actors can often be difficult to determine, but we do know that protection provided by the noblemen became necessary. As I have pointed out elsewhere, at least 14 women can be designated as patrons of drama, determined on the basis of dedications of dramatic texts to them.[7] Shakespeare's fellow actors gathered the play texts for the great Folio edition of 1623; and they chose to dedicate the volume to William Herbert, Earl of Pembroke, and his brother Philip, Earl of Montgomery. William was Lord Chamberlain in 1623, and Philip would shortly succeed him. The dedication makes clear their interest in and support of Shakespeare. William Herbert, we may recall, gave Jonson an annual stipend for books; and Jonson dedicated *Catiline* (1611) to him.

Text dedications provide one of the principal means for understanding patronage of drama by noblemen. Out of roughly 600 dramatic texts printed from Elizabeth's reign to 1642, some 200 contain dedications, the number of such dedications doubling with each successive reign. Dedications single out, for example, the earls of Hertford, Somerset, Dorset, Rutland, Middlesex, Holland, Carnarvan and Peterborough, as well as Pembroke and Montgomery. This partial list reflects the status and support that the dramatists sought.[8] Even allowing for the sometimes formulaic nature of the dedications and granting that sometimes the dramatist clearly did not know the patron, I find impressive the number of noblemen sought out for recognition or gratitude. In a time of well-established traditions of paying audiences and solid court support, dramatists nevertheless reach out to another group, the nobility, for patronage. Instead of ending such a practice when James put all companies under royal patronage, dramatists increasingly sought noble patrons, at least on the basis of text dedications; only occasionally did they seek money. Rather, dramatists probably desired status and legitimacy for their texts and themselves. With increasing numbers of play texts being printed, dramatists desired a status for them as literature. Having a noble dedicatee seems part of that pattern.

Having briefly examined paying audiences, the court, the guilds, and noblemen as patrons of drama, I turn finally to Thomas Heywood, and specifically to his drama of the 1630s. Here we will find evidence of all these groups, especially the guilds and noblemen. Heywood's career in the theater spanned 50 years, from 1590 to 1640; in several ways his career, more diverse than, say, Shakespeare's, included a wide variety of dramatic forms and various acting companies. With performances in the 1630s, Heywood obviously received support from audiences. His play *Love's Mistress* had court performances, being first performed at court in 1634 to celebrate the king's birthday. Thus Heywood benefitted from these groups of patrons. Although enjoying the monetary rewards of theatergoing audiences, Heywood, like other dramatists, did not overlook other sources of patronage; dramatists thus did not radically depart from systems of patronage seen elsewhere in Renaissance societies.

In the 1630s Heywood wrote seven Lord Mayor's Shows, his only excursion into this form of civic pageantry. Guild records again reveal something about the negotiation between the dramatist and the guild committees. Heywood and his artificer Gerard Christmas typically submitted joint proposals for the pageants. Payment of £200 for the 1631 show, *Londons Ius Honorarium*, comes in fact to Christmas with no separate entry for Heywood. Presumably Christmas paid Heywood some portion of this handsome sum. In 1635, Heywood collaborated with John Christmas, Gerard's son, to underbid the team of John Taylor and Robert Norman who had insisted on a payment of £190. But Heywood and Christmas submitted a proposal for the pageant to the Ironmongers with a price tag of £180. So the negotiations went throughout the 1630s. The guilds provided lucrative incomes to dramatists and others involved in staging these pageants. Unfortunately, the guild records do not clearly show exactly what Heywood earned. One infers that it sufficed to keep him eager to have his projects accepted.[9]

If the records do not specify Heywood's income, his pageant texts nevertheless do reveal much about his dealings with the guilds, offering a useful perspective on how one dramatist dealt with his patron. For example, in the 1631 text, Heywood praises the guild members for understanding what he proposed. He informs us that he appeared before the Masters, Wardens, and committees of the Haberdashers and made his proposal. In 1633 Heywood negotiated with the Clothworkers. In describing the working arrangement, Heywood commends the committee's "affability and courtesie, especially unto my selfe being at that time to them all a meere stranger, who when I read my (then unperfect) Papers, were as able to judge them, as attentively to heare them" (64–65). Because the guild had its own reputation to think about, as Heywood notes, they were inclined to be generous in expenditure and concerned about the dramatist's conception of the pageant. Apparently Heywood appeared before his prospective patrons with a sketch or outline (his "unperfect" papers); they heard him out and then decided to employ him for the mayoral pageant. In Heywood's pageant texts one catches a glimpse of the workaday world of a dramatist trying to sell his wares, secure a patron, and survive financially.

In the 1630s Heywood also sought the patronage of citizens and noblemen, although again it is impossible to know the precise form that such patronage may have taken. Six of Heywood's plays contain dedications to patrons. *Fair Maid of the West*, part 2 (1631), *The Iron Age*, part 1 (1632), and Heywood's additions to Marlowe's *Jew of Malta* (1633) have dedications to his friend Thomas Hammond of Gray's Inn. Heywood claims that *Fair Maid* has passed muster with everyone, including Charles I and his queen Henrietta Maria. He suggests that Hammond is willing to pay for the pleasure of this drama, unlike those whom Juvenal complains about, who want to enjoy but do not want to pay.[10] In a prefatory epistle to the *Jew of Malta*, Heywood writes of Hammond: "Sir, you have been pleased to grace some of mine owne workes with your curteous patronage; I hope this will not be the worse accepted; . . . none can clayme more power or priuiledge than your self [over me]."[11] Similar ideas also prevail in *The Iron Age*. The implication seems fairly clear that Heywood may have received financial support from Hammond.

Heywood dedicates part 2 of *The Iron Age* to Thomas Mainwaring. Interestingly, Heywood comments on Mainwaring's presumed enjoyment of the play: "I much deceiue myselfe, if I heard you not once commend it, when you saw it Acted; if you persist in the same opinion, when you shall spare some sorted houres to heare it read, in your paynes, I shal hold my selfe much pleased."[12] Unlike the situation of patronage from guilds, this search for support comes after performances and focuses instead on publication of the play text as a book. The dedication of *The English Traveller* (1633) to Sir Henry Appleton includes recognition of apparently close family ties between the Heywoods and Appletons. Heywood writes: "Neither Sir, neede you thinke it any vnderualuing of your worth, to vndertake the patronage of a Poem in this nature, since the like hath beene done by Roman *Laelius, Scipio, Macaenas*, and many other mighty Princes and Captaines, Nay, euen by *Augustus Caesar* himselfe.[13]

This conscious reference to earlier patterns of patronage puts Heywood squarely in line with well-established systems of patronage: the argument hinges on precedence. This point Heywood pursues in the dedication of *Love's Mistresse* (1636) to Edward Sackville, Earl of Dorset and Lord Chamberlain. Heywood begins by noting the favorable reaction that this play has enjoyed at court: "It having pleased Her Most Excellent Majestie to grace this (though unworthy) Poem so often with her Royal presence, I was imboldened the rather (though I dare not commend) yet to commit it to your Noble Patronage" (*Heywood*, 5:83). Having cited precedents for such patronage, Heywood concludes: "If your Honor shall dayne the acceptance of a playne mans love, an obseruance in this Presentment, as you grace the worke, so you shall much incourage the Author" (84). Sackville, who had received dedications of other literary works from Camden, Davenant, Drayton, and Southwell, certainly represents an ambitious target for patronage. As Lord Chamberlain, Sackville presumably helped to get the play performed in the first place.

The nobleman who seemed to have the most to do with the final decade of Heywood's career was Henry Carey, Earl of Dover. Carey was the grandson of Elizabeth's Lord Chamberlain, made Baron of Hunsdon in 1619 and finally Earl of Dover in 1628. By 1641, he became Speaker of the House of Lords. Several writers, including Henry Peacham, dedicated books to Carey; Heywood dedicated *Englands Elizabeth* (1631) and *Pleasant Dialogues and Drammas* (1637) to him. The latter includes additional evidence of Heywood's connection to the Earl.

In dedicating *Englands Elizabeth* to the Earl, Heywood makes special mention of the earl's grandfather, "the most constant Friend and faithful Assistant in all her [Elizabeth's] troubles and dangers."[14] Heywood follows this statement with an exposition of the Lord Chamberlain's service. He says of the Earl of Dover: "It hath pleased your Lordship to censure fauourably of some of my weak labours not long since presented before you, which the rather encouraged mee, to make a free tender of this small peece of service" (sigs. A7v–A8). And he closes: "wishing to you and to all your Noble Family, not onely the long fruition of the blessings of this life present; but the eternal possession of the Ioyes future" (sig. A8v). Obviously some kind of knowledge of patron and artist precedes this 1631 publication, for this dedication seems both a statement of gratitude for past support and a plea for future patronage.

That curious collection entitled *Pleasant Dialogues and Drammas* (1637) contains a dedication to Henry Carey, an anagram on his name, and speeches spoken in his honor on the occasion of dramatic performances—including a masque. These items give ample testimony to Heywood's desire for patronage from the Earl. Heywood describes his collection as he dedicates the text to Carey: *"This is a small Cabinent of many and choyse, of which none better than your Noble selfe can judge, some of them* [the items] *borrowing their luster from your own vertues, vouchsafe therefore (great lord) their perusal, being devoted to your sole patronage, whilst the presenter wishing unto you and all yours, a long fruition of terrestriall graces."*[15] By 1637 Heywood enjoyed a well-established relationship with this patron. One may therefore readily understand the theme of the anagram on Carey's name: "Ever raigne rich . . . / . . . in your blest posterity / You shall raigne rich" (264). This serviceable if undistinguished verse nevertheless makes its point: indebtedness to Carey and hope for future patronage.

Heywood also wrote prologues and epilogues to the performances of plays at the Earl of Dover's home in Broadstreet in London. One assumes that these took place sometime in the mid-1630s. Thus Heywood not only dedicates books to his patron; he also offers entertainment for some kind of dramatic performances. The first included in *Pleasant Dialogues* is a Prologue and Epilogue spoken at a play performed in the Christmas season, perhaps 1635. Hospitality speaks, "*a frollick old fellow: A Coller of Brawne in one hand, and a deepe Bowle of Muscadel in the other*" (242). He complains about the decline of entertainment; fortunately, the earl's household welcomes all with generous society. Hospitality says: "But harke, a Cock crowd, and I heard a Swan / Ecchoing to him, that here did live a man, / Noble, and of that high and ancient straine, / To call back *Hospitality* againe" (243). The Swan, Heywood notes, forms part of the earl's heraldry, and the Cock, the countess's. The Epilogue also describes the household as one where "hospitality hath grace."

Similar themes pervade the Prologue and Epilogue, given at a dramatic performance at the Earl of Dover's London house on Candelmas night in an unspecified year. The speaker refers to the auspicious union of the Earl and Countess, and praises them:

> In this blest state both of you, and yours, now stand
> As first dispos'd, so strengthened by that hand
> Which as it makes, protects; you have begun
> To grace the City with your presence: run
> That happy course still: you and your lov'd wife
> Have to dead hospitality given new life. (244)

The Epilogue wishes that countless blessings "and the Courts best grace, / Attend the great Lord of this place." Doubtless Heywood hopes that the earl's bounty may extend to him, as presumably it already has.

For Henry Carey, Heywood on New Year's Day, probably 1637, prepared a masque, a fragment of which remains. This was Heywood's only attempt at this, another dramatic form. Given the speeches that Heywood had already written for the earl and the dramatic performances, the preparation of a masque seems a logical extension. The performance took place at the earl's house at Hunsdon; and the masque itself, we infer, contained the nine Muses. Once more alluding to the heraldry of the earl and countess, Heywood makes much of the swan and cock. The speaker says: "Long may your bounty last, and we rejoyce, / To heare both City and the Country voyce / Your hospitality" (246). The figure Truth actually presents the masquers in a speech filled with mythological allusions. This fragmentary masque illustrates another way in which Heywood sought to serve his patron, Henry Carey.

The case of Thomas Heywood in the 1630s makes clear that systems of patronage, familiar in the Renaissance, remained intact; they had not been set aside by a paying theater-going audience. Rather, here in the last decade before theatrical activity ceased, we find a dramatist reaching out to all the principal groups of patrons for support. Heywood's relationship with Henry Carey, Earl of Dover, intensifies, giving striking evidence of at least this dramatist's desire for noble patronage. Heywood's situation is not unique. Instead of radical departure from systems of patronage, the dramatists represent an expansion of those systems, so that even with theaters established and flourishing, and with occasional support from the court or guilds, dramatists nevertheless seek and secure the patronage of noblemen, the oldest pattern of patronage.

FOUR

Women as Patrons of English Renaissance Drama

In the attempts to reassess the position of English women in the society of late Tudor and early Stuart times no one, to my knowledge, has looked very closely at their relationship to one of the most popular endeavors: namely, the theater. We know, of course, that the theater did not allow women as actors on the regular stage; and yet they performed frequently in other dramatic entertainments, principally masques. Several writers have detected a decline in the status of women after the death of Elizabeth and the advent of the antifeminist Jacobean court, but I do not think that the issue is that simple.[1] Indeed, two essays find evidence of "modern feminism" and the development of "women's rights movements" in the literature.[2]

Somewhere between these two opposing arguments lies the truth. Clearly James did not care much for women, but women maintained positions of prominence at Court and in the arts nevertheless. And curiously, Puritanism contributed to the supposed emergent feminism — an argument that has been advanced by Juliet Dusinbere.[3] As Dusinbere observes, "The drama from 1590 to 1625 is feminist in sympathy" (5), true not only of Shakespeare but of almost all his contemporaries. Nor does the status of women diminish appreciably with the death of Elizabeth; I would argue, in fact, that a significant index exists of the importance of women for the drama, not as actors in plays — for that is another subject — but rather as sponsors and patrons of theatrical activity.[4]

We find a number of obvious ways in which women impinge on English drama of the Renaissance. Clearly they constituted a large part of the audience, whether in the public theaters or at private performances, and we have from one an eyewitness account of theatrical events. The Lady Anne Clifford kept a diary, revealing much about her intellectual life — her reading of Montaigne, Chaucer, Spenser, the *Arcadia*, Ovid, Augustine — and her social life, including her attendance at dramatic performances.[5] She attended several masques, saw Fletcher's *The Mad Lover* in 1617, and noted the burning of the Banqueting House at Whitehall in January 1619.

Women could also sponsor theatrical events. When Queen Elizabeth journeyed on progress in 1592, the dowager Lady Russell, widow of Francis Russell, second Earl of Bedford, acted as hostess for Elizabeth's stop at Bisham in August. She provided dramatic entertainment of a typical sort, common to many progress shows for the queen.[6] Pastoral figures, such as Pan and Ceres, welcoming and praising the sovereign, dominated the brief pageant entertainment. As one scholar has noted: "Lady Russell had invited all the wit, the talent, and distinction, which she could convene, for the entertainment of her royal mistress, who prolonged her stay at Bisham several days."[7]

Even women dramatists appear, though we have no evidence of performance of their plays or of the intention to have them performed. Mary Herbert, Philip Sidney's sister and a translator and writer of some skill, produced a brief pastoral dialogue, *Thenot and Piers in Praise of Astraea* (1592), and *Antonie* (1592), a translation of Robert Garnier's French play. And *Mariam, the Fair Queen of Jewry* (1613 text, written 1602–05) by Elizabeth Cary (wife of Henry Cary, Viscount Falkland) has the distinction of being the only extant play written by a woman in this era that was not a translation. Proficient in several languages, Elizabeth Cary made a number of translations, primarily of religious writings, but also of the epistles of Seneca.[8]

Though they never appeared on the public theater stage, women did appear regularly in private performances of masques, not only joining in the final dances but also impersonating some of the symbolic and mythological figures in the masque proper. The list of masque "actresses," as impressive as it is long, contains some 46 in Jonson's masques alone, starting with Queen Anne and, later, Queen Henrietta Maria, and including Lady Anne Clifford and others.[9] A perplexing comment in Jonson's *Conversations* suggests that perhaps he planned to use women in a pastoral play of some sort:

> [H]e heth a Pastorall jntitled the May Lord, his own name is Alkin Ethra the Countess of Bedfoords Mogibell overberry, the old Countesse of Suffolk ane jnchanteress other names are given to somersets Lady, Pemb[r]ook the Countess of Rutland, Lady Wroth.[10]

Henrietta Maria provoked controversy because of her theatrical activities. She encouraged plays and masques at Court, and she often performed in the masques. In February 1626, she and her ladies performed a French pastoral at Court, "at which there was some murmuring":[11] Racan's *Artenice*. "Queen Henrietta's speaking like a common player in the first part of her performance and the masculine dress of some of

the ladies . . . raised the eyebrows."[12] In January 1633, after
months of preparation and rehearsal, the queen performed
in Walter Montagu's pastoral, *The Shepherd's Paradise*.[13]
This stirred William Prynne's blood and pen, leading to his
Histrio-Mastix and thus to his prosecution. Tradition and
the Puritans notwithstanding, one could have seen women
performing in dramatic shows.

During the period from the accession of Elizabeth to the
closing of the theaters, patronage of the drama took several
forms, beginning with the crucially important sponsorship of
the Court itself. The Court remained the single most significant institution for the support of drama, including within its
bureaucracy a Master of the Revels, and ultimately, in the
reign of King James, placing all the principal acting companies under royal patronage. City governments and trade guilds
were also active, producing and financing civic pageants, such
as royal entries and Lord Mayor's shows. The Inns of Court
made their contribution by sponsoring drama and preparing
masques for special occasions. With the advent of public
theater buildings in the latter part of the sixteenth century a
new group of patrons emerged: namely, the paying, theater-
going audience. What this meant to the flourishing of drama
becomes simply incalculable: it created a class of professional
dramatists and actors, able to earn their living exclusively from
theatrical endeavors. The final major group of theater patrons
comprised a diverse and wide-ranging collection of noblemen
and courtiers, including women, who served, like Leicester
and the Lord Chamberlain, as sponsors of acting companies
or caused certain dramatic shows to take place. Though they
lost some of their prominence when James took over the
companies, such aristocrats nevertheless remained important
in both direct and indirect ways by their continued patronage
of drama.

Recent scholarship has come a long way toward understanding the functioning of the early English theater. We can dis-
card the misleading and naive view of W. J. Lawrence, who

once claimed: "In those days all writing done for pay was looked upon as soiled in the process, and unworthy of patronage."[14] Such a simplistic approach Virgil Heltzel countered more than half a century ago in his essay, "The Dedication of Tudor and Stuart Plays."[15] But Heltzel had his own excesses, as when he claimed that "during the entire reign of Queen Elizabeth and for some years after, the ordinary stage play was not thought worthy of patronal favor and none was dedicated" (74). Heltzel thought 1613 a kind of turning point, after which dedications of regular drama increased. But before then Jonson had dedicated *Volpone* (1607) to the universities, *Catiline* (1611) to William Herbert, *The Alchemist* (1612) to Mary Wroth, and special issues of *Cynthia's Revels* (1601) to Camden and the Countess of Bedford, while Chapman had dedicated the *Tragedy of Byron* (1608) to Walsingham and *The Widow's Tears* (1612) to John Reed, to cite the most obvious examples. And neither Lawrence nor Heltzel called attention to the number of women as dedicatees of the dramatic texts. By a study of such dedications we can gain some understanding of the nature of women's significance as patrons.[16]

Why did some dramatists dedicate their plays to women? The answers remain problematic. If we expect in each case to pinpoint some deed, some beneficence, that led the dramatist in gratitude to dedicate his play to a particular woman, we shall be both frustrated and disappointed. But obviously writing a play and dedicating it to a patroness in hope of some immediate financial reward does not seem to have ranked very high on the list of purposes. Several other themes run through the dedications. In some instances the dramatist wished to become known to the woman, with the implied expectation of some benefit. But many dramatists simply sought recognition, hoping that the patroness's name would lend a kind of luster to their effort. Some writers acknowledged previous benefits from the patroness. Others used the dramatic text as the occasion to celebrate an event or to celebrate and honor the woman. In those cases where the woman was herself a writer, the dedication became a means of tribute to a fellow writer also serving the muses. And some dedications seem to exist in order to provide the writer, either the dramatist or his publisher, the opportunity to defend drama, either in the particular or in the abstract. These ideas and purposes will become apparent as we turn to a study of the women singled out as patrons of drama.

The 14 women that I have identified as patrons of drama — that is, as recipients of dramatic dedications — range from the well known to the relatively obscure. To determine the circumstances that might have led to the dedication or the context for it remains vexing. Four of the women share a dedicatory statement with someone else. The 1591 revision by Robert Wilmot of *Tancred and Gismund*, for example, praises Mary, Lady Petre (wife of John, Baron Peter) and Anne, Lady Gray (wife of Baron Gray of Groby) for their rare virtues as noted by many people "(which are not a fewe in Essex)."[17] Wilmot wishes to be known to them and has "deuised this waie . . . to procure the same." He says, "I shall humblie desire ye to bestow a fauourable countenance vpon this little labor, which when ye haue graced it withall, I must & will acknowledge my selfe greatly indebted vnto your Ladyships." Calling them a "worthy pair," Middleton dedicates his *The World Tossed at Tennis* (1620) to Mary Howard and her husband Charles, Baron of Effingham. Obviously these are Middleton's friends, and he offers this drama to them to celebrate their wedding: "Being then an entertainment for the best — / Your noble nuptials comes to celebrate."[18] John Ford hopes that Mary and John Wyrley will look with favor on *The Lady's Trial* (1639), which he offers "to the mercy of your *Iudgements*: and shall rate *It* at a higher value . . . if you onely allow *It* the favour of *Adoption*."[19] In these brief examples one observes three different motivations for the dedications: to become known to the patron, to honor a special event, and to have the play received favorably.

Bridget Radcliffe, the Countess of Sussex, receives Thomas Kyd's adulation in the dedication to his translation of Garnier's *Cornelia* (1594), in what seems a rather blatant appeal for reward. Though Kyd first modestly refers to his work as "rough, vnpollished," he warms to the task and finally declares: "A fitter present for a Patronesse . . . I could not finde."[20] He knows of the countess's "noble and heroick dispositions" and her "honourable fauours past (though neyther making needles glozes of the one, nor spoyling paper with the others Pharisaical embroiderie)," and he thus presumes upon her "true conceit and entertainement of these small endeuours, that thus I purposed to make known my memory of you and them to be immortall." Whether the countess rewarded Kyd is uncertain, but she became the dedicatee of other literary works, including Greene's *Philomela*.[21]

Philip Massinger cites the precedent of Italy, where women have granted patronage and protection to writers (though he need not have looked across the waters), as justification for sending his play *The Duke of Milan* (1623) to Katherine Stanhope (wife of Philip Lord Stanhope, eventually Earl of Chesterfield). He leaves these "weake, and imperfect labours, at the altar of your fauour" because "there is no other meanes left mee (my misfortunes hauing cast me on this course)" than to let the world know "that I am ever your Ladyships creature."[22] Lady Katherine also received dedications of a few other works, primarily religious writings, all after Massinger's desperate plea for assistance.

Though we know little of Samuel Brandon, the author of *Virtuous Octavia* (1598), he seems to have been acquainted with Lady Lucy Audley (Audelay), wife of George, first Earl of Castlehaven, to whom he dedicated this play. He proclaims her "Rare Phoenix" and "Rich treasurer, of heauens best treasuries."[23] And he closes: "These lines, wherein, if ought be free from blame,/ Your noble *Genius* taught my Pen the same."

Certainly Ben Jonson knew Mary Wroth, to whom he addressed three poems, *Epigrammes* ciii and cv and *Under-wood* xxx, and his play *The Alchemist* (1612). Mary Wroth, a niece of Philip Sidney and wife of Sir Robert Wroth, characterized by Jonson to Drummond as "unworthily married on a jealous husband,"[24] and praised by a number of writers, including Chapman in his translation of the *Iliad*, also performed in Jonson's *Masque of Blackness*. Not surprisingly, then, Jonson dedicates one of his finest dramas to her, praising her value, uncommon "in these times."[25] And Jonson's relatively brief statement provides him the occasion to glance at those who indulge in fulsome praise: "But this, safe in your iudgement (which is a SIDNEYS) is forbidden to speake more; least it talke, or looke like one of the ambitious Faces of the time: who, the more they paint, are the lesse themselues." Intentionally or not, Jonson draws a link between the dedication and the play proper, whose character *Face*, essential in the grand con game of alchemy, takes on many guises, each one making him less himself. Jonson's satiric bent, which has full rein in the play, surfaces in the dedication to the patroness. We note that *Epigramme* ciii emphasizes Mary Wroth's Sidney connection and *Epigramme* cv finds in her "all treasure lost of th'age before," both themes in *The Alchemist*, suggesting that they may all have been written about the same time.

In the final decade before the theaters close, Joseph Rutter, who according to Bentley became a disciple of Jonson in his old age, celebrates the virtues of Lady Theophilia Cooke (Coke) in the translation of the second part of *The Cid* (1640). He recalls a conversation and wishes that the French author of the play (Corneille) had her wisdom; he offers the play to her patronage "lest I be thought indiscreet in placing it else-where, or unmindfull of what I owe you, though this be the least part of that returne which is meant to you."[26] In 1635 Lady Theophilia had three other works dedicated to her. Reflecting apparent long experience with the Willoughby family, William Sampson selects Ann to be patroness for his *The Vow Breaker* (1636): "it properly prostrates it selfe to you, for a patronesse."[27] He praises her "Candor, beauty, goodnes, and vertues: against those foule mouthd detractors, who . . . sought to villifie an unblaunchd Laune, a vestall puritie, a truth like Innocence." In part Sampson is responding to his critics, "ignorant Censurers (those Critticall Momes that have no language but satirrick Calumnie)." But he closes with a wish for Ann Willoughby: "continue ever in that noble pedigree of vertues, . . . heaven keepe you from faunning parasites, and busie gossips, and send you a Husband, and a good one." (She eventually married Thomas Aston.)

A personal relationship in these cases makes the women a natural choice for patronage of the drama. The dramatist James Shirley more explicitly than others confronts the issue of selecting a patroness instead of a patron. In the dedication of *Changes, or Love in a Maze* (1632) to Dorothy Shirley (no relation) he acknowledges "custom, that to men/ Such poems are presented; but my pen/ Is not engag'd, nor can allow too far/ A Salic law in poetry, to bar/ Ladies th'inheritance of wit."[28] But, as the evidence shows, by 1632 singling out women as dedicatees of drama, if not commonplace, was not uncommon.

Elizabeth Cary, referred to above as a dramatist, received the dedication for *The Workes of Mr. Iohn Marston* (1633); she gained recognition from the publisher of the volume, William Sheares. He uses the dedication as a means of defending drama and touting the virtues of the plays contained in the collection. He does not understand why plays "should appeare so vile and abominable, that they should bee so vehemently inveighed against."[29] The term "plays" provokes: "The name it seemes somewhat offends them, whereas if they were styled Workes, they might haue their Approbation also" (sig.

A3ᵛ). Hoping to have "pacified that precise Sect," Sheares has styled the collection *The Works of Mr. JOHN MARSTON*. He next praises Marston, "equall unto the best Poets of our times," as "free from all obscene speeches" and who is "himselfe an enemie to all such as stuffe their Scenes with ribaldry, and lard their lines with scurrilous taunts and jests" (sigs. A3ᵛ, A4). This defense makes one wonder if Sheares has read the plays carefully and observed the language of, for instance, *The Dutch Courtesan*. Because of Elizabeth Cary's status as a writer "well acquainted with the Muses," Sheares becomes "imboldened to present these Workes unto your Honours view" (sig. A4). Indeed, the report flatters Lady Elizabeth as "the Mirror of your sex, the admiration, not onely of this Iland, but of all adjacent Countries and Dominions, which are acquainted with your rare Vertues, and Endowments" (sig. A4ᵛ). Sheares does not seem to speak from personal knowledge of Cary; and can we suppose that he knew that she had become a Catholic? It is difficult to see how such a dedicatee would quieten the "precise Sect." In any event, he obviously thought her reputation sufficient to enhance his publishing venture. She had, after all, been the dedicatee of several other works, beginning with Drayton's *Englands Heroicall Epistles* (1597).

The final two women patrons of drama are the best known: the Countess of Bedford and the Countess of Pembroke. Lucy Russell, wife of Edward, third Earl of Bedford, received more dedications than any other woman associated with the drama; these dedications, coming from such writers as Daniel, Davies, Drayton, Florio, Chapman, and Jonson, range over a 44 year period, 1583 to 1627, suggesting her continuing prominence and importance for writers. The fortunes of John Donne also closely intersected with those of the countess.[30] Hers is an explicit case of reward and support to a number of writers. With regard to the drama, she particularly supported Jonson and Daniel.

Because of her prominence at Court and her influence with

Queen Anne, the countess doubtless paved the way for Jonson's masques. She herself performed in *The Masque of Blackness, Masque of Beauty, Hymenaei*, and *The Masque of Queens;* "she organized *Lovers Made Men* for Lord Hay in 1617."[31] In a special issue of *Cynthia's Revels* (1601), Jonson included an address praising the countess. Because it is brief and not often reprinted, I quote the entire dedication, entitled "Author *ad Librum*," found in the copy in the William Andrews Clark Library, Los Angeles:

> Goe little Booke, Goe little *Fable*
>   vnto the bright, and amiable
> *LVCY* of *BEDFORD;* she, that Bounty
>   appropriates still vnto that *Country;*
> Tell her, his *Muse* that did inuent thee
>   to *CYNTHIAS* fayrest *Nymph* hath sent thee,
> And sworne, that he will quite discard thee
>   if any way she do rewards thee
> But with a *Kisse*. (if thou canst dare it)
>   of her white Hand; or she can spare it.

One can be reasonably sure that Jonson hoped for and indeed received more than a simple kiss for his dramatic text. *Epigrammes* lxxvi, lxxxiv, and xciv also celebrate Lucy Russell.

In jail for his part in *Eastward Ho*, Jonson apparently wrote a letter to the countess, or at least so his modern editors, Herford and Simpson, conjecture. He begs for help: "if it be not a sinne to prophane yor free hand with prison polluted Paper, I wolde intreate some little of your Ayde, to the defence of my Innocence."[32] Jonson marvels that he is in jail: "our offence a Play, so mistaken, so misconstrued, so misapplied, as I do wonder whether their Ignorance, or Impudence be most, who are our adversaries." He closes with the implied request for help: "What our sute is, the worthy employde soliciter, and equall Adorer of youre vertues, can best enforme you" (1:198). Whether the addressee was indeed the Countess of Bedford, which seems most plausible, and

whether she assisted, we do not know; but Jonson gained release from prison, and surely such influential friends as the
countess could only help his case. We may have here, in fact,
an unusually effective instance of patronage, in which the patroness aids the cause of drama by helping gain the release of
the dramatist from prison. But then, implicit in the role of
patron resides the task of protector.

The Countess of Bedford helped Samuel Daniel consid-
erably. She, "who had charge of the Queen's masque for the
first Christmas of the new reign, recommended Daniel to the
Queen";[33] and this led to Daniel's *The Vision of the Twelve
Goddesses*, performed on 8 January 1604 at Hampton Court
and dedicated to the countess. Daniel presented his pastoral
The Queen's Arcadia before the queen and the countess at
Christ Church, Oxford in August 1605. "He long continued
to profit by Lady Bedford's introduction to the Queen, for she
appointed him together with John Florio, to be a Groom of
her Privy Chamber."[34]

In the authorized text of the masque, Daniel offers a statement of 210 lines, certainly the longest dedication of a dramatic text. He provides a lengthy account of "the intent and
scope of the project," describing all the mythological figures,
their iconography and function, and thereby greatly enhances
the understanding of the masque. Rather than get involved
in the complex and sometimes contradictory iconological interpretation of figures, Daniel says that "we took their aptest
representations that lay best and easiest for us."[35] He provides
this extended account because he does not want the experience to slip into oblivion, for "(by the unpartial opinion of all
the beholders, strangers and others) it was not inferior to the
best that ever was presented in Christendom" (30). And equally
important, the dedication offers the means whereby Daniel
"might clear the reckoning of any imputation that might be
laid upon your [the countess's] judgment for preferring such a
one to her Majesty in this employment" (30). Not only did

the countess make it possible for Daniel to write the masque; she also performed the role of Vesta in the entertainment.

Daniel's literary and dramatic fortunes intersect also the patronage of Mary Herbert, Countess of Pembroke, renowned for her support of writers. Pearl Hogrefe sums up Mary Herbert's contribution to literature: "She gave practical help and encouragement to many writers when she became the Countess of Pembroke and lived at Wilton House; she influenced the writing of her brother, Philip, during his brief life; she edited and published all his prose and his poetry after his death; she published her own translations from French and Italian and had an outstanding part in turning the Psalms into Elizabethan lyrics."[36] Understandably she received a number of dedications of literary works from such writers as Daniel, Spenser, Davies, Breton, Morley, and Fraunce.

The drama contains several acknowledgments of her patronage. Abraham Fraunce dedicates *Amyntas Pastoral* (1591) to the Countess, saying, "If *Amyntas* found fauour in your gracious eyes, let *Phillis* bee accepted for *Amyntas* sake."[37] Fraunce for the most part discusses and defends poetic form. If we may strain the point slightly and allow Sidney's *Arcadia* (1598 edition) as partially a dramatic text because it includes *The Lady of May*, a progress entertainment of 1578, then Sidney's dedication of the romance to his sister may be included. His moving statement credits her with being the inspiration for his work: "For my part, . . . I could well find in my heart, to cast out in some desert of forgetfulnes this child, which I am loth to father. But you desired me to do it, and your desire, to my heart is an absolute commandement. Now, it is done onely for you, onely to you."[38] Most of it, he says, he wrote in her presence. The chief protection for his work, Sidney writes, will be "bearing the liuerie of your name" (sig. ¶3ᵛ). In the most personal statement in any of the dedications examined here, Sidney closes: "And so . . . you will continue to loue the writer, who doth exceedingly loue you, and moste moste heartilie praies you may long liue, to be a principall ornament to the family of the *Sidneis.*" This is, of course, exactly what Mary Herbert did. She was no ordinary or conventional patron for her brother's work: she inspired it and brought it to light by editing and publishing it.

More typically, William Gager addresses the countess in his *Ulysses Redux* (1592). He does not know her personally: "*Nimis inverecunde facio, illustrissima Domina, qui tibi, ne de facie, vix de nomine, cognitus, literis tamen meis Celsitudinem tua[m] interpello*" (I am perhaps acting audaciously, most illustrious lady, who am known to you if not by appearance then at least by name, thus to intrude upon your ladyship with my writings).[39] But he decides to be audacious, has heard much about her, and has admired her brother and the whole family, "*totem etiam Sidneiorum gentem.*" Because of her extraordinary spirit and candor, he has sought some means to be known to her, "*vt aliqua tibi honesta ratione innotescerem*"; and nothing could be more honest than literature, "*ac praesertim poetica.*" Gager also recalls the indebtedness of many poets to her ("*debent Poete nostri*" [sig. A2]) and makes a valuable observation about patronage: it aids the giver as well as the recipient by providing glory. The dedication closes with Gager's wish that she will favorably receive his *Ulysses* and with confidence that she will: "*Quare peto a te, Nobilisima Comitissa, vt Vlysi, non in Ithacam, sed in scenam iam primum venienti, tanquam altera Penelope, saltem manum tuam exosculandam porrigere digneris. Quod te prestituram, plane confido.*" (Therefore, most noble Countess, I ask you to be another Penelope and deign at least to extend your hand to be kissed by Ulysses as he comes, not to Ithaca, but now for the first time onto the stage. And I have full confidence that you will do so [Sigs. A2V–A3]). Her expected act of favor Gager describes as "*humanitate.*"[40]

At the time that Gager wrote his academic dramas, the countess led a whole group of writers, including Kyd and Daniel, in translating Garnier's tragedies. Why Mary Herbert should have wished to make these French classical plays available in English remains unclear, but one can reasonably speculate that this program of translation and these particular dramas fit the ideas found in Philip Sidney's *Apologie*.[41] At any rate, the true course of English drama passed them by; theirs, as it turned out, represented a program of the past, not the future charted by Marlowe and Shakespeare.

Having already dedicated *Delia* and *Rosamond* to the countess, Daniel seemed a prime candidate for carrying the English Garnier banner and hewing to classical principles of dramatic construction. By 1594, Daniel had become "deeply immersed in the Wilton atmosphere and *Cleopatra* is Pembroke work in a much fuller sense than *Delia* and *Rosamond* are. Daniel is keenly aware that this verse drama marks a new and probably decisive stage in his literary career."[42] The play makes an excellent example of what the "Pembroke school" aimed at: "a shapely and complete artefact that could be fingered piece by piece and admired for its skill and polish."[43] How many other literary figures of this era self-consciously set out to shape the direction of dramatic form with a clear-set system of principles? The Countess of Pembroke became a patron of extraordinary quality, even if theater history may in retrospect see the effort as a failure.

In the dedicatory statement prefaced to *Cleopatra* (1594), Daniel touches on several issues as he directs his thanks and praise to the Countess. He begins with an acknowledgment of the countess's involvement with — and inspiration for — his translation:

> Loe heere the worke which she did impose,
> Who onely doth predominate my Muse:
> The starre of wonder, which my labours chose
> To guide their way in all the course I vse.
> Shee, whose cleere brightnes doth alone infuse
> Strength to my thoughts, and makes mee what I am;

> Call'd vp my spirits from out their low repose,
> To sing of state, and tragick notes to frame.[44]

He admits that his drama directly responds to the countess's own *Antonie*: "thy well grac'd *Anthony*/ . . . Requir'd his *Cleopatras* company" (14, 16). And he acknowledges her support: "thou so graciously doost daine,/ To countenaunce my song and cherish mee" (29–30). Thus he must labor to be worthy of this investment: "I must so worke posterity may finde/ How much I did contend to honour thee" (31–32). As Daniel closes this extended statement, he voices what must have been a common idea for those who sought in patronage, if not financial reward, at least recognition:

> But, (Madam,) this doth animate my mind,
> That fauored by the Worthyes of our Land,
> My lynes are lik'd; the which may make me grow,
> In time to take a greater taske in hand. (109–12)

But Daniel also provides an apology for the Pembroke endeavor on both aesthetic and moral grounds. Their cause, no less than "To chace away this tyrant of the North:/ *Gross Barbarism*" (34–35), first encountered and done battle with by Philip Sidney, thereby embolded others to wrest "that hidious Beast incroching thus" (40). The references to "darkness," "foe," and "Monsters" assure a stridently moral tone to the effort of poetry, making this no ordinary defense of drama as seen, for example, in the comment by William Sheares affixed to the Marston edition. In a nationalistic vein Daniel defends their style against the disregard of their European counterparts, "That they might know how far *Thames* doth out-go/ The musique of Declyned Italie" (77–78). He wishes that the work of Sidney and Spenser could be better known, enchanting the world "with such a sweet delight" (91), thus demonstrating "what great ELIZAS raigne hath bred./ What musique in the kingdome of her peace" (93–94).

Cleary Daniel needs the patronage of the countess far more

than she needs him: "Although thy selfe dost farre more glory giue/ Vnto thy selfe, then I can by the same" (51–52). He praises her translation of the Psalms, "In them must rest thy euer reuerent name" (61). By such artistic efforts and by, one supposes, her acts of patronage the countess has achieved a fame that will be known "When *Wilton* lyes low leuell'd with the ground" (66). And, in words reminding us of Shakespeare's *Sonnets,* Daniel says: "This Monument cannot be ouer-throwne,/ Where, in eternall Brasse remaines thy Name" (71–72).

Later editions of *Cleopatra* provide an interesting insight into the waxing and waning of patronage. As Joan Rees points out, Daniel omitted the verse dedication in the editions of 1605 and 1607; but by the 1611 text the dedication, slightly revised, reappeared, suggesting that the countess had resumed her patronage of Daniel.[45] Though he covers much of the same ground, some changes occur, as one would expect in a statement written nearly 20 years later. He acknowledges their renewed relationship: "And glad I am I haue renewed to you/ The vowes I owe your worth, although thereby/ There can no glory vnto you accrew."[46] The dedication begins by calling attention to the obvious fact of the countess's gender, a point not emphasized in the 1594 verses:

> Behold the work which once thou didst impose
> Great sister of the Muses glorious starre
> Of femall worth, who didst at first disclose
> Vnto our times, what noble powers there are
> In womens harts, and sent example farre
> To call vp others to like studious thoughts . . . (sig. E3).

Why Daniel should make this point in 1611 remains uncertain; perhaps in the era of the male-dominated Court noting the remarkable accomplishments of women and of the countess in particular became important.

This study of women patrons of the drama may be seen as

verifying Daniel's comment that noble powers exist in women's hearts, powers that led to the creation and active support of the drama, that inspired some dramatists to do their work, that provided financial support, that offered the much-desired but sometimes elusive quality of favorable recognition. Assessing the contribution of women to the flourishing of drama during the Renaissance cannot be a simple matter of tallying monies expended, but rather it must take into account reputations secured, possibilities gained, doors opened, and the more intangible qualities of guiding and supporting spirits. Without understanding the role of women as patrons we have a partial and incomplete picture of theatrical activity in this, its richest period.

FIVE

Bacon's *Henry VII*

٨

Commentary on King James I

Francis Bacon wrote *The History of the Reign of King Henry the Seventh* during 1621 after his fall from power and during his initial period of disgrace. He had, of course, contemplated some such history for a long time; and his exile from the Jacobean court allowed him time to complete this project. Exactly how much he researched his subject remains a matter of debate. But this history of Henry VII exists as an exceptional example of Tudor-Stuart historical writing. Given Bacon's fascination with questions of history, broached in *The Advancement of Learning* (1605) and expanded in *De Augmentis Scientiarum* (1623), one might reasonably expect to find an example of Bacon's practice of history. *The History of Henry VII* exists as Bacon's only finished full-scale history of an era, although other fragments survive.

A favorite scholarly pastime, at least since the late nineteenth century, has been to detect Bacon's "errors" in his history — that is, how and where he got things wrong. Sometimes, for example, he apparently duplicated the error of a source. He does not, however, stand alone among historians on this score. In any event, modern historical research affords a clearer view of the accuracy of Bacon's account. None of this detracts, however, from Bacon's considerable achievement. Part of the recognition of his accomplishment derives from understanding the different influences that impinge on Bacon's writing of *Henry VII*. I intend, for example, to assess the degree to which Bacon's portrait of King Henry's relationship to his wife, Queen Elizabeth, derives from the life of the Jacobean court as a model or influence.

Over 100 years ago, James Spedding took Sir James Mackintosh to task because Mackintosh interpreted *Henry VII* in light of Bacon's perceived desire to flatter King James and thereby to regain some favor that he had lost. With rising incredulity, Spedding questions the idea of Henry as a model king. Spedding writes: "Now Henry was in his entire character and in all his ways, both as a man and as a king, the very contrast and opposite to James himself. Both indeed professed to love peace; and both were constant, without being uxorious, to their wives. But there the resemblance ends."[1] Well, not quite. A fair number of other parallels exist, but that is not the issue. The very matter of the relationship of the two kings to their wives, which Spedding finds as a similarity, constitutes the problem that I will examine. I will argue that Bacon's assessment of Henry's relationship to Elizabeth derives not from any sixteenth century source but from Bacon's observation of James's treatment of Queen Anne.

Many of Bacon's contemporaries made some kind of link between the first Tudor and the first Stuart king. Bacon himself, in the dedication of *Henry VII* to Prince Charles, writes: "I have endeavoured to do honour to the memory of the last King of England that was ancestor to the King your father and yourself; and was that King to whom both Unions may in a sort refer: that of the Roses being in him consummate, and that of the Kingdoms by him begun."[2] Bacon echoes a commonplace, one that James had enunciated in an address to his first Parliament on 19 March 1604. In this important speech, whose theme is peace and union, James reinforced a patriarchal and spiritual understanding of his position as ruler. At one moment, for example, the king insisted: "I am the Husband, and all the whole Isle is my lawfull Wife; I am the Head, and it is my Body. . . ."[3] Earlier in the speech, James explored the concept of peace, epitomized in his person. That peace derives in part because of the tacit union of kingdoms that he has achieved, making him recall Henry VII:

> First, by my descent lineally out of the loynes of *Henry* the seuenth, is reunited and confirmed in mee the Vnion of the two Princely Roses of the two Houses of LANCASTER and YORKE, whereof that King of happy memorie was the first Vniter, as he was also the first ground-layer of the other Peace.[4]

In other words, as Henry VII united warring houses, so James now unites the kingdoms of England and Scotland. James boasts: "But the Vnion of these two princely Houses, is nothing comparable to the Vnion of two ancient and famous Kingdoms, which is the other inward Peace annexed to my Person." For political purposes, James makes explicit a link back to Henry VII, reminding hearers of his claim to the throne from both English and Scottish descent.

Just four days before James's address to Parliament he had made a royal entry through the streets of London on 15 March, one of the most spectacular civic pageants of the English Renaissance. This pageant, delayed because of the plague of the previous year, brought together the talents of leading dramatists — Ben Jonson, Thomas Dekker, and Thomas Middleton — actors, musicians, and architects. Among the seven triumphal arches stationed throughout the city stood one erected by the Italian merchants living in London. The front of the arch, as described in Dekker's text, included the arms of England and Scotland and this scene:

> In a large Square erected aboue all these, King *Henry* the seuenth was royally seated in his Imperiall Robes, to whome King *Iames* (mounted on horsebacke) approches, and receyues a Scepter.[5]

Other figures underscore the theme of peace and union. In fact, the whole arch on both sides refers to James's accomplishments. Visually and dramatically realized in London's streets a few days before James addressed Parliament, this tableau-vivant makes the political link between Henry and James. Since James passed through this arch, he had the opportunity to see this portrayal of his lineal descent. The real James looks at the representation of himself and Henry, just as he would 20 years later on the pages of Bacon's history.

In October 1605, the Lord Mayor's Show, *The Triumphes of Re-United Britannia* written by Anthony Munday, called attention to James's supposed connection to Brutus, the mythical settler of Britain. As the kingdoms had been divided under Brutus, so they were reunited by James. This civic pageant, honoring the installation of the new Lord Mayor of London, focuses much of its attention on the union of the kingdoms. Brutus, represented as a character in the pageant, consistently sings the praises of James's accomplishment. In one speech he connects the fate of James to Henry VII:

> *Albania, Scotland*, where my sonne was slaine
> And where my follies wretchednes began,
> Hath bred another *Brute*, that gives againe
> To *Britaine* her first name, he is the man
> On whose faire birth our elder wits did scan,
>   Which Prophet-like seventh Henry did forsee,
>   Of whose faire childe comes *Britaines* unitie.[6]

As Amphitrita says near the end of the pageant: "And Scotland yeelded out of *Teudors* race,/ A true borne bud, to sit in *Teudors* place" (15). Therefore, early in James's reign the popular imagination firmly established a link to his Tudor precursor. Bacon did not have to invent such a connection.

Exiled from court in 1621 and desiring a restoration to favor, Bacon began to write his history of Henry VII's reign. Martin Elsky, writing of Bacon's earlier career, observes: "His decision to write as an author rather than a courtier was for him an expression of alienation."[7] He adds: "Bacon turned to writing as a response to failure at court; writing was a manifestation of his distance from the center of political life" (189). A similar argument can be made for the Bacon of the early 1620s. Bacon's letters make clear his hopes of regaining favor with James, whether his *Henry VII* would be the means or not. The dedication of the history to Prince Charles reinforces the idea that Bacon had an eye focused on the court. That simply makes good sense, and the text also fulfills an earlier promise to write such a history.

On 8 October 1621, Bacon wrote to King James:

> I have therefore chosen to write the Reign of King Henry the 7th, who was in a sort your forerunner, and whose spirit, as well as his blood, is doubled upon your Majesty.
>
> I durst not have presumed to intreat your Majesty to look over the book and correct it, or at least to signify what you would have amended. But since you are pleased to send for the book, I will hope for it.[8]

By the following January, Thomas Meautys could write to Bacon and tell him that the king had indeed read the book and had passed it on to others. Meautys informs Bacon that the book "may go to press when your Lordship please, with such amendments as the King hath made, which I have seen, and are very few . . ." (7:325). Apparently James's suggestions focused primarily on word choice. Letting James have a chance to read and amend the book before publication was smart politics and unabashed flattery. James the author-king enjoyed opportunities to function as critic. Because Bacon made explicit in his letter to James that Henry VII is a "forerunner" of the king, all the more reason to have him examine the history and approve it.

After an unexplained brief delay in publication, Bacon's *Henry VII* finally appeared toward the end of March 1622. On 20 March, Bacon wrote to Buckingham: "I am bold likewise to present your Lordship with a book of my History of King Henry the seventh" (7:356). At the same time, he wrote also to King James:

> These your Majesty's great benefits in casting your bread upon the waters (as the Scripture saith) because my thanks cannot any ways be sufficient to attain, I have raised your progenitor of famous memory (and now I hope of more famous memory than before) King Henry the 7th, to give your Majesty thanks for me; which work, most humbly kissing your Majesty's hands, I do present. (7:357)

Bacon signs the letter as "Your Majesty's poor beadsman." James as king not only recalls his Tudor ancestor, but he also through Bacon's writing has some involvement in the production of a history of Henry's reign. Therefore, Bacon exploits the link between James and Henry, making it secure and inevitable. Stripped of political power and place, Bacon now has only his writing to represent him. If he entertained hope that *Henry VII* would restore him fully to the court, he would be disappointed.

My focus centers on how Bacon depicts the relationship of Henry to his wife Elizabeth. Early in the account Bacon records their marriage, noting that the celebration exceeded that of the king's own coronation, "which the King rather noted than liked."[9] Bacon offers this assessment of their relationship:

> And it is true that all his life-time, while the Lady Elizabeth lived with him . . ., he shewed himself no very indulgent husband towards her though she was beautiful, gentle and fruitful.

> But his aversion toward the house of York was so predominant in him, as it found place not only in his wars and counsels, but in his chamber and bed. (79–80)

Perhaps with such analysis we can understand the delay in Elizabeth's coronation, which did not take place until two years after the wedding. Bacon comments on the delay: "which strange and unusual distance of time made it subject to every man's note that it was an act against his stomach, and put upon him by necessity and reason of state" (96–97). Necessity and resentment run as themes throughout Bacon's analysis of Henry and Elizabeth.

Bacon records Elizabeth's death in childbirth, not long after the death of their son Prince Arthur. Silence characterizes Henry's reaction to her death, at least in Bacon's account. Providing a summary estimate of Henry, Bacon observes the distance that he kept in personal relationships. Bacon adds: "For he was governed by none. His Queen (notwithstanding she had presented him with divers children, and with a crown also, though he would not acknowledge it) could do nothing with him" (242). A few pages later Bacon offers this final comment: "Towards his Queen he was nothing uxorious; nor scarce indulgent; but companiable and respective, and without jealousy" (244). This portrait does not flatter Henry; but the issue is: how accurate is this report and assessment of Henry's relationship with Elizabeth? Has Bacon correctly followed his sources in reaching his conclusions?

F. J. Levy in his edition notes some of the gaps of evidence in Bacon's account, concluding that "Bacon cannot be considered an original source for the reign of Henry VII, nor did he have available evidence that has since been lost" (52). Levy adds: "Henry's relations to his wife and mother-in-law were not as Bacon reported them: he elaborated some dubious hints without seeking positive evidence." In the standard modern biography of Henry VII, S. B. Chrimes writes: "Little precision can be given to any estimate of Henry's relations with his queen, for lack of appropriate material. . . . Bacon's facile phrase that 'towards his queen he was nothing uxorious' has no justification."[10] "There seems," Chrimes points out, "good reason to suppose that she was an admirable and wholly acceptable spouse in the king's eyes." Contemporary accounts praise Elizabeth's beauty and ability.

Judith Anderson states the matter succinctly: "In light of Bacon's sources, Henry's hostility to Queen Elizabeth is without any basis in fact."[11] As Anderson observes, "The fiction of Henry's hostility to his Queen is clearly an important one for Bacon" (186). Thus, "To the continuing dismay of modern historians, Elizabeth . . . becomes for Bacon the focus and symbol of a deep and repeatedly aggravated aversion Henry has to the house of York." The logical expansion of this perspective is "to extend this aversion to the privacy of the King's chamber and bed." In a word, Bacon has his own agenda, thereby permitting him to create a fiction to suit his own purposes. We can rid ourselves of the idea of Bacon as objective historian. Unwittingly, perhaps, he spins a fiction through the web of his historical narrative.

Analyzing Bacon's personal connection to Henry VII's history, Anderson claims: "Surely one reason Bacon enters so naturally into Henry's analyses is that they merge with or grow out of his own" (201). And "to imagine the writer of the *Henry* as simply unaware, self-deceived, and confident of his own objectivity is, on the basis of the evidence we have examined, unwarranted — indeed, plainly wrong." That is, Bacon exists somewhere inside his *Henry VII.* Without discounting the possibility that Bacon has some sort of axe to grind, I will suggest instead that on the question of Henry's relationship to Elizabeth, Bacon, consciously or not, incorporated the evidence of his observation of James and Anne. Bacon's "fiction" may bear a contemporary relevance to what he had witnessed at the Jacobean court. It may well be that Bacon read backwards from his current moment to the early sixteenth century, where, finding little evidence about the royal couple, Bacon filled in the gaps from his own experience.[12]

"He was nothing uxorious"; so Bacon wrote about Henry. But, as we now see, this cannot be understood as an accurate statement about that king's relationship to his queen. It does, however, serve as a reliable assessment of James's relationship to Anne. Though the Oxford English Dictionary attests the word *uxorious* as first being used in 1598, it gains much currency in the seventeenth century and is applied to James. Contemporary commentators provide insight into this husband-wife relationship. Francis Osborne reports an outward display of affection, presumably shortly after the royal couple's arrival in England in 1603: "He [James] that evening parted with his queene, and to show himself more uxorious before the people . . . than in private he was, he did at her coach side take his leave, by kissing her sufficiently to the middle of the shoulders."[13]

Commenting on this marriage, William Sanderson wrote in 1656: "A matchless pair, drawing evenly in all courses of honour, and both blessed with fair issue, because never loose from eithers Bed."[14] Bishop Godfrey Goodman (1583–1655), writing about 1650 in reaction to Anthony Weldon's unfavorable account of James, tried to make the best possible case for James and Anne, observing that at least they did have children. He writes: "It is true that some years after they did not much keep company together. The King of himself was a very chaste man, and there was little in the Queen to make him uxorious; yet they did love as well as man and wife could do, not conversing together."[15] By "not conversing together" the good bishop presumably means not having sexual intercourse, a now obscure meaning of "converse." Other commentators regularly point out the extended absences of James from Anne and of course their separate residences. Only a tortuous kind of logic could lead Sanderson to claim that they were never "loose from eithers Bed" and that they were a

"matchless pair." The James who had written love poems to
Anne, who had sailed across dangerous seas to fetch his bride
home to Scotland, who had her crowned Queen of Scotland
and later Queen of England, lost all interest in her as his wife;
she remained a convenient political symbol of a family and
the necessary means to assure him and the kingdom of an
heir. James, after all, made clear that he had married for political reasons; the first blush of love for this woman lasted
about as long as morning dew.

I will cite just a few representative examples of James's attitude toward Anne. In late summer 1607, their young daughter Mary became ill and eventually died, having been preceded
in death by her sister Sophia; thus both children born in England died. Neither parent attended the dying child. Mary was
buried on 18 September without solemnity or a funeral. After
Mary's death, James sent Robert Cecil to console Anne, as
indicated in a letter from Sir Roger Aston to Salisbury, dating
from mid-September: "[James] desires you to bend all your
force to persuade her Majesty that this burial may not be a
second grief: it is not for charge, but only for removing of the
grievous present and the griefs to come. He is going this morning to Chesson [Cheshunt] Park to hunt."[16] James remained
always certain of his priorities: hunting took precedence over
most activities of government or of family life. At the very
least, this incident reinforces the idea of James's lack of devotion to Anne.

Anne had to endure the emergence of Robert Carr as the
center of James's attention; and she shed no tears when he
eventually fell, the victim of the Overbury murder scandal.
But she had moved, along with other family members, to the
outer limits of James's affection. Arthur Wilson outlines several possibilities for Anne's animosity toward Carr, including "an apprehension that the King's love and company was
alineated from her, by this *Masculine conversation* and inti-
macy."[17] Ironically, Anne became a pawn in the triumph of

George Villiers, eventual Duke of Buckingham. Her relationship to Buckingham, curiously, remained fairly cordial, perhaps reflecting his charm and her acceptance of the inevitable. In 1617, when James decided to make a trip to his native Scotland, Anne angled to become named Regent of England. That responsibility went instead to Francis Bacon. Anne, not invited to make the trip to Scotland, traveled with James as far as Ware in March 1617 but then returned to London, leaving James to travel on with his retinue, which included Villiers.

A constant thread runs through contemporary reports of the last years of Anne's life: her many illnesses seem as much emotional as physical. The question of a Spanish marriage for Prince Charles did occupy Anne's attention in 1618, the last major political and familial issue in which she became involved. To the Venetian Ambassador, Anne expressed her apprehension about the Spanish match: "She herself did not see a necessity for such haste, the Infanta being so young and the Prince in a state to wait four or five years. She added that these precocious marriages were generally failures."[18] Since Anne was herself not quite 15 years old when she married James, does she include her own "precocious" marriage among these? Given her melancholy state in her last few years, one would not be surprised if she viewed her marriage as a failure. The Venetian Ambassador Piero Contarini analyzed the queen's position in 1618: "She is unhappy because the king rarely sees her and many years have passed since he saw much of her. She possesses little authority in the court and cannot influence the king's favour" (15:420). During her final illness in January 1619, the letterwriter John Chamberlain observed that James did not visit her at Hampton Court where she lay. In fact, Anne died without seeing James; only Charles was available to support her.

The Venetian Ambassador, in a poignant image, captures much of Anne's predicament: in physical death Anne had "released herself from the prison of a perpetual death" (15:494).

In this same report Antonio Donato refers to the beauty and popularity that Anne had enjoyed. But that had changed: "But of late her Majesty had to bear a change of fortune, suffering countless bitter things and great pain. She lost her health and fell out of favour with the king" (15:494–95). On the day of her death, James wrote to her brother Christian IV of Denmark: "She who was a most excellent wife to us and a most dear sister to you has now died, and our common loss has apportioned grief to both of us."[19] James adds: "Many pledges of both love and virtue remain after her life, whence she has left us a great longing for her." This statement, if nothing else, reveals that James writes for public consumption: we have much reason to question the "great longing" that James presumably felt for Anne. Akrigg, as editor of James's letters, in fact characterizes this letter as "thoroughly mendacious."[20]

After an embarrassing several weeks' delay as James hunted for money with which to bury Anne, the funeral finally took place without James's presence. As a political force, Anne had negligible impact; as a mother she endured much frustration and incompleteness; as a wife she suffered neglect and disregard. Donato's terse assessment speaks volumes: "Her Majesty's death does not make the slightest difference in the government of these Kingdoms."[21] In fact, less than a month after her funeral, James made an entry into London in June, dressed gaily in pale blue satin with silver lace and a blue and white feather — resembling more a "wooer then a mourner," Chamberlain noted.[22] No funeral blacks for James, nor mourning. James also displayed an unseemly eagerness to get his hands on his wife's legacy, most of which she had verbally committed to Prince Charles. In fact, he gave a sizable portion of the legacy to his beloved Buckingham. Everywhere we look we can draw only one inescapable conclusion: he was nothing uxorious.

Probably Bacon had drawn the same conclusion from his own observation of this royal couple; certainly plenty of evidence existed for this assessment. So powerful an image of estrangement and lack of devotion doubtless struck Bacon as it did his contemporaries. Clearly, Bacon intended his *Henry VII* to flatter James by the complimentary representation of his precursor; thereby he hoped to win favor and possible restitution to the court. James had no reason to think automatically of the link of his behavior toward Anne with that of Henry and Elizabeth; of course, he would have had no factual information about the earlier couple's relationship. Because he read Bacon's manuscript and offered comments, we have to assume that he approved of what Bacon had written. The problem, then, is with Bacon. Surely he must have known that he had scant or no reason to say what he reported of Henry's ill treatment of his queen. I doubt that he wanted to mock James; that would have been at odds with his purpose for writing. Instead, I think that he probably did not recognize that he was projecting backwards.

Looking back at Henry VII and Elizabeth, Bacon imposed the fiction of Henry's lack of loving loyalty to her, drawing on the reality of his experience with King James. Such a probable case answers the puzzle of why with no evidence Bacon had reached such an assessment in his *Henry VII*. In 1621, the recollection of Anne and her place in James's esteem would have been still quite fresh. In *De Augmentis*, book II, Bacon defines the task of civil history: "To carry the mind in writing back into the past, and bring it into sympathy with antiquity. . . ."[23] To be more precise, Bacon might have added that we take the mind of the *present* back into the past, sometimes without noting the difference.

SIX

Masculine Interpretation of Queen Anne, Wife of James I

For at least the past 100 years, a masculine bias against King James I's wife Anne has existed in historians' assessments of her, reaching a kind of crescendo climax in the exclamation of David Harris Willson in 1956: "Alas! The King had married a stupid wife."[1] Writing in the middle of the eighteenth century, William Harris, while offering a relatively sympathetic view of Anne, made the following astute observation: "I have been the longer upon the character of this princess [Anne], because it has been little known; our historians contenting themselves to speak one after the other, without examination, whereby, for the most part, it cometh to pass, that they tend little to improve or instruct; and, which is worse, fix such ideas of things and persons as are difficult to be eradicated, tho' ever so false."[2] Such fixed ideas about Anne dominate twentieth century historical analyses of her, and these ideas reflect a masculine ideology in their representation of her. This paper explores the ideology behind the analysis of Anne, noting how feminist writers provide an alternative view. Scholarly responsibility requires a revised view of Anne. I begin with the nineteenth century in order to provide an appropriate context, proceed to the twentieth, and then circle back to the seventeenth century.

Samuel Gardiner, in one of the standard historical accounts of the early Stuart period (1883–84), actually has little to say about Anne, which may in itself be a kind of commentary. Gardiner writes: "The Queen's death was of no political importance. Her character was too impulsive to give her much influence with her husband, and she seldom attempted to employ it with any settled and deliberate purpose. Her real sphere was the banquet and the masque."[3] Acknowledging the kind regard that most people had for the queen, Gardiner nevertheless adds: "But by the mass of the nation she was as completely forgotten as though she had never lived." Poignant truth governs that final judgment. In a nutshell Gardiner has hit on three themes that permeate much twentieth century historical analysis on this subject: Anne was impulsive, frivolous, and insignificant. I suggest that these terms create an image of Anne that derives from a masculine-based ideology; that is, historians seldom use these terms to characterize males who occupy prominent positions.

These ideas echo in the assessments made by Charles Williams (1934) and Godfrey Davies (1941). Williams suggests rightly that the marriage of James and Anne could not be called happy, though in some ways it was not an unhappy marriage — that depends, of course, at what moment one captures their relationship. Anne "wanted to enjoy herself"; she "liked as much festivity and dancing as she could get."[4] Anne, Williams writes, pursued in England "the same bird of happiness which she had sought in vain in Scotland. Masques, progresses, schemes of building, occupied her" (265). Her influence was negligible. James did not interfere with her "strong

tendency towards Catholicism." Davies continues in this vein
by suggesting that James "did not upbraid her for her vacilla-
tions in religion."[5] Anne's shifting religious views become yet
another example of her frivolous nature. Davies asserts: "He
[James] always treated Anne good-naturedly, tolerated her ex-
travagances, forbore to grumble at her frivolity" (41). Certainly
if one knows anything about the fierce struggle over the nurturing of Prince Henry, one can scarcely claim that James
always treated Anne benignly.[6] Part of the difficulty in their
marriage, Davies notes, was that they had little in common:
for example, Anne "had no interest in his [James's] theological
or other treatises and discourses" (42). A possible implication
of Davies's judgment is that Anne lacked the intellectual power
to engage in serious theological discourse.

Partly by default, Willson's 1956 biography has become the
standard one of James, and it encapsulates the pervasive bias
against Anne. For Willson, Anne is "folly incarnate" (118),
"prying and meddlesome" (157), and even in the face of death
"frivolous to the last" (403). Sounding rather like Charles
Williams and Davies, Willson asserts that Anne "could not
share his [James's] intellectual interests, and she confirmed
the foolish contempt with which he regarded women" (95).
She could not share such interests because she obviously
lacked intelligence; she was, in Willson's succinct phrase, "a
stupid wife." Although other historians comment on James's
apparent toleration of Anne's Catholicism, Willson shifts the
point slightly. He writes: "Very likely she adopted Catholicism in the half-trifling way in which idle persons sometimes
occupy themselves with a new faith. Her conversion did not
make her serious or devout, nor did it strengthen her character" (95). I do not think that the scanty evidence gives us
any basis for knowing why Anne embraced Catholicism: one
could just as readily and convincingly argue that she changed
for theological or spiritual reasons — unless, of course, one
has already decided that she was at best frivolous. Absent

clear indications, one cannot know, for example, if her refusal to take the communion sacrament during the coronation ceremony in England derived from pettiness or from principle.

Willson continues his catalogue of Anne's qualities: "She possessed high spirits and a playful sprightliness, but these qualities were shallow and vacuous. . . . Her love for gaiety and dancing, for games, masques and pageants, was childish rather than courtly" (94). I detect a rigid puritan spirit informing Willson's judgment. What exactly does it mean to have a "courtly" love for gaiety and dancing? Perhaps courtly as opposed to childish suggests "manly" virtues. Anne's tastes were "foolish and expensive." "She had a quick temper, high words came easily, and in her childish tantrums she could be violent, spiteful, indiscreet and quite ingenious in her efforts to annoy" (95). At last we have the "hysterical" woman analysis. If any of this be true, one can agree with Willson's conclusion: poor James, who had to put up with such a woman. I do not deny that Anne on occasion may have been all of these terrible things — as was James himself; rather, I direct attention to how the historian has stacked the cards against her, reflecting, I think, a conscious or unconscious male prejudice.

I do not know if William McElwee had a chance to use Willson's biography; but it does not matter: he captures the spirit and phrases of the earlier historians. Anne made, according to McElwee, "a perfectly good ordinary wife."[7] Unfortunately, James needed more than an ordinary wife; but Anne "had neither the character nor the intellect to deal with the special needs of James, who was very far from being an ordinary husband" (67). Interestingly, in such an analysis the woman carries the responsibilities for meeting her husband's needs. In the struggle over the nurture of Prince Henry, McElwee sees an ulterior motive on Anne's part: an attempt to move to the center of the political stage. But McElwee concludes: "Anne had strong prejudices, no scruples, and very little intelligence, and the more remote she was kept from politics the better" (79). Had she become custodian of Henry, she might have been "tempted to all sorts of dangerous madness." Despite worries about Anne's intriguing and meddlesome nature, McElwee later says that she had not "a spark of ambition, with hardly any interest in politics and the personalities which surrounded her"; therefore, she settled down "to enjoy the rest of her life as luxuriously as possible" (123). "Her life was already given up largely to selfish pleasures" (169). After the deaths of the two daughters, Sophia and Mary, born in England, James and Anne largely went their separate ways — that is, after 1607 — even though "Anne was still only 33, pretty in her fair-haired, vacuous way . . ." (169). McElwee concludes: "Her propensity for intrigue, her hysterical intolerance of opposition, and her dabblings with Rome had made it necessary to exclude her as much as possible from politics" (169). Although McElwee has some trouble deciding about Anne's precise place in the political world, he remains consistent in viewing her as lacking intelligence, being impulsive and often hysterical, and living in extravagant self-indulgence.

Writing about the royal marriage, Akrigg (1962) notes that it had not turned out well. "Anne had proved to be both dull and indolent, though showing a certain tolerant amiability so long as her whims were satisfied. She was interested in little that was more serious than matters of dress . . . Her chief delight lay in court balls and masques."[8] James, Akrigg adds, "must often have found his wife tiresome with her querulous demands and her moodiness" (22). By the time King Christian IV of Denmark visited his sister in England in 1606, he found a "somewhat bony sallow woman, sharp-nosed and tight-mouthed, a discontented wife and a purposeless woman" (79). At least Akrigg acknowledges James's role in helping Anne become a "discontented and frustrated woman" (264). Akrigg concludes: "Anne, however, would probably have been a much happier woman (though never a model of stability and good sense) had she been married to a more normal husband. The Queen's irresponsibility and petulance, her ineffectual meddling which alternated with languid indifference, were more consequence than the cause of the unsatisfactory relationship between herself and her husband" (265). But even this sensible perspective about Anne must share space with a reference to her "heedless prodigality" (264) and her "doing or saying something nice, even if in a rather feather-brained sort of way" (265).

The post-1970 period contains some of the same biases. Otto Scott (1976) underscores Anne's frivolous and intolerant character when he observes that Anne "liked anyone that James disliked and was always swayed against her husband's opinions."[9] Anne had developed "a talent for nagging, weeping, scolding, and amateurish plotting" (233); at the same time her "intelligence had not improved . . ." (224). When she got her way, her intransigence would soften. Scott concludes: "Relations between James and his wife, uneasy at best, grew even more strained. Anne was a meddler and could not resist annoying her husband deliberately . . ." (258). Prince Henry's love of the visual arts and festival, Roy Strong attributes (1986) to his mother: "On the whole Anne lived for pleasure, passing her time moving from one of the palaces assigned to her to the next."[10] Sounding what has become the well-established party line, Strong adds: "she deliberately avoided politics, devoting herself instead to dancing, court entertainments and the design and decoration of houses and gardens. She also presided over her own circle, one noted for . . . extravagance . . ." (16). Writing about a crisis in Scottish history in the 1590s, Maurice Lee (in 1990) describes Anne as "young, silly, and meddlesome, [who] was beginning to get on his [James's] nerves."[11] Therefore, 100 years after Gardiner, male historians still voice very much the same attitudes toward Anne. The needle has been stuck on her stupidity, frivolity, extravagance, silliness, impulsiveness, and finally insignificance.

James remains the victim who tolerated this unpleasant woman, a woman who in the historians' view placidly, unthinkingly, and self-indulgently sought the sweet bird of happiness.

To be fair, one has to note that some of this male bias may ironically draw inspiration from the first woman historian to write about the Stuart period, Catherine Macaulay [Graham], who published *The History of England from the Accession of James I to the Elevation of the House of Hanover* in the 1760s. Macaulay writes about Anne: "She was a woman of a vain, haughty, and violent temper. The court-amusements took their bias from these qualities; they were pompous and gaudy, without any degree of taste or propriety. The direction of the revels were the bounds of Anne's empire."[12] Macaulay's perspective derives in part from her use of certain mid-seventeenth century sources, such as Anthony Weldon, which had an especially bleak view of the Jacobean court. Also, Macaulay's own ideology operates here: she believes the Stuarts to have been obstructors of justice and enemies of "Liberty," as is made obvious in Macaulay's Introduction (vii–xviii). She champions any and all who fought "against tyranny which had been established for a series of more than one hundred and fifty years" (ix). From this ideological stance, one that seeks to make the world safe for the Hanoverians, Macaulay could do no less than write unflattering comments about Anne.

Although acknowledging some of Anne's flaws, Ethel Williams in 1970 implicitly challenged the male bias operating among historians. And yet, as we saw above, her more evenhanded perspective has not been adopted in all quarters. Instead of writing about Anne's "heedless prodigality," Williams writes simply: "Two of Queen Anne's greatest pleasures were fine clothes and expensive jewelry. Unlike her mother, Queen Sophia, she had no idea of the value of money."[13] This analysis, grounded in evidence, avoids the pejorative adjectives common among male historians. Whatever Anne's "prodigality" might have been, her husband clearly rivalled if not exceeded her. In ways that most male historians have not, Williams emphasizes the damage done to the relationship of James and Anne by James's policy of excluding Anne from the care and nurture of their children. His failure to understand or appreciate these maternal instincts "was the rock upon which King James's marriage foundered" (56). This judgment, which I share, appropriately moves away from merely outlining Anne's stupidity, frivolity, and hysterical intolerance as causes for the breakdown of the marriage. Too many historians have overlooked or downplayed the fundamental struggle over their children that governed the life in the royal family, especially in the last decade in Scotland. Possibly this conflict serves as the basis of John Chamberlain's observation in a letter to Dudley Carleton, 28 February 1603: "New troubles arise dayly in Scotland, but the worst of all is the domesticall daungers and hartbreaking that the Kinge findes in his owne house."[14] Williams concludes that Anne "was a devoted mother" (186), a point that James could not fully comprehend or respect.

Like other historians, Williams believes that Anne embraced Catholicism. But instead of impugning Anne's motives or seeing this action as but another example of her frivolous nature (the half-trifling response of an idle person), Williams outlines the probable reasons for Anne's change. For example, Anne "found the bleakness of Calvinism intolerable" (109), and she resented the attacks upon her from some of the Scottish clergy. Therefore, when her Lutheran chaplain joined the Presbyterians, Anne may have been inspired to move also, but in the opposite direction. In any event, sometime late in Scotland, Anne apparently became a Catholic. Nothing in the scant evidence leads one inevitably to see this action as whimsical and petulant, which some male historians posit. Instead, Williams makes a point underemphasized by her historian colleagues: "Yet Anne was most careful not to allow her religion to interfere with her husband's policy in any way. In public she attended Church of England services with her husband" (111). I think that finally we cannot know why Anne accepted Catholicism; but surely historians skew judgment when they indulge in a kind of name-calling — a disservice to Anne and to historical analysis.

Williams observes that Anne remained popular with her subjects. "The people recognised her courage, dignity and sympathy with those less fortunate than herself" (182). Her kindness of heart led her to help those in trouble; Williams notes particularly Anne's help given to Arabella Stuart when she ran afoul of James's objection to her marriage to William Seymour. Also, Williams points out that "Queen Anne was a much shrewder judge of character than modern historians will admit" (156). (Williams could have said modern "male" historians.) For example, she "saw that Frederick [her future son-in-law] was not very intelligent, but he was intensely ambitious. . . ." Certainly history bears out Anne's assessment of Frederick, as one recalls his disastrous acceptance of the Bohemian crown, the loss of his German principality, and his ensnarement in the Thirty Years' War. Anne also feared the advancement of James's last favorite, George Villiers; she thought that "although Villiers had perfect manners, intelligence and great charm he would prove ambitious and headstrong" (170). She warned George Abbot, Archbishop of Canterbury, who was promoting Villiers, that he would rue the day of Villiers's acceptance into the post of groom of the bedchamber. Years later the Archbishop "with the advantage of hindsight remarked, 'Noble Queen, how like a prophetess or oracle did you speak'" (171). But one looks in vain among male-biased historians for any emphasis on Anne's shrewd powers of judgment. Ethel Williams offers a necessary corrective, a softening of the harsh and unrelenting portrait of Anne provided by other historians. Even Williams's restrained language opens the possibility for a fairer assessment of Anne. She modulates the tone of the discussion, moving away from a male bias.

Antonia Fraser and Caroline Bingham develop this feminist perspective on Anne. Fraser believes that Anne's alleged
"lack of brains" has been exaggerated. And she says simply:
"for all the dour criticisms which have been made of Anne's
frivolity, it is difficult not to conclude that James was fortunate
in his selection."[15] Fraser explicitly addresses the question
of Anne's love of pleasure and her extravagance in pursuing it: "However, since the fruits of this passion, such as
her patronage of Inigo Jones, are so admirable in themselves,
it is pleasant to find that in modern times Queen Anne has
made up in approval of art historians what she has lost in the
disapproval of more political pundits" (55). This sound perspective counters the sympathy for James for having married
a stupid wife; and it puts into helpful context the matter of
her indulgence in festivities, although subsequent historians
still emphasize Anne's living only for pleasure. Caroline
Bingham argues that Anne's delight in entertainments and
indulgence in friendships came partly as the result of there
being little left for her to do, given her relationship with
James.[16] And Bingham writes in an earlier book: "her intelligence is usually the subject of slighting comment, yet . . . she
was evidently a facile linguist, and she became a discerning
patron of the arts."[17] Anne eventually accepted the "role of a
virtuous wife to an inattentive husband . . ." (126). Bingham
also finds her to be an astute judge of character and capable of
influence on the affairs of court. The alternative feminist view
of Anne comes like a breath of fresh air against the stagnant,
male-dominated prevailing wind.

Assessing the position of women in Jacobean England,
Barbara Kiefer Lewalski includes an initial chapter in which
she focuses on Queen Anne.[18] Contrary to much that we have
found in male historians about the frivolous court masques
that occupied Anne's attention, Lewalski argues that such
masques served as vehicles "for self-affirmation and for subversive intervention in Jacobean politics" (15). Even Anne's

separate household represented "female resistance to Jacobean patriarchy" (18). Lewalski notes Anne's intervention in behalf of Walter Ralegh, whom she admired. And she writes that "Queen Anne's more direct forms of resistance centered on her children and household, the Roman Catholic religion, court appointments, theater patronage, and political maneuvering" (20). Instead of idle indulgence and pettiness, Lewalski finds in Anne an oppositional stance that "offered a patently subversive royal example to Jacobean patriarchal culture" (43). In effect, Lewalski stands on its head the typical perspective of male historians: where they find submission, she finds subversion.

A major breakthrough for male interpreters of the queen comes in the article by Leeds Barroll, who writes altogether sympathetically about Anne, emphasizing her political adroitness and her cultural activity.[19] Barroll concentrates on the queen's formation of her own court in the early years in England and "the political influence of her court upon English culture" (192). Examining Anne's political activity in Scotland, Barroll emphasizes her political skill, whether one agrees with her tactics or purposes. Arguing against Roy Strong's stance in his book on Prince Henry, Barroll suggests that "the queen and her court not only came to constitute a centre of patronage, but they also established an important connection with the heir apparent, Prince Henry" (205). Finally, "it was the queen's cultural activity that is most significant" (207). In other words, Queen Anne must be taken seriously. Her interest in and support of the arts, often viewed as further signs of her frivolous behavior, should be seen positively, as an area of serious contribution.

Masculine views of Anne in the early seventeenth century were on the whole sympathetic. One senses that in reading, for example, John Chamberlain's letters and diplomatic dispatches. Although not entirely flattering, the report of the Duke of Sully, a special representative of the French government who came to England in mid-1603, does suggest that Anne possessed energy and interest. Sully writes: "The character of this princess was quite the reverse of her husband's; she was naturally bold and enterprizing; she loved pomp and grandeur, tumult and intrigue. She was deeply engaged in all the civil factions, not only in Scotland, . . . but also in England. . . . The king could not be ignorant of this, but he was so weak as never to be able to resist. . . ."[20] This analysis doubtless exaggerates Anne's involvement in political intrigue, but it does suggest that she was far from placid. Anne's conversations with the French Ambassador, Harley de Beaumont, reveal a perceptive and knowledgeable mind at work. She readily understood the danger of some of James's policies and the pitfalls of a morally lax court. Arthur Wilson attributes to Anne the control of a faction opposed to Robert Carr, Earl of Somerset: "she became the head of a great *Faction* against him."[21] We recall that she warned about the dangers of Buckingham's rise in favor.

The Venetian Ambassador Nicolo Molin reported in 1607 that Anne was gracious and "moderately good looking" and that she enjoyed dancing and festivities. He added: "She is intelligent and prudent, and knows the disorders of the government, in which she has no part. . . . She is full of kindness for those who support her, but on the other hand she is terrible, proud, and unendurable to those she dislikes."[22] The Earl of Mar and others could testify to the last point. But at least the ambassador recognized the queen's intelligence. Antonio Foscarini reported to Venice in December 1618 that Anne "is a princess endowed with the utmost kindness and affability" (*CSP Ven*, 15:392). She is "passionately attached" to her brother Christian IV and to her son Prince Charles. Piero Contarini added in 1618 that Anne is "a lady of great goodness and virtue" (15:420). But she "is unhappy because the king rarely sees her and many years have passed since he saw much of her." One notes that these seventeenth century reports more readily square with the analysis of female historians writing in the twentieth century. The piling on of pejorative terms about Anne, so characteristic of male historians, does not exist here. Instead, the earlier male voices speak of Anne as intelligent, vivacious, full of spunk, knowledgeable about politics, a nurturing mother, and yet victim of her husband's neglect.

Poignantly, Antonio Donato reports to Venice about Anne's death on 2 March 1619:

> Freeing others from the trouble of living longer, she has released herself from the prison of a perpetual death. Her Majesty died three days ago in the palace at Hampton Court . . . without seeing the king, who was at Newmarket. She breathed her last amid a few attendants in a country place, without the help of those remedies which might have lengthened her days even if they did not cure her. (*CSP Ven*, 15:494)

Her only consolation came from Prince Charles, who attended her. At the end of her days, Donato adds, "at the age of 44, she had nothing but to lament her sins and to show herself, as she was always believed to be, very religious and sincere in the worship of the true God" (495). Donato also captures Anne's status in 1619: "Her Majesty's death does not make the slightest difference in the government of these kingdoms . . ." (495). The final indignity came from the ten-week search by James to find sufficient money for Anne's funeral, which finally took place on 13 May without James's presence.

Perhaps the time has come to release Queen Anne from the "perpetual death" of masculine bias. Ample materials exist in seventeenth century sources to provide a fair assessment of her without resorting to the fixing of certain unfavorable terms that cannot easily be eradicated, as William Harris had noted in the eighteenth century. Patriarchal ideology seems to have taken root among historians in the nineteenth century — that is, among those writing about Anne — and it has not altogether disappeared. Surely contemporary developments in

historical thinking should compel us to examine our own ideology as we seek to analyze and write about historical persons
and events. A feminist perspective on Anne offers a corrective
to the dominant view and opens the subject for additional investigation and analysis, along the lines of Leeds Barroll's and
Barbara Lewalski's perspectives. On this subject the scholar
has both a responsbility and an opportunity to revise previously accepted and transmitted ideas about a historical figure.
At such moments revisionism appropriately serves the inter-
preter's task.

SEVEN

Thomas Middleton and Anthony Munday

ε**a**

Artistic Rivalry?

Artistic lives have intersected in varied, challenging, and sometimes productive ways: consider T. S. Eliot and Ezra Pound,
Nathaniel Hawthorne and Herman Melville, or Coleridge and
Wordsworth. In the early seventeenth century Francis Beaumont and John Fletcher seem a fixture of artistic collaboration. We know that Thomas Middleton worked with Thomas
Dekker in *The Roaring Girl* and with William Rowley in *The
Changeling*, to cite two well-known examples. Yet such artistic collaboration may involve rivalry — think of Ben Jonson
and Inigo Jones working on the court masques. Their relationship eventually collapsed. Nearly 180 years of scholarship
has documented Middleton's presumed contempt for his lesser
contemporary Anthony Munday. I intend to swim against this
scholarly tide. I will question the evidence of their antipathy;

and I will shift the ground from rivalry, which in their relationship has come to have only negative connotations, to collaboration.

By investigating the Middleton-Munday relationship, I will be asking about how we practice scholarship. We may also ask how we *know* what we know in scholarship. Typically we know on the basis of our own investigation and research, or by accepting the testimony of a host of witnesses that has preceded us. Scholarly authority may displace the need for personal investigation. Two essential problems emerge in the Middleton-Munday debate: unsubstantiated or unjustified interpretation of texts and uncritical transmission of presumed information about the writers. I argue that a nineteenth century fiction about the two dramatists readily became fixed as a truth and that it has been faithfully perpetuated through the twentieth century, largely unexamined and unquestioned. Although this essay concentrates on the relatively minor Middleton-Munday problem, it has implications for an array of other scholarly issues that remain insufficiently investigated, having their "truth" asserted and assumed rather than substantiated.

This examination of the ideology and practice of scholarship begins with the dramatist's own attitude. I will discuss how the nineteenth century myth came about and how scholars in that century regularly reinforced and even added to the fiction. I think that this development has much to do with a nineteenth century scholarly interest in topical readings of texts and a major preoccupation with the concept of attack, abetted by the scholars' own nervous anxiety about personal attack from fellow scholars. A "war of the theaters" mentality informs much of the scholarly commentary, leading to a preoccupation with this subject at the end of the century. Removed from the fervor of such battles, twentieth century commentators on the Middleton-Munday rivalry have exhibited less ideology and more benign neglect of the issue, resulting in an uncritical acceptance of what the nineteenth century created and fought over.

Where does the Middleton-Munday antipathy come from? In which of Middleton's plays or prose works does he malign the hapless Munday? What about external evidence? Scholarship has focused on two passages from two of Middleton's texts, both pageant texts providing entertainment for the new Lord Mayor of London: *The Triumphs of Truth* (1613) and *The Triumphs of Love and Antiquity* (1619). Far too often texts of civic pageants fall victim to puzzlement or yawning indifference. Not surprisingly, when a nineteenth century scholar establishes a position based on a pageant text, we have been ready to accept rather than investigate. The general position has been: if scholars want to read those texts, more power to them. My recent editing of Middleton's civic pageants for the forthcoming *The Complete Works of Thomas Middleton* has forced me to think anew about the pageants and to wrestle with some editorial problems I had not explored earlier. This has landed me squarely in the middle of the Middleton-Munday relationship.

The "offending" passages follow so that we may see the cause of the fuss. On the title page of *The Triumphs of Truth* we find this curious description: "All the shows, pageants, chariots, morning, noon, and night triumphs. Directed, written, and redeemed into form, from the ignorance of some former times, and their common writer."[1] The opening passage in the text proper refers to the contribution of the Grocers, the sponsoring guild, whose generosity has enabled "streams of art to equal those of bounty" (14) and therefore made possible this entertainment which surpasses that to be found anywhere. But Middleton complains that not all writers have risen to the challenges of art and knowledge:

> the miserable want of both which, in the impudent common writer, hath often forced from me much pity and sorrow; and it

would heartily grieve any understanding spirit to behold many times so glorious a fire in bounty and goodness offering to match itself with freezing art, sitting in darkness, with the candle out, looking like the picture of Black Monday. (16–22)

The opening lines of *The Triumphs of Love and Antiquity* return to the question of art:

If foreign nations have been struck with admiration at the form, state, and splendour of some yearly triumphs wherein art hath been but weakly imitated and most beggarly worded, there is fair hope that things where invention flourishes . . . should receive favour. (2–7)

These passages constitute the only evidence for Middleton's contempt of Munday. Two key moments in the *Truth* passages apparently clinch the case: the reference to the "common writer" and even the "impudent" common writer, and the allusion to "Black Monday." The conclusion? Middleton must have Anthony Munday in mind. Similarly, if Middleton writes about art weakly imitated and "most beggarly worded," he must mean Munday. As an editor of Middleton, I confess that I do not know that Middleton refers to any specific writer. Is Munday somehow the only writer who lacks adequate art and knowledge? Is he the only one guilty of "freezing art" which sits in the dark "looking like the picture of Black Monday"? Some scholars have pounced on the word "Monday"; surely that points inevitably to Anthony Munday. Do we know any other writers from the period with such a name? But as Shakespeare intends the reference to Black Monday in *The Merchant of Venice* and as Middleton intends it in his *The Black Book*, such an allusion refers to the Monday after Easter.

Rather than referring to a specific dramatist, Middleton seems only to be trying to make the world safe for his efforts. Since this Lord Mayor's Show is his first, perhaps he responds to some kind of Bloomian "anxiety of influence." In any event, his ideology consists of drawing attention to his accomplishments at the expense of lesser (unnamed) artists. In the "Epistle Dedicatory" addressed to the new mayor, Middleton refers to the "oppositions of malice, ignorance, and envy" (23) that he has presumably overcome, preserved "to do service to your fame and worthiness, and my pen only to be employed in these bounteous and honourable triumphs" (26–28). Instead of the letdown of a Black Monday or the limitations of a freezing art, Middleton offers streams of art equal to the occasion.

Therefore, if Middleton's comments in these two texts do not lead us automatically and indubitably to think of Munday, how have scholars come to such a conclusion? The next section of this paper provides a catalogue of scholars from the nineteenth and twentieth centuries who have in effect accepted the premise of Middleton's low opinion of his rival Munday. I will establish the atmosphere that permeated much nineteenth century scholarship, a climate that enabled and encouraged speculation about personal attacks by Renaissance dramatists upon their contemporaries.

So far as I have been able to determine, the first person to see the connection between the comments in *Truth* and Munday was William Gifford in his 1816 edition of Ben Jonson. Gifford offers his commentary on the character Antonio Balladino as modeled on Munday in Jonson's *The Case Is Altered*:

> It would be unjust to dismiss Anthony Munday without adding that he appears to have been an industrious and worthy man. . . . Anthony kept pace with the times, and was not outstripped till a gigantic race of men arose, who were destined to render competition desperate and success hopeless. He died in a good old age.[2]

Gifford adds that Munday regularly received ridicule: "The *Triumphs of Truth*, written by Middleton, to celebrate the entrance of Sir T. Middleton into the mayoralty, has many reflections on 'the pageant poet' of the city" (6:328n). Gifford cites the offending passages at the beginning of the pageant as proof. In a fit of generosity and consideration he finally says: "There is more of this; but I forbear" (6:328n).

Because Gifford begins the tradition of Middleton-Munday rivalry, I want to take a closer look at what ideas inform his view. First, he exhibits certain prejudice about pageants, which he characterizes as "not a little risible" (325n) and as entertainments "which amused and edified the *apprentices* on festivals and holidays" (my emphasis). Gifford suggests that Munday experienced the wrath of Catholics because of some of his writing; and this left him "embittered many years of his life by the personal assaults to which it exposed him." Exactly where Gifford gets the evidence of Munday's bitterness he does not say. He hints that Jonson's satiric attack on Munday in *The Case Is Altered* came about because Jonson took offense at Francis Meres's designation in *Palladis Tamia* (1598) of Munday as "our best plotter." The connection of Munday and Jonson to the idea of the "war of the theaters" lurks behind Gifford's interpretation. Once scholars posit the reality of such a war, it becomes easy, if not necessary, to include as many dramatists as possible in order to heighten the signficance of this event. That is, Gifford buys into the idea of vicious attack, one dramatist upon another: hence it seems a small step to insist that Middleton must have Munday in mind in the pageant texts.

Also, Gifford clearly thinks himself under attack, or at least that Jonson is under attack. He therefore adopts a combative tone in many of his commentary notes, railing against those, for example, who with their "wanton and outrageous calumny" (2:458n) would assert the "malignity" of Jonson. In writing about *Poetaster*, Gifford singles out former scholars: "Messrs. Steevens and Malone content their spleen, in general, with harping on the 'malignity of Jonson to *Shakspeare:*' their zany, Mr. Thomas Davies, takes up the idle calumny" (2:459n). Exasperated at the perceived attacks on Jonson, Gifford blurts out: "The commentators are absolutely mad" (2:545n). He castigates "sheer ignorance" (1:xxxiv) and "solemn absurdity" (1:xxxvii). He so dislikes some of Steevens's commentary that he suggests that the prototype of Steevens "sat for Macilente" (2:458n) in *Every Man out of His Humour*. He asks: "can any folly equal that of construing every application of a written passage into an insult upon the original?" (2:175n). At moments Gifford clearly violates his own rhetorical question as he also forgets the interpretive caveats enumerated by the Scrivener in the Induction's covenant between the audience and the author in *Bartholomew Fair*.

John Nichols, in his edition of *The Progresses of King James* (1828), seconds Gifford's idea but goes him one better by insisting that the reference to Black Monday indeed refers to the writer, Middleton's "rival City Poet."[3] Middleton considered Munday only competent to provide apparel for the pageant. Nichols adds: "This virulent attack, however, appears to have experienced no greater attention than such violence deserved, since Munday was employed in the three following years." Suddenly "virulence" and "violence" enter the scholarly vocabulary. Nichols, the first to comment on *Triumphs of Love and Antiquity*, writes: "This Author [Middleton] had before shewn his own self-conceit, and his jealousy of his rival Anthony Munday, in the preface to his Pageant of 1613" (3:571n). The opening lines of the 1619 pageant text suggest to Nichols that Middleton intends to refer to Munday, henceforth to be designated as "rival."

In the year of Nichols's edition, John Payne Collier published an edition of several of Anthony Munday's plays in which he offered a "corrective" to the view of the Middleton-Munday relationship articulated by Gifford. Collier writes:

> Mr. Gifford was of opinion that Middleton meant to censure
> him [Munday] in his *Triumphs of Truth*, as the "impudent com-
> mon writer" of city pageants; but this is hardly consistent with
> the mention Middleton introduces of Munday at the close of
> that performance. Besides Dekker wrote the pageant for the
> year 1612, immediately preceding that for which Middleton
> was engaged.[4]

A scant ten years after Gifford, Collier provided the necessary
corrective to Gifford's position. But Collier's view remains the
single voice of opposition to what became the prevailing, indeed only, understanding of the relationship between the two
dramatists.

The first modern edition of Middleton, that by Alexander
Dyce in 1840, adopts wholesale and by quotation the view
enunciated by Nichols, asserting that in *Truth* Middleton
clearly means to impugn Munday. Dyce does acknowledge
Collier's demur, only to doubt it: "In the remarks prefixed to
Munday's *Downfall of the Earl of Huntington . . .*, I am surprised to find Mr. Collier doubting if Middleton alludes to
him here; and I can only suppose that when Mr. C. wrote those
remarks, his recollection of the present passage was somewhat imperfect."[5] Dyce develops the theory that the "ill will
which the dramatists appear to have borne towards him" arose
from Francis Meres's praise of him in *Palladis Tamia*. Dyce
writes of the opening lines of *Love and Antiquity*, as "Alluding to the pageants of Munday" (5:275n). Thus, Middleton's
first editor merely brushes aside a scholar who has a contrary
view, asserting that the benighted soul obviously does not recall the text correctly. We find ourselves in the presence of
that all-too-common and bracing view that "all sensitive readers" will agree with the stated position. If not, then clearly
something is wrong with the other person. It also seems rather
unlikely that other dramatists would be so upset by Meres's
praise of Munday that they would set out to disparage him
and knock him down a peg or two. We also notice that once

Dyce takes care of Collier, no one else even raises Collier's objection to the interpretation: the power of complete editions.

Writing the first study of Lord Mayor's Shows, Frederick W. Fairholt in 1843 joins the swelling chorus of those who see Middleton as castigating Munday. In fact, Fairholt says that *The Triumphs of Truth* "is principally remarkable for the attack upon Anthony Munday, the rival city poet, contained in it."[6] This certainly damns the pageant with faint praise. Fairholt writes that the "attack commences on the title-page, . . . and it is continued in the first page of the pamphlet" (32–33). He closes his quotation with the "Black Monday" passage and comments: "This virulent attack failed in depriving Munday of future employment" (34). Fairholt also adds in a note that the 1619 pageant "again alludes to Munday." None of the scholars gives much thought to why these alleged virulent attacks seem to have had no impact on Munday's career. Could it be that no one at the time understood Middleton's texts to contain such an attack on Munday?

A. H. Bullen's edition of Middleton, the last full-scale edition before the one currently underway, solidifies the Middleton-Munday rivalry. Commenting on the opening passage in *Truth*, Bullen writes: "Middleton is sneering at the rival city-poet Anthony Munday, who produced the pageant for the three following years."[7] And Bullen adds somewhat gratuitously: "Meres in *Palladis Tamia*, 1598, absurdly dubbed Munday 'our best plotter.'" In discussing *Love and Antiquity*, Bullen observes that Middleton "is again glancing at Antony Munday" (7:315n).

Three books in the 1890s tie into the controversy directly or indirectly; their common denominator derives from their discussion of the "war of the theaters." They offer a culmination of the century's concern for this alleged war, primarily among Jonson, Marston, and Dekker. These investigations heighten topical understandings of the drama and its reflection of personal and professional attacks. Josiah Penniman and

Roscoe Small write books on the subject, all designed to create an importance for the battle.[8] One comes away from these
books convinced that both more and less exist here than meets
the eye in this "war." Outside a few examples, the evidence
does not point to a large-scale struggle. On the contrary, this
"war" and the attendant issues of topical interpretation of texts
seem more complicated than these writers let on. Interestingly,
neither Penniman nor Small has anything to say about
Middleton's presumed attack on Munday. But Small, for example, notes Jonson's critical portrayal of Munday and offers
an explanation: "it is more likely, however, that Munday had
cast reflections on Jonson in some of his lost plays written about 1598" (198). A page later Small names which lost
Munday plays contain attacks on Jonson. Attack seems to be
everywhere, even in lost plays. Such an atmosphere or ideology encouraged finding slighting references in Middleton's
pageant texts.

Frederick Fleay's *Chronicle of the English Drama 1559–1642*
(1891) certainly embraces speculation about the war of the
theaters even as Fleay writes about Middleton's contempt for
Munday. Fleay observes: "Munday is distinctly alluded to as
'the impudent common writer' wanting in knowledge, and
'freezing Art sitting in darkness with the candle out and looking like the picture of Black Monday.'"[9] And then Fleay adds
what no one else had dared even to conjecture: Munday "is
further personated as Envy on a rhinoceros. Zeal is Middleton."
The pageant rapidly becomes an allegory not just of the moral
struggle between Truth and Error but of the battle between
Middleton and Munday. Interestingly, Fleay has adopted
Gifford's basic position even though he elsewhere refers to
Gifford as being "rash and inaccurate as usual" (2:69). In this
scholarly charged atmosphere Fleay also takes on Bullen and
his edition of Middleton. Feeling maligned by Bullen, Fleay
lashes at his "libellous attack" and adds: "If gratitude has no
influence on the heart of this New Shakesperian, surely respect

for 'his own credit' in every sense should restrain his effeminately facile pen" (2:374). Scholars imitate Renaissance dramatists in creating vitriolic wars among themselves.

As we cross into the twentieth century things do not get any better, although the sniping among scholars disappears — at least on this subject. Building on the nineteenth century fiction, no one stops to ask questions about why we believe the presumed antipathy between Middleton and Munday. Writing about the London guilds, George Unwin comments on various pageant entertainments, including Middleton's. He refers to Munday as Middleton's "rival" and alludes to Middleton's "unkind remarks" about Munday.[10] Robert Withington, in the first comprehensive study of English civic pageantry, devotes considerable space to a discussion of Lord Mayor's Shows. Referring to the 1613 pageant, Withington writes: "In his introductory remarks, Middleton takes advantage of the opportunity to sneer at his brother-poet, Munday."[11] One suspects, without altogether being able to prove, that each scholar has some awareness of what others have said about this problem; therefore, each stretches to find some new way to express it, "sneer" being the latest verb.

In the only full-length study of Anthony Munday, Celeste Turner in 1928 offers a rousing defense of him. She sees the Munday-Middleton rivalry in elitist terms; that is, Middleton uses his Gray's Inn education to belittle Munday. Unfortunately, regarding her argument, one has to point out that Middleton did not attend Gray's Inn; rather, he spent some time at Oxford University. Turner comments on *Truth* and its opening lines: "In the preface to this pageant of 1613, he openly flaunted his Gray's Inn education in the face of the 'impudent, common writer.'"[12] And writing about *Love and Antiquity* she observes: "In the Skinners' menagerie of furry beasts for 1619, the Gray's Inn graduate [Middleton] scoffed at those previous yearly triumphs [Munday's 1618 pageant]" (166). Middleton "voiced in after years" the opinion of Munday as an impudent common writer, Turner says (141). But in her version of literary history some poetic justice emerges from this situation: Munday "lived long enough to see Middleton buried at Newington Butts in July, 1627, six months after *The Triumphs of Health and Prosperity*, and to see Mrs. Middleton petitioning the city for funds to sustain her during her final year of life" (168). Middleton may have scoffed at Munday, but Munday outlived him and had the last laugh. We have now encountered a rather strange scholarly approach; one might call it ghoulish. Instead of investigating the scholarly problems, the writer personalizes the matter in favor of her writer, who just happened to live longer than Middleton. What would Turner's argument be had Munday not lived that long?

The first attempt to interpret Middleton's civic pageants as a group came in R. C. Bald's mid-1930s article. Of *The Triumphs of Truth* Bald writes: Middleton "had the assistance of his more experienced rival, Anthony Munday, of whom he speaks so disparagingly in his descriptions of the pageants."[13] He suggests that "this particular partnership does not seem to have been a happy one" (73). Bald leaves the matter rather open-ended, as if several pageant texts contain incriminating and insulting remarks about Munday. He does not pause to examine what Middleton actually says. As a defense of Middleton's artistic accomplishment in pageants, Bald's article leaves much to desire. In fact, he writes at one point: "Any serious artistic achievement in these shows was prevented not merely by the prescribed themes but by the fact that it was impossible to regard the show as a whole" (74). I believe that Bald has adopted the wrong critical stance and therefore has pursued the wrong critical questions: clearly he embraces some concept of *unity* as the all-important one. That raises the wrong expectations for these pageants. He concludes by quoting a brief passage from a song sung by the Seasons in the indoor *Honourable Entertainments*: "Here, and here alone, in the course of his City employments did Middleton breathe

the spirit of poetry into his work" (78). Turner hits Middleton over the head with his presumed education, and now Bald can find virtually nothing good to say about the pageants, indeed finding only one small moment of memorable poetry. No wonder it has been difficult to sort out the Middleton-Munday relationship.

In the magnificent Malone Society *Collections III*, which provides many pertinent records from the London guilds, the editors, D. J. Gordon and Jean Robertson, comment in the Introduction: "In his [Middleton's] printed description of the Show for 1613 he took the opportunity to disparage Munday."[14] In the headnote for the guild records for 1619, they indicate that the Skinners's records show that "Anthony Munday, whom Middleton speaks slightingly of in his pageant . . . also submitted a plot for the pageant" (99). Robertson continues in this vein in her 1956 article in which she mentions the rivalry among pageant dramatists: *"On peut citer, notamment, les attaques délibérées de Dekker et de Middleton contre Munday, qui fournissait bien d'autres choses que les textes de ses spectacles."*[15] She cites specifically *Triumphs of Truth* as evidence of Middleton's antipathy toward Munday, noting Middleton's *"ferveur qu'il réservait pour cette occasion"* (272) and its target Munday. Robertson quotes the notorious passage that includes the reference to Black Monday. Also in 1956 in an exchange of letters in *TLS*, Peter Phialas focused on *Love and Antiquity*, which, he argues, provides another instance of the keen competition between Middleton and Munday. Phialas adds: "That Middleton resented the competition is made clear by his disparaging allusion in the opening of his pageant, . . . a glance aimed at Munday, who had written the pageant for the preceding year."[16]

Two critical studies of Middleton carry on the by now well-established tradition: only a few verbs and adjectives change to protect the "originality" of the scholars' contributions. Richard Hindry Barker's *Thomas Middleton* (1958) warms to the task, claiming that Middleton "was anxious to outdo one of his predecessors, Anthony Mundy" and therefore on the 1613 title page and in the first paragraph of the text "he goes out of his way to sneer at Munday's achievements."[17] Barker expresses his incredulity that at the end of *Truth* Middleton cites the contributions of three people, including Munday "(of all people!)" (18). David Holmes discusses Middleton's pageants not at all, although intending to write about Middleton's "art." Instead, we find in Appendix C a reference to the text of *Truth*, identifying the "common writer" as "Anthony Munday."[18] Holmes does provide an unusual analysis: "The facetious context of this rather pointed innuendo keeps it outside the realm of spleen." Such disregard for Munday makes Holmes wonder how Middleton could have later sought the "assistance of a man of Rowley's patently modest gifts." I smell a non sequitur.

Writing in 1981, M. C. Bradbrook explores the politics of pageantry. Bradbrook writes about Middleton and Munday: "Old Anthony Munday, who had been attacked by Middleton, although he had had some share in the Triumph of 1613, came back a last time for the Fishmongers' Triumph of 1615."[19] Several problems arise in this statement, starting with the by now familiar one of Middleton's attack on Munday in 1613. But further, Bradbrook has confused Munday's 1616 pageant, which he wrote for the Fishmongers, with his 1615 show; in her description she clearly intends the 1616 entertainment. And, of course, Munday wrote additional shows in 1618 and 1623. In commenting on Middleton's avoiding an attack on the rebellious poor in his writing, Gail Kern Paster draws a distinction between this attitude and that of "his rival Anthony Munday."[20]

Smugness has no place in this saga of scholarly dereliction. These scholars of the nineteenth and twentieth centuries lack only me to help swell their ranks. I now know of my own guilt. In my book on English civic pageantry, I write of the

1613 pageant that Middleton "disparages [Munday] in his text."[21] And I add for the 1619 pageant: "Middleton pauses long enough in the opening sentences of this text to hurl a few barbs at his rival Munday" (189). In my 1985 edition of Munday's pageants, I include this headnote for his *The Triumphs of the Golden Fleece* (1623): "The rivals [Middleton and Munday] meet again as uneasy companions."[22] At least I now understand why and how I came to such views: mainly I inherited them uncritically.

The sections on Munday and Middleton in the appropriate volumes in the *Dictionary of Literary Biography* perpetuate some of the problems. Philip Ayres, writing about Munday's pageant career, says: "After 1616, to Munday's disappointment, Thomas Middleton, his one-time collaborator in play writing, replaced him as the favored author of the pageants, and Munday returned to reediting romances."[23] I know of no evidence that suggests that Munday felt disappointment, and in fact he wrote two more pageants after 1616. T. H. Howard-Hill writes: "The most experienced pageant master of the Jacobean era was Anthony Munday, whose virtual monopoly Middleton interrupted."[24] Of the entertainments in 1616, Howard-Hill says that "the rival dramatists were obliged to work together." But in that year Middleton wrote the pageant for the investiture of Prince Charles as Prince of Wales, and Munday wrote the Lord Mayor's Show, *Chrysanaleia*. They did not exactly work together, although the two pageants shared at least a barge between them. Howard-Hill says that the two wrote the 1621 pageant together, but the evidence remains less than clear on that. In any event, by 1987 the sense of rivalry between Middleton and Munday runs no risk of dying out; only the language to describe it has calmed a bit.

But another side of this story exists: professional cooperation between Middleton and Munday. The first entry in Henslowe's *Diary* for Middleton shows him as collaborator with Munday, Drayton, and Webster in writing *Caesar's Fall,*

payment being made in May 1602.[25] The first payment to
Munday dates back to 22 December 1597, when Henslowe
paid him and Drayton for *Mother Redcap*. At the least
Middleton and Munday knew each other as fellow playwrights
in Henslowe's stable of writers. Munday had by 1602 already
established himself as a writer of plays, translator of prose
romances (French and Spanish), author of prose fiction and
ballads, and he had begun writing pageants, producing the Lord
Mayor's Show of 1602 (no text survives). As Philip Ayres
claims: "Few Elizabethan and Jacobean authors produced as
varied a canon as did Anthony Munday."[26] He collaborated on
plays for Henslowe with Chettle, Drayton, Dekker, Webster,
and Middleton.

We pick up the trail of Middleton and Munday next in 1613
in Middleton's first Lord Mayor's Show, *The Triumphs of Truth*,
the very one in which Middleton presumably disparages
Munday. At the end of the pageant text Middleton singles
out for praise the contributions of Humphrey Nichols, John
Grinkin, and Munday. Of the latter he writes: "and those fur-
nished with apparel and porters by Anthony Munday, gentleman" (770–71). If we look at the Grocers' records, the
sponsoring guild, we gain further evidence of Munday's involvement in this pageant. In early February 1613, Munday's
name crops up as the guild begins exceptionally early planning. A committee intended to consider also "the Device or
project in writing set down by Mr Munday and offered to be
read to the Court concerning matter of triumph against that
time" (i.e., the time of the pageant, 29 October, the mayoral
inaugural day).[27] Those last words may strike us as, uninten-
tionally, suggesting the eventual title for the pageant. Therefore, by early February, Munday had already submitted some
kind of proposal for the show. The Grocers, who had not since
1598 presented a pageant for one of their members elected to
become mayor, seem particularly eager as they anticipate in
late September the election of their member and a namesake
of the dramatist, Sir Thomas Middleton.

Grocers' records of April 1614 reveal the expenditures for this the most expensive mayoral pageant of the Stuart era. Middleton received £4 "for the ordering overseeing and writing of the whole Device and also for the apparelling the personage in the Pageant" (87). Munday, on the other hand, received £149 "for the device of the Pageant and other shows, and for the apparelling and finding of all the personages in the said shows (excepting the Pageant) and also for the Portage and Carrying both by land and by water" (87). From the size of Munday's payment he obviously had to make his own expenditures for apparel and transportation; thus, we cannot determine precisely what he netted for his services. John Grinkin, the principal artificer or craftsman who built the pageant structures, received a payment of £310, from which he would have been expected to pay for a wide range of materials.

In light of the guild records and Middleton's explicit citation of Munday in the text, it becomes difficult to accept the idea that Middleton's references to the "impudent common writer" must refer to Munday. If anything, it might have been Munday who felt slighted, given his early involvement in planning the pageant but the guild's eventual choice of Middleton to become the author of the show. All evidence points therefore in the direction of cooperation between the two dramatists. Guild records confirm more fully than do pageant texts that such entertainments came into existence only as the result of extensive collaboration among appropriate committees of the guild, playwrights, and artisans. Munday's name, for example, crops up in a number of records even though his work may or may not be recorded in the text. Indeed, Munday is the only playwright to be involved in the production of someone else's Lord Mayor's Show in the Stuart period.

The year 1616 provided a new means of such cooperation, a unique blending of planning for a Lord Mayor's show and the pageant entertainment for the investiture of Prince Charles as Prince of Wales. The Fishmongers commissioned Munday to write the mayoral show, which he entitled *Chrysanaleia*, performed on the usual 29 October. Middleton wrote *Civitatis Amor* as the pageant entertainment that greeted Charles on the Thames at first Chelsea and then, Whitehall. Because the prince's installation would take place just a few days later, the Corporation of London summoned the appropriate members of the Fishmongers to discuss the possibility of sharing some materials. The City of London intended to confer "with them how their pageant and other devices may be altered and used for show at the meeting of the prince aforesaid, and for Chambers to be provided, and placed against that day and take consideration of some speeches to be made and then acted to the Prince."[28] Records of the Fishmongers reveal that the master of the king's barges appealed to the company for payment of barges, used both for the Lord Mayor's Show and for the prince's pageant. Doubtless the close proximity of time for the two events (itself rare) and the city's involvement with both led to this cooperation.

For the Grocers in 1617 Middleton wrote *The Triumphs of Honour and Industry*, and for the Skinners in 1619, *The Triumphs of Love and Antiquity*. Munday's name appears in the appropriate guild records for both pageants. Middleton received £282 for writing the 1617 show, which included expenditures for all the materials and transportation. We also find this record: "Paid and given in benevolence to Anthony Munday gentleman for his pains in drawing a project for this business, which was offered to the Committees £5" (*Collections III*, 93). For similar reasons Thomas Dekker received a payment of £4. Such payments underscore the competitive nature of these entertainments. The records for the Skinners in 1619 include the following item: "Lastly Anthony Munday, Thomas Middleton and Richard Grimston poets, all showed at the table their several plots for devices for the shows and pageant against Simon and Judes tide and each desired to serve the Company" (99). Obviously, the guild eventually chose Middleton — all the more reason to question the assumption that in his 1619 text Middleton somehow attacks Munday. Presumably one could make just as strong a case that he impugns the artistic merit of Dekker or Grimston. No one has made such an argument.

In 1621 Middleton, Munday, and Garret Christmas received a payment of £140 from the Drapers for the pageant, *The Sun in Aries*. Because Munday's name appears in the group, T. H. Howard-Hill suggests that Middleton and Munday wrote the show together, apparently basing this assumption on the guild records. But as we see, three names appear together without specifying who did what. No other evidence exists to give Munday credit for helping write the pageant. But in 1623 Munday clearly does write part of the pageant, the entertainment on the Thames, which he entitled *The Triumphs of the Golden Fleece*. Munday got paid £35 for "an Argoe," according to the Drapers records. The collaboration in 1623 takes a rather different turn, resulting — uniquely — in two different texts for the mayoral pageant: Munday's and Middleton's *The Triumphs of Integrity*. At the opening of his text Middleton refers to the show on the river, describing it as "a proper and significant masterpiece of triumph called the Imperial Canopy, being the ancient arms of the company, an invention neither old nor enforced" (ll. 16–19). Surely these rather glowing terms belie the supposed antipathy that Middleton felt for Munday. Munday's last pageant effort gets an appropriate sendoff.

I know of no reference to Middleton in Munday's writing, but he does reproduce a speech written by Middleton for the New River Entertainment in 1613. The account of the event and the speech appear in the 1618 edition of Stow's *Survey of London*, which Munday revised. In fact, Munday has gone to some trouble to include this material, as evidenced by the bibliographical note at the bottom of the first page: "Let this half sheet be plac'd between Folio 20. and 21."[29] Munday provides apparent firsthand information about the New River project, which Sir Hugh Myddleton, brother of the new Lord

Mayor, completed in 1613, successfully bringing a new supply of water from Hertfordshire to Islington, nearly 40 miles
of canal that took several years to complete. Munday insists:
"I myself . . . did divers times ride to see it, and diligently observed, that admirable Art, pains and industry were bestowed
for the passage of it" (sig. *1v). He then records the entertainment on Michaelmas Day (29 September) that celebrated the
completion of the water project and for which Thomas
Middleton wrote the pageant. Munday describes the troop of
laborers who represent all those who had worked on this difficult project. Finally he offers the speech given on that occasion at the cistern in Islington, according, Munday writes, "as
it was delivered to me" (sig. *2). With only a couple of minor
variations he reprints the speech as found in Middleton's text,
itself forming part of the expanded version of *The Triumphs
of Truth*. By devoting four pages to this effort, Munday clearly
wants to call attention to this event and Middleton's pageant,
even though he does not cite Middleton by name; perhaps that
seemed unnecessary. In any case, one can argue that Munday
pays Middleton the supreme compliment of reproducing the
only speech given in the entertainment. Such a response again
raises serious question about the existence of some bitter rivalry between these two writers. In light of this 1618 edition
of Stow's *Survey*, why would Middleton, in his next pageant
(1619), allegedly attack Munday? I argue that he did not.

Surely part of the problem of interpreting the relationship
of Middleton and Munday emerges from our failure to understand or acknowledge the nature of collaboration in Renaissance drama. Jeffrey Masten has written astutely on this
subject, particularly with regard to Beaumont and Fletcher.[30]
Masten reminds us: "Collaborative dramatic texts from this
period thus strikingly denaturalize the author-text-reader continuum assumed in later methodologies of interpretation"
(338). Stephen Orgel had earlier asserted that "most literature
in the period, and virtually all theatrical literature, must be

seen as basically collaborative in nature."[31] Collaboration obviously takes many forms, most clearcut, for example, when
we observe the situation in 1623 in which Middleton and
Munday each produce a separate text. Other examples remain
more uncertain. But surely if Munday provides apparel for the
actors and arranges transportation, as he did in 1613, he has
collaborated with Middleton in producing, "writing," *The Triumphs of Truth*. If collaboration, then we need not go to in-
ordinate lengths to posit an adversarial relationship, some
petulant quarrel for which evidence simply does not exist.

Indeed, we can often know more about collaboration in the
pageants than in the public theater because extant guild or
city records provide information. Most discussions of rivalry
among dramatists derive from a text-centered interpretation.
Nineteenth century scholars either did not know of this additional information; or they chose to ignore it, preferring their
own theories of jealousy, ill will, virulent attack, sneering,
and disparaging comments. Ultimately reductive, such an
approach and ideology rendered impossible any attempt to
understand collaboration. On the subject of the Middleton-
Munday rivalry, twentieth century scholars have chosen to
imitate rather than investigate. We stand on the verge of
parody.

To redeem ourselves we must regularly and faithfully question the received knowledge passed to us from earlier scholars. Second, we need to underscore the idea and practice of
collaboration, made particularly manifest in pageant texts and
the accompanying evidence from guild records. Margreta de
Grazia and Peter Stallybrass have concluded: "We need, in
other words, to rethink Shakespeare in relation to our new
knowledge of collaborative writing, collaborative printing, and
the historical contingencies of textual production."[32] Third,
we might shift the meaning of "rivalry" so that it does not
always mean attack or quarrel. James Shapiro has shown how
this can profitably be done as he redefines the rivalry among

Marlowe, Jonson, and Shakespeare to refer to their struggles with "influence."[33]

Middleton's sneering at his hapless rival Munday survives as a fiction that itself grows out of a romantic cult of the proprietary single author, a triumph of the individual author who dismisses, erases competitors. But the fact of collaboration forces us to think differently, even as we understand Shapiro's paradox: "the very frequency of collaboration in the public theater appears to have heightened sensitivity to the distinctive voices of individual dramatists" (8). Clearly scholars writing about the theater have to negotiate this paradox, hearing the distinctive voices yet hearing the surrounding ones as well.

If Middleton seems not to have had Munday explicity in mind in the 1613 text, if no other evidence exists of a quarrel between the two, if they in fact collaborated on this pageant and several others, and if Munday conspicuously incorporates a Middleton pageant text into his 1618 revision of Stow's *Survey*, then I think we can safely surrender the nineteenth century myth of their unpleasant rivalry — just in time for the twenty-first century.

EIGHT

Did a "War of the Theaters" Occur?

In 1973, Norbert Platz declared: "The War of the Theatres by which nineteenth century literary historians were so much fascinated, is dead and buried, and nowadays hardly anyone who is interested in the Elizabethan period wants to resurrect it."[1] But Platz's report of the war's death has been greatly exaggerated. I want to resurrect the topic of the War of the Theaters; and I intend to focus primarily on its nineteenth century history. Although the alleged skirmish, principally among the dramatists Jonson, Marston, and Dekker, occurred roughly in the 1598–1602 period, it gained a new and important lease on life in the nineteenth century.[2] Indeed, one could argue that the War of the Theaters *belongs* to the nineteenth century. That, in fact, will be the heart of my position. I want to see this "war" as a product of nineteenth century scholarship, itself often beset with a kind of Darwinian ethos, even before Darwin. Early in the century (1814), for example, Isaac Disraeli published three volumes of his *Quarrels of Authors*, including a long section on "Jonson and Decker."[3] This atmosphere, caught up in scholarly politics, triggers an exaggerated response to the limited evidence available, leading, I believe, to an inadvertent fictionalizing of the war. In the name of providing a "history" of the War of the Theaters, nineteenth century scholars instead provided a fiction, a narrative that itself constitutes a war. I suggest alternatives to such an imagined war.

My rallying point centers on Algernon Swinburne's trenchant commentary on the habit of character identification in a number of the plays. Swinburne writes in 1889 in *A Study of Ben Jonson*: "But such absurdities of misapplication and misconstruction, once set afloat on the Lethean waters of stagnating tradition, will float for ever by grace of the very rottenness which prevents them from sinking."[4] Swinburne adds: "Ignorance assumes and idleness repeats what sciolism ends by accepting as a truth no less indisputable than undisputed." I intend to dispute the largely undisputed "truths" of the war, beginning with an examination of the evidence and nineteenth century reaction to and interpretation of it.

Nearly two decades after the war, Jonson visited William Drummond in Scotland and indulged in endless conversations with him. A rapt listener, Drummond recorded many of Jonson's comments. In these *Conversations* we find Jonson's statement in 1619 that "he had many quarrells with Marston beat him & took his Pistol from him, wrote his Poetaster on him the beginning of ym [them] were that Marston represented him in the stage."[5] This juicy bit of gossip, first made publicly available in 1842, has been seized on by students of the war. For many, Jonson's statement confirms the reality of a war, suggests a possible reason for its beginning, puts the blame squarely on Marston, and reveals how artistic wrangling led to physical violence. As one recent critic puts the matter: "The controversy it generated easily spilled over into physical violence, when Jonson not only parodied but also assaulted and robbed Marston for subjecting him to public ridicule."[6] Since Jonson's account constitutes the only "evidence" of physical violence, we must be careful about implying that the war "easily spilled" into such examples.

Although seemingly irresistible, Jonson's account of his dealings with Marston should be taken with several grains of salt. We encounter here a fundamental problem in evaluating evidence: how much and how far should we trust comments made by one participant in an artistic squabble? Should we believe that Jonson actually took Marston's pistol and beat him? This sounds wonderfully virile on Jonson's part, and we know that he had a famous temper. But the idea also resonates fully with his self-serving, self-aggrandizing quality. In one sense, Jonson can safely make the comment to Drummond, who, slightly in awe of Jonson, has no way (perhaps no desire) to validate the report.[7] We get only Jonson's version of things. That alone should prompt suspicion. But, it has been argued, this "proof" joins all the other "proofs." I, for one, remain doubtful.

I see the report to Drummond and the material that comes at the end of the *Poetaster* text as elements of Jonson's self-fashioning, his attempt to shape an understanding of whatever kind of war occurred. The 1602 quarto text of *Poetaster* contains only a brief note to the reader, indicating that Jonson had intended an "Apology" "with his reasons for the publishing of this booke: but (since he is no lesse restrain'd, then thou depriu'd of it, by Authoritie) hee praies thee to thinke charitably of what thou hast read . . ." (261). We do not possess any independent evidence confirming that some "authority" restrained Jonson from publishing the Apology. We can only speculate about his reasons for the publishing. Instead of seeing Jonson as victim, I think of him as perpetrating his own fiction. His cryptic comment allows us, even encourages us, to imagine the wrongs that he has experienced, compounded by the restriction of authority on him: he shows us a man more sinned against than sinning. We cannot be certain that some kind of Apology appeared as part of the performance; Jonson aims at readers.

The Folio of 1616 contains the full-fledged "Apologetical Dialogue," which, some scholars have been quick to claim, must have been the item allegedly suppressed in the earlier text. We cannot know. In some ways we find ourselves in the trap of the deposition scene in *Richard II*. This disputed evidence can prove little. But we do know that Jonson devoted much effort to shaping the Folio volume to suit his purposes, artistic and personal. In other words, the Apologetical Dialogue may not have been around in the earlier period as part of the War of the Theaters. In the address "To the Reader," Jonson insists that it "was only once spoken upon the stage, and all the answer I ever gave to sundry impotent libels then cast out (and some yet remaining) against me and this play" (261). In the late nineteenth century A. W. Ward suggested that Jonson himself spoke the Apology on stage, a view endorsed by the most recent editor of *Poetaster* (261). But this compounds difficulties and probably only adds to the fiction about this play. Jonson further makes a distinction between "their manners that provoked me then, and mine that neglected them ever." He busily constructs a self-righteous persona.

The Apologetical Dialogue, as interesting and revealing as it may be, cannot be used as evidence for the War of the Theaters. I suspect that Jonson wrote it long after *Poetaster*'s performance, in any event in time for the Folio. Jonson looks to posterity and wants to set the record straight in a written form designed for readers. In the dialogue itself, the "Author" figure sums up in a disingenuous way his position: "I, at whom they shot, sit here shot-free, / And as unhurt of envy as unhit" (263). Polyposus and Nasutus question him closely and rehearse the charges leveled against him. He characterizes the writing of *Poetaster*: "I can profess I never writ that piece /

More innocent, or empty of offence" (265). The Author accepts only one charge brought against him, that he wrote slowly. This rhetorical strategy lends a kind of credibility to his position. In the midst of the discussion, the Author also says: "But sure I am, three years / They did provoke me with their petulant styles / On every stage" (266). Many commentators have fastened on the statement of "three years" as providing a beginning point for the War of the Theaters. But again, I think we have to be skeptical.

Jonson writes the dialogue to serve his purposes, not to provide an accurate account of events. The dialogue therefore exists as fiction, not as history. It provides us a portrait of Jonson as beset by "hornets" and "screaming grasshoppers," innocent of all wrongdoing. Had he pursued his enemies, he would have indulged "a feminine humour, / And far beneath the dignity of a man" (270–71). The idea of Jonson as "manly" and others as "effeminate" crops up in nineteenth century criticism. C. H. Herford put it best: Marston's "childish vanity . . . made his quarrels numerous, virulent, and brief. This effeminate figure was in the end caught by the spell of Jonson's personality, and became a devoted disciple; but his first contact with the most masculine of Elizabethans produced only a prolonged explosion of ill-will."[8] Small wonder that the Herford and Simpson edition of Jonson refers to the Apologetical Dialogue as offering a "manly and sufficient justification."[9] In the dialogue Jonson touches all the bases; he knows a good fiction when he sees one.

He creates a romantic myth of the long-suffering author; and he sends this document out to readers, who, in 1616, are far removed from the presumed event, so that they can agree with the author. He provides them an appealing narrative, one that dovetails nicely, I think, into his later remark to Drummond. The Dialogue also fits the overall purposes of the 1616 Folio, a collection that Jonson shapes to suit his self image. Recent commentators have underscored the "constructedness" of the Folio, a publication consciously changed to reflect how Jonson wanted to be presented to a reading public. As Timothy Murray has observed, "As shown by 'The Catalogue,' the folio flaunts but one image: its own *intra*textuality or Jonson's own version of his textual history."[10] This reshaping Loewenstein also notes: "it becomes clear in these texts that the assertion of the authority of the text, its counterauthority with respect to performance, entails Jonson's contentious jealousy of his own cultural authority."[11] I suggest that this authorial jealousy extends to *Poetaster* and the writing of the Dialogue for 1616 publication.

I do not mean to imply that Jonson made *everything* up, but rather that he exaggerated whatever events had taken place. The reality of some kind of quarrel finds support in Dekker's "To the World" preface to his *Satiromastix*. Dekker in fact coins the term "Poetomachia" to characterize the squabble, "lately commenc'd betweene Horace the second [i.e., Jonson], and a band of leane-witted Poetasters."[12] Horace, Dekker insists, "hal'd his Poetasters to the Barre, the Poetasters untruss'd Horace: how worthily eyther, or how wrongfully, (World) leave it to the Jurie." Dekker writes: "Read his *Arraignement* [i.e., *Poetaster*] and see." The evidence for the War does not get more explicit than this; whether this evidence confirms a "war" is the question. The tone of Dekker's address sharpens at the end: "let that mad Dog *Detraction* bite till his teeth bee worne to the stumps: *Envy* feede thy Snakes so fat with poyson till they burst" (310). The genial tone of the play itself counters this harshness, itself a pose. The Epilogue, spoken by Tucca, teases the audience: "if you set your hands and Seales to this, *Horace* will write against it, and you may have more sport" (385). And then the Poetasters "will untrusse him agen, and agen, and agen." One can certainly read Dekker's comments as implying that he and others have at least one eye firmly fixed on the box office. One can almost smell a collusion.

The plays themselves constitute the other major "evidence"

for the War of the Theaters. Perhaps Gerard Langbaine, in one of the earliest works of dramatic criticism, set the stage for probing the plays for what they can reveal of literary or topical history. Writing in 1691, Langbaine says of Dekker's *Satiromastix* that "This Play was writ on the occasion of *Ben Johnson's* [sic] *Poetaster*, where under the Title of *Crispinus*, Ben lash'd our Author, which he endeavour'd to retaliate by Untrussing *Ben* under the title of *Horace Junior*."[13] Langbaine adds: "I heartily wish for our Author's Reputation, that he had not been the Aggressor in this Quarrel; but being altogether ignorant of the Provocations given him, I must suspend my Judgment, and leave it to better Judges to determine the Controversy" (295). The critic shows suitable caution, a quality to be ignored by later scholars.

Poetaster and *Satiromastix* thus immediately arise as dramas that yield information about the poetic war. But even as Cyrus Hoy has to admit of Dekker's play: "The result is a dramatic medley that has been the despair of critics since Swinburne."[14] One might, in other words, have wished for a more successful play to "answer" *Poetaster*. Nineteenth century scholars added several other plays to the war, including Marston's *Histriomastix, What You Will*, and *Jack Drum's Entertainment*; and Jonson's *Every Man Out of His Humour*, and *Cynthia's Revels*. The list, of course, varies, largely depending on the imagination of the scholars. We recall that the "evidence" consists mainly of Jonson's comment to Drummond about Marston, the "Apologetical Dialogue" that appears attached to the text of *Poetaster* in the 1616 Folio, and the plays themselves. Part of the discussion here will sketch the trajectory of that creative musing that began to find hints of the War everywhere.

I choose as my starting point of nineteenth century scholars William Gifford and his 1816 edition of Ben Jonson.[15] This edition and its various revisions became the standard edition of Jonson until the twentieth century edition prepared by

Herford and Simpson. Gifford had one burning passion: to make the world safe for Jonson. He wanted to do for Jonson what the eighteenth century had done for Shakespeare in terms of scholarship and editing. Indeed, partly he determined to serve as an apologist for Jonson against what he saw as unfair attacks on Jonson's character, perpetrated by several eighteenth century editors of Shakespeare, especially Edmond Malone. This desire logically led Gifford into the controversy of the poetic war. He therefore focuses on the attacks on Jonson by his fellow playwrights, embraces a system of character identification, accepts certain evidence, and launches his own personal and professional war on fellow scholars.

About *Poetaster*, Gifford writes that the Children of the Queen's Chapel performed the play in 1601. Then in order to state Jonson's purpose and justification for this play, Gifford quotes approvingly a generous portion of the "Apologetical Dialogue" (1:lvii). He begins the quotation from the section about the "three years" in which the others did provoke Jonson. Gifford also adds that "The players, who had so long provoked him with their petulance on the stage, felt the bitterness of his reproof" (lix) — another conclusion drawn from the Dialogue. In Gifford's account we may also find the seed of the idea that Jonson spoke the part of the Author on stage: "Jonson was induced, after a few representations, to add to it, what he calls an Apologetical Dialogue, in which he bore the chief part. It was spoken only once, and then laid aside by command" (lxi). In any event, all of these ideas derive from the "evidence" of the Dialogue. But Gifford does not make clear in his Introduction that the 1602 quarto text does not contain this Dialogue; he does in the edition of the play include a note: "This Apology was first printed in 1616" (2:539n). This observation, of course, does not confront the question of when the Dialogue may have been written. As indicated above, Jonson may have written it explicitly for the 1616 Folio, where, in any event, it appears for the first time. Therefore, Gifford has uncritically accepted as reliable the Dialogue as "evidence" for the War of the Theaters. He will not be the last to do so.

Gifford writes simply: "As Marston and Dekker had headed the cabal against him, he [Jonson] introduced them under the respective names of Crispinus and Demetrius" (1:lvii). Here begins the identification of specific characters with specific playwrights, altering the single identification that Langbaine had made at the end of the seventeenth century. In his edition of *Poetaster* Gifford carries on the matter of the identification. For example, he notes at one point: "the Crispinus of Jonson is Marston, to whom every word of this directly points. This will derange much confident criticism; but I shall be found eventually in the right. Decker I take to be the Demetrius of the present play . . . I know not the origins of our poet's quarrel with either; but he denies, and I believe with truth, that he made the first attack" (2:453n). (Disraeli and Langbaine, for example, before Gifford, had identified Crispinus with Dekker.) Gifford, of course, wants to believe that Jonson did not attack first; the basis for this conclusion comes mainly from having accepted the "evidence" of the Apologetical Dialogue.

Late in act V of *Poetaster*, Gifford comments: "I have already observed, in opposition to the whole string of commentators, that Crispinus is Marston: if any doubts of it should remain after what has been advanced, the lines which follow will be more than sufficient to remove them" (2:517n). He refers to the peculiarly Marstonian language, "many of the uncouth and barbarous terms which characterize Marston's poetry." Gifford hesitates to search for many such terms from Marston because the "labour would be neither pleasant nor profitable." He chides other commentators who have accepted Marston's statement that he is "'free from licentiousness of language.' The fact is not so; he is extremely gross, and impure." Obviously, a strong moral sense guides Gifford's approach to editing Jonson, trying as ever to secure Jonson's reputation as a better person than his attacking contemporaries. As Gifford says at the end of his commentary on *Poetaster*: Jonson "was hourly growing in reputation with the wise and good; and in his three succeeding comedies soared to a height which his persecutors never reached, and where he consequently suffered but little molestation from their hostility" (2:551n).

Dekker comes in for severe scrutiny, both as one identified with the character Demetrius in *Poetaster* and as the author of *Satiromastix*. Commenting on act III, scene i of Jonson's play, Gifford says that "Decker attempts to ridicule this little ode, but without success: It is easy to parody any thing into nonsense; but to make the public believe that it comes from such men as Jonson, when it is done, exceeds the power of a hundred Deckers. This is some consolation" (2:431n). In the play's reference to Demetrius as a "dresser of plays," Gifford writes: "Here the allusion is too plain to be mistaken, except by those who can see nothing with their own eyes. *Demetrius* is unquestionably *Decker*" (2:461n). Gifford frequently employs the rhetorical strategy of dismissing any possible objection to his conclusions by implying myopia or stupidity on the part of any who might disagree.

Gifford complains about Dekker's approach to writing *Satiromastix*: "Decker writes in downright passion, and foams through every page. He makes no pretensions to invention, but takes up the characters of his predecessor, turns them the *seamy side without*, and produces a coarse and ill-wrought caricature" (1:lxiii). Given the genial nature of *Satiromastix*, it is difficult to see Dekker as "foaming" through every page. But Gifford wants to establish Dekker as "aggressor, and that, in conjunction with others, he had been ridiculing Jonson on every stage for *three years* before he sat down to write the *Poetaster*" (1:lxivn). "Yet," Gifford adds with smug indignation, "this is your 'harmless' fairy!" In his final note in the commentary on *Poetaster*, Gifford takes Dekker to task yet

again for his considerable "want of judgment" in borrowing characters from *Poetaster*. And he concludes: "But, indeed, the whole plot of the *Satiromastix* is absurd" (2:551n).
Throughout his observations Gifford maintains the view that
Jonson is innocent of all wrongdoing, that he is the supreme
"moral satirist."

In addition to Gifford's uncritical use of evidence, his identifying of certain characters with playwrights, and his overall
sense of an unfair attack on Jonson, he also establishes a kind
of war within the war. The subject may be the War of the
Theaters, but for Gifford that topic expands to include a war
on his fellow scholars. One idea feeds on the other; indeed, I
argue that because nineteenth century scholars loved attacking *each other*, the War of the Theaters naturally received
much attention, expansion, and fictionalizing. The theatrical
war of the late Tudor period became a pretext for a scholarly
war of the nineteenth century. Under the screen of discussing
the Elizabethan theatrical war, one could also skewer other
critics. At moments Jonson, Marston, and Dekker seem to
have pointed the way.

Gifford saves some of his harshest scorn for Edmond Malone,
himself no stranger to scholarly rivalry and battle, as the most
recent biography of Malone makes clear.[16] In a word, Gifford
did not invent such attacks; but he did possibly perfect them.
His edition of Jonson becomes the battleground, the place
where scores can be settled even if, as in the case of Malone,
the offending scholar is already dead. Gifford raises to a dubi-
ously high art the practice of editing with a vengeance: the
text of the literary author opens the door to other kinds of
battle. Many nineteenth century editors of literary works followed in Gifford's wake. War begets war.

Relying on the Apologetical Dialogue from *Poetaster*,
Gifford reports that Jonson "treats their [other playwrights's]
clamours, however, with supreme contempt, and only regrets
the hostility of *some better natures* whom they had drawn

over to their side . . ." (1:lix). Gifford adds: "By *better natures*, the commentators assure us that Shakspeare [sic] was meant, and Mr. Malone quotes the passage in more than one place to evince the *malignity* of Jonson — as if it were a crime in him to be unjustly calumniated!" Nothing sets Gifford off so much as the idea of the "malignity of Jonson"; indeed, one whole section of volume 1 of the edition focuses on this problem. Malone and other eighteenth century scholars who emphasized Shakespeare's genial nature at the expense of an irascible Jonson stir Gifford's ire. Responding to Malone's idea that "Shakespeare put Jonson down," Gifford says: "But with Mr. Malone's leave, if it went as far as either, Shakspeare was greatly to be blamed, for Jonson had given him no offence whatever" (1:lxn). "Let Mr. Malone," Gifford continues, "answer for the unforgiving temper with which he has dishonoured Shakspeare; — I believe nothing of it" (lxin). In a nice rhetorical sleight of hand Gifford turns the tables on Malone by assuming the role of defending Shakespeare.

In the commentary notes for *Poetaster* Gifford stays busy with his own war. Malone appears, but so do George Steevens and Thomas Davies. All earn Gifford's rebuke. Gifford lumps them altogether in one scintillating and scornful note: "Messrs. Steevens and Malone content their spleen, in general, with harping on the 'malignity of Jonson to *Shakspeare*': their zany, Mr. Thomas Davies, takes up the idle calumny, and embellishes it with ingenious additions of his own. Jonson, it seems, not only abused and insulted Shakspeare, but all the actors of his theatre" (2:459n). Gifford ridicules Steevens's suggestion that Jonson acted Hieronimo in *The Spanish Tragedy*: "At the time alluded to, *old* Ben might probably be about twenty years of age: but Steevens is too ready to trust the calumnies of any of Jonson's enemies" (2:445n). Gifford calls Davies "our egregious critic," whose ideas Gifford dismisses: "But enough of such deplorable folly" (2:460n). The final commentary note for *Poetaster* takes one last, withering slap at Davies: "Mr.

Davies, with whose perspicacity the reader is already acquainted, is pleased to affirm that the *Poetaster* is one of the lowest productions, and that Tucca is a wretched copy of Falstaff" (2:550n). About Tucca as a copy of Falstaff Gifford says that "none but Davies" could maintain such an absurd idea. Clearly Gifford regards his fellow scholars and critics as poetasters.

Criticism of and reaction to Gifford run throughout the nineteenth century as most who write about the War of the Theaters have to take Gifford into account. For example, Frederick Fleay adopts many of Gifford's ideas about the war; but that does not keep him from taking exception to some findings: "Gifford, rash and inaccurate as usual, says that Marston in *The Scourge* ridiculed Jonson's words, 'real, Delphic, intrinsicate,' &c., 'which are all to be found in his earliest comedies;' but when *The Scourge* was written not one of Jonson's extant comedies had been published, and scarcely one acted."[17] Whatever one may think of Gifford's work, to call it "rash and inaccurate as usual" smacks of the theatrical war itself. Ironically, more often than not Fleay agrees with Gifford. And because Gifford had devoted considerable energy to attacking Malone, James Boswell, in the edition of Shakespeare (1821) based on Malone's work, gives 18 pages to defending Malone against Gifford's charges.[18] Grosart chides Gifford for ignoring the implications of Jonson's comment to Drummond, "which he loses no opportunity of foolishly and perversely caluminating."[19] Robert Cartwright accuses Gifford of "wilful obstinacy" and warns: "We must receive with some caution the statements of Gifford, who instead of being the dispassionate biographer, sinks himself into the blind advocate."[20] I suggest that Gifford, in discussing the war and in editing *Poetaster*, set the stage for ongoing recriminations among scholars, a practice that characterizes much of nineteenth century scholarship. In such an atmosphere, expanding the Elizabethan theatrical war became a natural if not inevitable step.

In the 1873 edition of Thomas Dekker, Shepherd argues that Dekker had received provocation from Jonson. *Poetaster*, Shepherd insists, "had been flung like a fire-brand among the wits and witlings, among the poets and the smaller fry who only aspired to that name. Dekker was chosen as the champion of all these, and acquitted himself of the office in a most effective manner."[21] One might question how "effectively" *Satiromastix* responds to Jonson's play. But Shepherd has raised the dubious idea that the downtrodden playwrights chose Dekker as their "champion." Finally, Shepherd expresses regret "that two men so gifted should have prostituted their genius to the expression of such narrow jealousies and hatreds" (xv). He quotes approvingly a large section from Disraeli's *Quarrels* that clearly argues that Jonson was the "aggressor" in the war. This position overlooks Gifford's argument.

A. H. Bullen in his edition of Marston (1887) says: "There seem to have been many quarrels and more than one reconciliation."[22] This rather vague statement opens the war to many permutations, ever expanding. Indeed, Bullen spends time enlarging the number of Marston's plays that may have been involved in the war. For example, he insists that *Antonio and Mellida* and *Antonio's Revenge* had been "ridiculed in that year [1601] by Ben Jonson in *Poetaster*" (xxvi). In the Induction to *What You Will*, "Marston again had his fling at Ben Jonson" (xlvi). Bullen asserts: "It was doubtless with Marston's approval that Dekker took up the cudgels against the truculent Ben" — in writing *Satiromastix* (xxxiv). Bullen offers no evidence to support such a claim. And Bullen accepts the idea that Marston in *Scourge* ridiculed Jonson with such words as "real, intrinsecate, Delphic" (xxx). Bullen had found this idea in Gifford, who receives no credit; and the connection to *Scourge* Fleay disputes a few years later. We begin to see not only how the war expands but also how it knows no clear scholarly boundaries. It becomes the site for creative imagination, unfettered by ordinary constraints of evidence, and the place for personal squabbles.

Two important books close out the nineteenth century: Josiah Penniman's *The War of the Theatres* (1897) and Roscoe Small's *The Stage-Quarrel between Ben Jonson and the So-Called Poetasters* (1899). These books nicely sum up the century's approach to the subject. To start with, Penniman expands the war to include 13 plays. Suddenly, *Every Man in His Humour* joins the fray. "Although it contains no mention of Marston," Penniman writes, it "was yet closely connected with the 'War,' on account of the violent attack on Daniel which it contains."[23]

Now why "Jonson attacked Daniel, whom so many of his other contemporaries praised, we do not know" (13). But the attack on Daniel leads to Marston's response in *Scourge* and "probably also in *Histriomastix*" (13). Symptomatic of many approaches to the War, Penniman begins to construct a perilous edifice with each little piece tenuously and precariously connected with and dependent on another equally fragile piece. For example, we have to believe that Matthew represents Daniel: "That Samuel Daniel was the man held up to ridicule there can be no doubt . . ." (30).

Penniman has his own quarrels with other scholars, although he expresses himself in measured terms. For example, he offers a long critique of Fleay's confusion about the identification of some characters and their possible connection to Dekker (46–47n). Penniman criticizes critics who "have assumed, apparently without a particle of proof, that he [Dekker] was involved in it [the war] from the beginning. . . ." One could wish that Penniman's exacting standard of "proof" had operated fully in his own approach. He accepts Gifford with some reservation: "Little has been added to our knowledge of the meaning of *Poetaster* since Gifford published his notes, which, although containing some mistakes, yet point out clearly the most important allusions and the true relationship of the chief characters" (107). Penniman does not spell out exactly the "mistakes" Gifford made, and his later (1913) edition of *Poet-aster* clearly reflects its indebtedness to Gifford. Some of Penniman's notes in the Introduction to the edition engage in a running battle with earlier critics (see especially xxii–xxiii), such as Disraeli, Gifford, and Small. In other words, Penniman functions true to form for nineteenth century scholars and editors.

Surely one of the reasons Penniman in the edition of *Poet-aster* takes Small to task comes from Small's criticism of Penniman in *The Stage-Quarrel*. (One wonders if Small intends anything by calling the affair a "quarrel" instead of "war"; perhaps he only wants to avoid Penniman's term.) Small asserts: "In dealing with the abundant evidence afforded by those comedies, modern critics have shown themselves sin-gularly inefficient."[24] Small then sets out to clarify the issues, challenging the work of many critics, including Fleay and Penniman especially. Of Fleay's work Small writes: "for Fleay's book, capitally important as it is, is both confusing and untrustworthy" (10). Penniman "has failed to give an intel-ligible account of the chronology, causes, and results of the quarrel and has gone far astray in untangling the personal relations of the men involved in it" (10). The pages that fol-low purport to show how these critics failed. Amusingly, the attack on Penniman forms, lo and behold, the outline of what Small now intends to accomplish. In the tangled discussion of, say, *Every Man out of His Humour*, we see how Small func-tions as he first sets aside the analysis of Fleay and Penniman as being inadequate (44–45) and then proceeds with his own version. On another issue Small asserts: "The attempt to find evidence of a quarrel between Jonson and Marston earlier than 1599 has caused some very queer guesses" (63). Fleay, Gifford, Herford, and Penniman all come under attack for finding a representation of Jonson in Marston's Satires. The nineteenth century closes much as it had begun: the Elizabethan theatrical war blends readily into nineteenth century scholarly skirmishes. At moments, who can tell the war from the war?

Small has "narrowed" the list of possible plays involved in the war to ten and includes Jonson, Marston, Dekker, Shakespeare, and Anthony Munday as participants. Small writes: "At all events, careful research fails to show evidence that any other man took part in it. The elaborate structure of modern criticism has no foundation either in early testimony or in valid reasoning" (199). Small's summary (199) of the whole war underscores just how tricky this business can be. The quarrel begins in Small's view with Munday's "probable" attack on Jonson in 1598, who then attacked Munday. And off we go with Marston jumping into the fray, although intending to compliment Jonson in the character Chrisoganus in *Histriomastix*. Jonson responds, and finally Dekker joins in with *Satiromastix*. Whether this "elaborate structure" retains persuasive validity becomes the sticking point. It has a kind of logic, provided that all the pieces fit together.

It also proceeds on some shaky assumptions. Small writes: "All this time the quarrel had been growing more bitter, and now Jonson made the climax with the Poetaster, about June, 1601, in which he vented his wrath upon Marston and Dekker" (127). Small's chronology requires questioning, as does his by now familiar use of the "Apologetical Dialogue" as evidence for the war. He also says: "We have seen that at the close of the sixteenth century, the time was ripe for personal satire upon the stage" (128). He adds: "Given such conditions, a quarrel must occur, in which all parties are partly in the wrong" (129). "No doubt the fires were smouldering all the time" (128), Small says. Such observations beg many large and important questions. Once asserting a presumed cultural atmosphere, then Small can move readily to a view that suggests inevitability: "a quarrel must occur." If it must, then the scholar can quickly supply a scenario, one that has, in my judgment, a large measure of fiction in it. We confront Small logic and less evidence.

This sketch of major nineteenth century scholars and their response to the War of the Theaters reveals several problems in their analyses, as I have already indicated. I want to return to the major issue of *chronology*. Several conclusions that these scholars reach depend on assumptions about the time at which the playwrights wrote specific plays. As we know, under the best of circumstances this can be problematic. But if one wants to establish a pattern of play and response, as nineteenth century writers do, then we have to be certain that play x preceded play y; otherwise, y cannot be a response to x. Here matters get very difficult, if not impossible. I want to focus on the specific case of the relationship of the writing of *Poetaster* to Dekker's "response" in *Satiromastix*.

Early on, Gifford established the basic scenario: namely, that Jonson somehow learned that Dekker intended to write a play lambasting him, and so Jonson took preemptive action by writing *Poetaster*. Dekker's play therefore becomes a re-sponse to Jonson. Gifford writes: "Marston and Decker were eager to revenge the imaginary insult, and readily consented to lead the attack now meditated against him. Of this Jonson obtained full information; for the secret was ill kept by the poets . . ." (1:lv). Jonson found it necessary to "draw up the *Poetaster*, in which together with the untrussing, the whip-ping, and the stinging, he anticipated and answered many of the accusations subsequently brought against him in the *Satiromastix*" (lvi). In other words, Jonson writes an "answer" before the other play even exists. He can do this, according to Gifford, because he "obtained full information" about Dekker's intended play. All of this hinges on the assumption that poets just cannot keep secrets. They talked, and Jonson wrote. The logic of this approach collapses for lack of evidence.

Interesting and seemingly innocent myths enjoy long lives.

For example, Penniman, writing in 1897, says: "An examination of *Poetaster* shows that it is not at all impossible that Jonson did not originally intend to mention Dekker, with whom he had no quarrel, but that after *Poetaster* was well advanced in preparation, . . . Jonson learned of the plan to 'untruss' him, and in order to forestall the attack added the lines of Demetrius" (113–14). In a 1905 edition of *Poetaster*, Herbert Mallory writes: the play "was probably undertaken, as it was certainly hurried to completion, in order to forestall a counterattack which Jonson had heard was to be made by the dramatists whom he had been satirizing."[25] Another product of nineteenth century scholarship, Felix Schelling's *Elizabethan Drama* (1908), echoes Gifford via Penniman, whose work Schelling follows closely. Schelling writes: "It seems, then, likely that Jonson had originally no intent to satirize Dekker, with whom he had no quarrel; but that, learning that that dramatist had been hired to 'untruss' him, he forestalled the attack by this addition to his satire."[26] Schelling slavishly imitates Penniman, hesitating even to change much of the language. Penniman and Schelling do not bother to offer an explanation of how Jonson could have learned of Dekker's plan: he just somehow "learns" and sets out to beat Dekker to the task by writing his play first.

The life of this myth extends well into the twentieth century. The Herford and Simpson *Ben Jonson* observes: "It was rumoured that they were preparing an elaborate revenge; and within a few weeks . . . Jonson, spurred to action, was at work . . ." (1:27). In his commentary notes on Dekker's *Satiromastix*, Cyrus Hoy writes: "The blow that *Satiromastix* was to administer to Jonson was well advertized before it appeared. Rumors seem to have reached him not long after the production of *Cynthia's Revels* in the winter of 1600–1601 that the attack was being prepared, and he promptly set about anticipating it with *Poetaster*." (1:181). Anne Barton offers a slightly different version of events: "By 1601, Dekker's suspicion that Jonson was prevaricating when he claimed always to pillory the vice, and never the individual, had ripened into certainty. Whatever the truth of the matter, Dekker saw the character of Anaides as a slur on himself. Rashly, he let it be known that he was preparing a riposte. Jonson responded by rushing out *Poetaster*. . . ."[27] Dekker himself now seems to blame, as he "rashly" let it be known what he intended.

Writing in 1989, David Riggs says: "In the early months of 1601, when Jonson was mulling over his response to *What You Will*, he learned that he had another enemy to contend with as well. Dekker had now begun writing *Satiromastix*. . . ."[28] Therefore, Jonson wrote *Poetaster* "well in advance of *Satiromastix*." Riggs does not offer a theory of how Jonson learned of his new enemy Dekker. David Kay more or less accepts the prevailing idea, dating back at least to Gifford, when he writes in 1995: "What began as a debate among private theatre playwrights soon broadened with Thomas Dekker's *Satiromastix* . . . produced jointly by the Lord Chamberlain's Men and the Children of Paul's some time in the late spring or summer of 1601."[29] He adds: "Jonson, in turn, got wind of their project and, in fifteen weeks, wrote *Poetaster, or His Arraignment* as a preemptive strike to neutralise their planned attack." Everywhere we turn scholars agree that Jonson learned — by whatever means — of Dekker's plan and responded accordingly and quickly. No one stops to ask just exactly *how* Jonson could have learned enough that would enable him to anticipate most of what Dekker intended to do. This information would be especially difficult to come by if we accept the premise of warring enemies. But chalk it up to poets who cannot keep secrets, or to a rash and talkative Dekker, or to something out there in the "wind." Or perhaps we can chalk it up to a fertile imagination that took root in the nineteenth century.

The other major problem with the nineteenth century's exploration of the war derives from the process of *character identification*, which becomes crucial. That is, such and such a character must be Jonson, or Marston, or Dekker — or indeed, a host of other possibilities. Imaginative forays might have gained from heeding Jonson's own words in the Induction to *Bartholomew Fair*, where the Scrivener reads the Articles of Agreement concluded between the spectators and the author. The spectator should not speculate about the characters in the play: "Or that will pretend to affirm, on his own inspired ignorance, what Mirror of Magistrates is meant by the Justice, what great lady by the Pig-woman, what concealed statesman by the Seller of Mousetraps, and so of the rest."[30] A fundamental question arises: can literature, especially the literature of this early period indeed provide the kind of evidence that scholars have desired and found? Where, again, should we draw the line between acceptable and unacceptable practices of ferreting out topical or historical information from fictional texts? These important questions, I suggest, nineteenth century scholars largely ignored. Their zeal refused to be bound by such constraints. The danger becomes obvious, as we see.

Two statements may sum up the century's approach to character identification. Grosart, who writes of Shakespeare's influence on Marston, acknowledges the difficulty of his task: "Opinions will differ. One catches sounds where to others all is silence. One discerns resemblance and analogies which another looking on never thinks of" (2:xviii). Grosart has put his finger on a fundamental problem: namely, the largely arbitrary quality of this endeavor. What if the sound is really silence, or vice versa? Robert Cartwright, in one of the most extraordinary books dependent on character identification, offers a breath-taking assessment: "However fanciful these opinions may appear, I hold them to be true, and have more delight in discovering these *imaginary* diamonds in the gardens of Shakspere, than picking up nuggets of gold in the fields of Australia" (26). *I believe, therefore I know*, Cartwright says.

The more fanciful, the more effort one expends in holding such opinions to be true. Such a position offers potential delight. Cartwright, and to a lesser degree Grosart, falls back on his own private vision, which creates problems for the rest of us. Such criticism risks becoming merely impressionistic and therefore incapable of rational disagreement.

Roscoe Small suggests that books by Cartwright and a German scholar, E. Hermann, are "as crazy as books can well be. They are now never quoted as authorities" (8). We may share Small's assessment without absolving others, such as Small himself, who routinely indulge their fancies in character identification. Richard Simpson, for example, speaks for many nineteenth century scholars: "Marston was modelling himself on Jonson when he wrote the first part of *Antonio and Mellida* in 1598; was quarrelling with him when he satirized him as *Torquatus* in the *Scourge of Villany*, 1599; was lashed by Jonson in 1599 as Clove; in 1600 in *Cynthia's Revels* as Hedon or Anaides; in 1601 in the *Poetaster* as Crispinus."[31] Cartwright, of course, has additional ideas, such as the identification of characters in Marston's *Antonio and Mellida*: "Piero is a satire on Jonson; Feliche, a gentle reminiscence of Macilente; and Bobadil and Master Mathew may be the prototypes of Matzagente and Castilio . . ." (35). Cartwright identifies Ovid in *Poetaster* with Shakespeare: "can it then be denied, can it for a moment be doubted, that Ovid in the *Poetaster* is intended for Shakspere?" (13). On one could go multiplying examples for almost all of the nineteenth century scholars; they differ in degree.

Even if they do not share Cartwright's extreme position, they also do not leave much room for doubt when they assert the connection between fictional characters and the actual playwrights. A rare instance of possible doubt emerges from the Folger Library's copy of Grosart's edition of Marston's poems. When Grosart writes that "'Torquatus' also of these 'Satyres' unmistakably points to Jonson" (2:xlix), a handwritten marginal note inscribes simply but emphatically: "Oh!!!." This exclamation about Grosart's assertion comes from the pen of Brinsley Nicholson, Grosart's friend. I like to read this comment as expressing doubt, even though I know I cannot be certain of the tone of this stark exclamation. As we know, candor and doubt exist in few nineteenth century studies of the War of the Theaters.

But skepticism must govern our approach to how earlier scholars understood the evidence of a war and how they constructed a narrative to fit it. Indeed, as I have argued, fiction-making overtakes restrained scholarship; expected boundaries explode, and imaginations run rampant. Wars stir within wars; the Elizabethan theatrical war generates a nineteenth century scholarly war, leading to competing narratives and competing scholars. In the task of evaluating whether a War of the Theaters occurred and if so how, we should not lose sight of another scenario for which sufficient evidence exists.

I refer to acts of *collaboration*, evident among Jonson, Marston, and Dekker.[32] For example, as the nineteenth century editor Bullen observes: "It is curious to note that in the very year (1601) when the quarrel between Marston and Jonson reached a climax, the two enemies are contributing poems to the *Divers Poetical Essays* appended to Robert Chester's tedious and obscure *Love's Martyr*" (1:xxxv–xxxvi). Of course, their contribution to this poetic miscellany does not in itself prove collaboration. More convincingly, Marston writes a glowing dedication to Jonson in his play *The Malcontent* (1602–04): "To Benjamin Jonson, the most discriminating and weighty poet, his frank and sincere friend, John Marston, disciple of the Muses, gives and dedicates this his unpolished comedy."[33] This hardly smacks of recent intense enmity. Dekker and Jonson collaborated in producing the spectacular royal entry pageant for King James's passage through the City of London, 15 March 1604.[34] Had nineteenth century scholars focused on acts of collaboration, they might well have tempered their enthusiasm for a personal war among the dramatists.

In fact, evidence of collaboration does not fit well with the narrative of a war. I suggest that the earlier scholars largely chose to ignore the competing evidence, giving themselves often to flights of fantasy.[35] Jeffrey Masten's recent book, *Textual Intercourse*, lays out a convincing argument for the prevalence and importance of collaboration in playwriting in the period. Masten writes: "collaboration was a prevalent mode of textual production in the sixteenth and seventeenth centuries, only eventually displaced by the mode of singular authorship with which we are more familiar."[36] Masten urges that "we no longer regard collaboration as an aberrant form of textual production in a period and genre in which it in fact predominated, and that we forego anachronistic attempts to divine the singular author of each scene, phrase, and word" (7). The nineteenth century's preoccupation with singular authorship occluded the possibilities of collaboration. Although here I do not precisely write about joint authorship in the War of the Theaters, I do think that the atmosphere and practice of collaboration informed any events that we can recover about such a war. If, on the other hand, a romantic ideology of authorship prevails with each writer being beset by other writers and hostile forces, then a more subdued and more accurate image of collaboration becomes impossible.

The nineteenth century "rescued" the War of the Theaters from relative obscurity and breathed new life and energy into it. But at what price? In answer to the question of "did a War of the Theaters occur?" I believe that minor skirmishes certainly happened. But the large-scale war as imagined by the likes of Gifford, Fleay, Penniman, Small, and others must be seen as an exaggeration. A zeal for narrative and an equally compelling zeal to engage in battle with one's fellow scholars distorted and inflated the scanty evidence available. Beside the scholars' intricate character identifications and certainty about chronology, we might inscribe Nicholson's succinct "Oh!!!"

NINE

Gilbert Dugdale and the Royal Entry of James I (1604)

Gilbert Dugdale, if not exactly a name to reckon with, makes an important, generally unrecognized, contribution to our knowledge of the spectacular civic pageant that welcomed James I through the streets of London on 15 March 1604. His text, short title *The Time Triumphant*, provides an eyewitness account of the happenings on the day of the royal entry.[1] Discussions of the civic pageant, mine included, have tended either to ignore Dugdale's text or to give him short shrift.[2] I will demonstrate here Dugdale's contribution to our understanding of the pageant, arguing that we must add him to the list of essential texts if we aim to get the fullest picture of this civic entertainment. Though at moments Dugdale can be maddeningly silent about events or frustratingly cryptic about what he saw and heard, I think this gives credibility to his report as an authentic one, not one whipped up in response to other printed accounts.

About Gilbert Dugdale we know little. John Nichols, who reprints Dugdale's text (somewhat inaccurately) makes the teasing suggestion that Dugdale may have had a connection with the theater.[3] Nichols's educated guess has some basis in fact. The evidence comes in Dugdale's other published work, *A True Discourse of the Practice of Elizabeth Caldwell on the Parson of T. Caldwell* (STC 7293, 1604). This full report of a scandal in Chester in which Elizabeth Caldwell conspired with her lover to kill her husband demonstrates Dugdale's journalistic skill and concern for detail, including capturing Elizabeth's final words before her execution. These qualities prevail also in Dugdale's report of the pageant. At the end of *A True Discourse*, Robert Armin, a member of the King's Men, affixes his name to a letter addressed to Lady Mary Chandos, widow of Lord Chandos. Armin writes: "But so it was, and for the better proffe that it was so, I haue placed my kinsmans name to it, who was present at all her troubles."[4] The kinship of Armin and Dugdale raises the probability of Dugdale's knowledge of the theater; perhaps the actor suggested to Dugdale that he try his reportorial talents on the dramatic event of the civic pageant.

The full title of Dugdale's 1604 quarto reveals its basic contents: *The Time Triumphant, Declaring in briefe, the ariual of our Soueraigne liedge Lord, King IAMES into England, His Coronation at Westminster: Together with his late royal progresse, from the Towre of London through the Cittie, to his Highness mannor of WhiteHall. Shewing also, the Varieties & Rarieties of al the sundry Trophies or Pageants, erected aswel, by the worthy Cittizens of the honorable Cittie of London: as also by certaine of other Nations, Namely, Italians, Dutch and French. With a rehearsall of the King and Queenes late comming to the Exchaunge in London.* This is obviously the work of a man who believes that one should judge a book by its titlepage. Because of a feud among the foreign diplomatic corps in London at the time of the pageant, we do not get any helpful description from the Venetian ambassador, a usually reliable source for such events.[5] Thus Dugdale's account assumes special importance, serving as presumably the only full-fledged report from a spectator. It therefore joins the three principal texts of the entertainment as essential items for a study of this pageant: Jonson, *Ben Jonson, his Part of King James his Royall and Magnificent Entertainment* (1604); Dekker, *The Magnificent Entertainment* (1604); Stephen Harrison, *Arches of Triumph* (1604). The textual relationship of these texts to one another has been ably discussed by Fredson Bowers.[6]

Before examining specifically what Dugdale reports about the entertainment, I want to look at some other matters in this quarto. Like the pageant itself, much in Dugdale's text praises King James and the royal family. The "Dedicatorie poem" observes that James has been led hither by God's grace, "to plant . . . peace, plenty and grace together" (sig. A2). As the pageant is glorious "in showe," so may the King in triumph establish his reign. The poet closes: "King IAMES live happie, happiest on the Earth: / That God all seeing, may so blesse thy Lande,/ That seeing all, may all thy evils withstande."[7] The poem that follows, the "poore subjects prayer," centers its concern on the royal family: "That pierles ANN," "Rare HENRY young,/ . . . The Royall heyre" (A3); "Yea all in all, all Ioy betide,/ King, Queene, and Children, Heauens pride" (A3v).

Dugdale begins his report by starting with the journey of Sir Robert Carey to Scotland to bring word to James of Elizabeth's death and of his proclamation as King of England. He tells of the parting of James from Anne in Edinburgh as the king began his journey to the new land: "the parting betwixt his Queene and him in the open streete, in the full eye of all his subjects, who spent teares in aboundance to behold it" (A4v). Concerning the entertainment at Berwick, Dugdale writes, "I neede not set downe both of the traine of *England* &

Souldiers there." But he does decide to recount James's response to a question posed by one who notes that the rain has given way to sunshine:

> it [the weather] presages somewhat sure, the King smiling, no great matter quoth he, onely this imagine, the first faire shew of Weather, my prosperous setting forwards by Gods sufferance. The latter shower, the vniuersall teares of my Cuntrey, to leaue their king: and this suddaine Sunshine the Ioy of Englande for my approach. (sig. A4v)

Dugdale as an eyewitness to this episode may be unlikely, but his rendering of it does demonstrate some of the skill and care evident in his report of the royal entry.

Concern for detail guides Dugdale's report of the coronation as he notes James's salutation to the people and theirs to him "when he tooke Barge at *WhiteHall*, on *S. Iames* his day" (B1). Much attention focuses on Anne, "*Englandes Tryumph*, the worth of women," described as "with her seemely hayre downe trailing on her princely bearing shoulders on which was a crownet of Gold" (B1). Her presence moved the subjects: "women weeping ripe cryed all in one voice, God blesse the Royall Queene, welcome to England long to liue & continew so." Only the presence of the plague — sign of God's omnipotent power according to Dugdale — dashed the glory of the day. Even so, the hearts of Londoners "were wilde Fire, and burned vnquenchable in loue, to his Royall couple."

Unexpectedly Dugdale provides reference to the patronage of acting companies by the royal family. Such action indicates James's concern for all people:

> but to the meane [James] gaue grace, as taking to him the late Lord chamberlaines seruants now the *Kings* acters: the *Queene* taking to her the Earle of *Worsters* seruants that are now her acters, the Prince their sonne *Henry* Prince of Wales full of hope, tooke to him the Earle of *Nottingham* his seruants who are now his acters, so that of Lords seruants they are now the seruants of the *King Queene* and *Prince*. (sig. B1v)

Apart from Dugdale's prematurely making Henry Prince of Wales, this fascinating report gives further plausibility to Dugdale's familiarity with the theater. As we know, James had brought the Lord Chamberlain's Men under his patronage shortly after his arrival in England; the patent dates from 19 May 1603.[8] But the dates for the other companies coming under the patronage of the Queen and Henry are much less certain. Chambers conjectures that after Christmas 1603, Nottingham's Men became Prince Henry's men, and Worcester's Men became Queen Anne's Men sometime in 1603–04 (the patent is undated; Chambers, 2:186; 2:229–30). Since Ralph Blore, the printer, entered Dugdale's book in the Stationers's Register on 27 March 1604, this would seem to be the latest possible date for the transfer of the actors to royal patronage. Dugdale's information thus helps pin down the limits of these dates. Rarely do writers at the time take note of royal patronage of the drama in such detail.

As the day of the pageant itself draws near, Dugdale records James's visit to the Exchange and the scene at the Tower. James apparently went to the Exchange in order to have a view of the arches and other preparations for his royal entry: "accompanied with his Queene in his Coach, he came to the Exchange, there to see for their recreation" (B1v). But the "hurly burly" of the crowd became so great that James and Anne had to retreat inside the Exchange. From there James had a view of the crowds, the merchants, and the pageant structures. Dugdale at some length chastises the citizens for so disturbing the king with their uncivil behavior. At the Tower, from which James would depart on the processional through London, Dugdale saw several famous prisoners: "I beheld the late Sir Walter *Rawly*, the late Lord *Cobham*, the late Lord Gray" (B2). (He apparently means "late" in the sense of "out of favor.") Dugdale's eye catches the decorations of the Tower, "prepared with that pompe as eye neuer sawe, such glory in the hangings, such Maiesty in the Ornaments of the chambers" (B2).

The first item relevant to the actual entertainment not recorded in the other printed texts comes in the report of the
Thames show, presumably on the day or evening before the
royal entry: a fireworks spectacle, which "passe pleasing"
(B2v), according to Dugdale. A castle or fort, built on two barges
and "planted with much munition," was attacked by "two
pinnases ready rigde armed likewise to assault the Castle"
(B2v). First repulsed from the fort, the boats then succeeded in
taking it, making a show, Dugdale observes, "worthy the sight
of many Princes: being there plast at ye cost of the Sincke-
ports" (B2v). According to Dugdale, James "all pleasd made
answere that their loue was like the wilde Fire vnquenchable."
    The day of the royal entry finally arrived, and Dugdale helps
establish something of the tone and context of that event. He
notes that the citizens of London along with foreign merchants
"erected Trophies of glory, Pageants of that magnificence
the like was neuer" (B1). Stephen Harrison's drawings testify
to the likely truth of Dugdale's claim. Dugdale notes that
"cost was quite careles, desire . . . was fearelesse, and content
flourisht in aboundance" (B2v). One would have thought,
Dugdale suggests, that the gods had summoned a Parliament
and all moved in triumph to Jove's court. The companies of
guilds lined the streets in their liveries, the "Whiflers they in
their costly suites and Chaines of Gold walking vp and downe"
(B2v). Further, "not a conduit betwixt the Tower and Westminster: but runnes Wine." Simply stated, "the eie of man
was amazed at ye pomp" (B2v). Harrison confirms some of
these details, also adding others, in his "Lectori Candido" on
the final page of his *Arches of Triumph*. He comments, for
example, on the conduits running with wine and the guilds in
their liveries lining the streets. Harrison also provides the only
evidence for how long the procession of the royal entry took:
"His Maiestie departed from the Tower betweene the houres
of 11. and 12 and before 5. had made his royall passage through
the Citie, hauing a Canopie borne ouer him by 8. Knights."[9]

Among the reasons that one brings together all the texts of and commentaries on this royal entry, in order to get a reasonably clear picture of what took place, is the comment made by Dekker at the close of his description. Dekker writes "To the Reader": "Reader, you must vnderstand, that a regard, being had that his Maiestie should not be wearied with teadious speeches: A great part of those which are in this Booke set downe, were left vnspoken: So that thou doest here receiue them as they should haue bene deliuered, not as they were" (*Dekker*, 2:303). Unfortunately, Dekker does not reveal which items he omitted. If we knew that, we would better understand at what rate the procession moved, for example, the average time spent at the arches, and so on. Dugdale's account of the arches and the dramatic action at the arches remains often brief, sometimes cryptic. His mere omission of something reported in Dekker does not necessarily prove a failure to give the speeches. I believe that Dugdale followed the procession from its beginning; but as it wound its way through the City of London, he lost track of it and could not get close enough to know precisely what was taking place. His report is strongest for the events at the beginning of the entry. If indeed the pageant took some five hours to complete, as Harrison says, one understands the potential weariness for Dugdale or any spectator.

According to Harrison, "the first *Obiect* that his Maiesties eye encountred (after his entrance into *London*) was part of the children of *Christs Church Hospitall*, to the number of 300. who were placed on a Scaffold, erected for that purpose in *Barking Church-yard* by the *Tower*" (Harrison, sig. K1). But Dugdale begins with the first arch located on Fenchurch street: "In *Fanchurch street* was erected a stately Trophie or Pageant, at the Citties Charge, on which stood such a show of workmanship and glorie as I neuer saw the like" (B2v). Viewing Harrison's drawing of this arch, one tends to agree, for it contains a stunning rendition of the City of London on its top. (For Harrison's engravings, see next chapter.) Jonson planned the device, the dramatic action, and speeches; according to him a silk curtain covered the arch until James arrived, the allegory emphasizing the mists of grief driven away by the bright and hopeful presence of James.[10] Dugdale makes no mention of such a curtain; instead, he focuses on the carving of London: "The Cittie of London very rarely and artificially made, where no church, house nor place of note, but your eye might easilye find out, as the *Exchange, Coleharber, Powles, Bowe Church, &c.*" (B2v). Dugdale testifies to the accomplishment of speeches and action on the arch, but he is not illuminating: "top and top gallant whereon were showes so imbrodered and set out, as the cost was incomparable who speaking speeches to the King of that excellent eloquence and as while I liue I commend." Presumably these would have been the speeches of Genius and Thamesis, found in Jonson's text.

Discrepancies among the texts of Jonson and Dekker and Harrison's drawings occur, as I have discussed elsewhere.[11] But Dugdale adds an episode at Fenchurch not found in the other versions. He writes:

> There also Saint *George*, and Saint *Andrew*, in compleat Armour, met in one combate & fought for the victorie, but an old hermits passing by, in an Oration: ioynd them hand in hand, and so for euer hath made them as one harte, to the ioy of the King, the delight of the Lords, and the vnspeakeable comfort of the comminallty. (sig. B2v)

Dekker records in detail (2:254–57) a supposed meeting between St. George and St. Andrew: "These two armed Knights, encountring one another on the way, were to ride hand in hand, till they met his Maiestie" (2:254). Along the way Genius of the City intercepts them, asks who they are, and seeing their unity, accepts them: "I clap my hands for Ioy, and seate you both/ Next to my heart: In leaues of purest golde,/ This most auspicious loue shall be enrold" (256–57). Though this bears a close resemblance to Dugdale's account — the hermit he refers to could be Genius — problems exist. Dekker says that the device of St. George and St. Andrew "was suddeinly made vp, . . . And this (as it was then purposed) should haue bene performed about the Barres beyond Bishops-gate" (254).[12] At the close of the account Dekker writes: "This should haue beene the first Offring of the Citties Loue: But his Maiestie not making his *Entrance* (according to expectation) It was (not vtterly throwne from the Alter) but layd by" (257). If laid by, then apparently picked up and used in conjunction with the Fenchurch arch. This we can reasonably assume, thanks to Dugdale's report.

Because his eye rests on the total scene of the pageant, not just the planned dramatic action, Dugdale comments on the most eminent spectators for the magnificent pageant, namely the royal family. Though Dekker and Jonson certainly note the presence of James, they say little of Queene Anne and Prince Henry. Dugdale's description of Anne, flattering as it may be, reveals an apparent ease in her attitude toward the crowds that James did not feel; some, like Arthur Wilson, suggest that James went through the royal entry with a frown on his face. Anne saluted her subjects "so humbly and with mildenes, . . . neuer leauing to bend her body to them, this way and that." As a result, "women and men in my sight wept with joy" (B2v). Prince Henry, "smiling as ouer-ioyde to the peoples eternall comfort, salute them with many a bende" (B2v–B3). Before the royal family went the Lord Mayor in a "Crimson Veluet gowne, bearing his inamiled golden Mace vpon his shoulder" (B3). Dugdale understands what any spectator would perceive, that the honored sovereign and family become every bit a part of the pageant, as much as the magnificent arches. This occasional drama makes sense, gains completion, only with the royal presence whom it honors. Workmen may spend six weeks erecting the arches, but they have meaning other than mere art objects only when the royal presence sparks dramatic life and action. The royal family plays its part on the vast stage of the City of London.

Dugdale sees the second arch, built by the Italian merchants in London and located in Gracechurch street, but offers a disclaimer: "let me tell you I was not very neare" (B3). He does see the principal figure on top of the arch: "in my eye it was super excellent Iustice as I take it, attired in beaten gold, holding a crowne in her hand guarded with Shalmes and Cornets, whose noyse was such as if the Triumph had beene endles" (B3). The figure is probably not Justice, although we can see why Dugdale so identifies it. Dekker, followed closely by Harrison, describes the figure: "a Person carued out to the life, (a woman) her left hand leaning on a sword, with the poynt downeward, and her right hand reaching foorth a Diadem, which she seemde by bowing of her knee and head, to bestow vpon his Maiestie" (2:263). Harrison's drawing so represents the person. Clearly Dugdale saw a character with a sword and decided it had to be Justice; but without the other usual emblematic properties — for example, the scales (as shown on the next arch) — the figure probably represents some other quality, perhaps submission, though none of the writers identify the quality. Only this time does Dugdale offer such an identification, which gains importance because a spectator with some apparent knowledge of iconographical representation has attempted to recognize the character, even if not located close to the arch and guessing. Dugdale reports further about the arch and the speeches given on both sides, "showes appointed with seuerall harmonies, of drums, trumpets, and musique of all sortes." He notes that the Italians spared no cost, "at whose charge this glorious prospect was so pompous and full of show to the wonder of euery beholder" (B3).

An old man, some "three-score & 19.," Dugdale writes, stood at a street corner near the Gracechurch arch. The episode of the old man occurs only in Dugdale's report. Though Nichols suggests that the old man may have been Dugdale himself (1:419n), no evidence exists of course. Dugdale does report apparently a full version of the old man's speech, which raises interesting questions about how he could know it. In any event, the man who has seen the change of four kings and queens and now welcomes the fifth, "as hopeful neuer to behold the like" (B3), determines to speak a few lines, ostensibly written by his son, in order to do his duty and show his love. Because this is a significant verbal addition to the pageant, I quote the speech in full.

> Peereles of honor, heare me speake a word,
> Thy welcom'd glory, and inthroan'd renowne:
> Being in peace, of earthly pompe and State,
> To furnish forth, the beauties of thy crowne.
> Age thus salutes thee, with a dawny pate,
> Threescore and nineteene, is thy seruants yeares,
> That hath beheld, thy predissestors foure,
> All flourishing greene, whose deaths the Subiectes teares,
> Mingled with mine, did many times deplore;
> But now againe, since that our ioyes are fiue,
> Fiue hundreth welcomes, I doe giue my King,
> And may thy change, to vs that be aliue,
> Neuer be knowne, a fifth extreame to bring,
> My honest hart, be patterne of the rest.
> Who euer praide, for them before now thee,
> Both them and thine, of all ioy be possest,
> Whose liuely presence, we all blesse to see,
> And so passe on God guide thee on thy way,
> Olde Hinde concludes, hauing no more to say.
>
> (B3–B3v)

The sincerity of the speech, not prepared by one of the dramatists, endears. Sadly, the press of the multitude and noise of the show "ouershadowd him" "so that the *King* past by" (B3v). But in response to the old man's zeal, Dugdale writes, "I haue publiquely imprinted it [the speech] that all his fellow Subiectes may see this old mans forwardnes" (B3v). Such

examples of spontaneity are absent in this royal entry in contrast to, say, Elizabeth's of 1559; and Dugdale hints at one of
the reasons: "beside ye *King* apointed no such thing but at
seueral stays & appointed places" (B3v). Typical of James, he
wanted no surprises.

Near the Royal Exchange stood the arch devised by the
Dutch merchants in London which appealed for continued
aid to the Low Countries in their struggle against the Spanish. As James arrived at the Exchange, he "smilde looking toward it, belike remembring his last being there" (B3v), a visit
reported earlier by Dugdale. James cast his eye on the arch,
Dugdale says, and "admirde it greatly." Dugdale notes the
heighth of the arch: "so hie as it seemed to fall forward." His
description of the arch both confirms some details and adds
others not found in the printed texts or drawing of the arch.
Dugdale writes: "On the top you might behold the sea Dolphins as droping from the clouds on the earth, or looking to
behold the *King*" (B3v).[14] Strangely, Dugdale notes the dolphins
but makes no mention of the allegorical figures prominent
about them. Dekker writes: "vpon a *Pedestal*, curiously closed
in betweene the tayles of two Dolphins, was aduanced a
Woman. . . . She figur'd *Diuine Prouidence*" (2:269). She clearly
stands atop the arch in Harrison's drawing. Dugdale adds the
matter of a ship, a scene not described by Dekker and not
apparent in the drawing. Dugdale observes: "pictures of great
arte and cost and glory as a double ship that being two: was so
cunningly made as it seemde but one, which figured *Scotland*
and *England* in one with the armes . . . in one Scutchin, sayling
on two seas at once" (B3v). This seems an unlikely thing for
Dugdale to have invented; thus his report has probable reliability. One notes on the arch in passing the obvious figure of
Justice, which Dugdale thought he had seen on the previous
arch; here he takes no note of it. He captures his delight in the
arch in a vivid image: "the glorie of this show, was in my eye
as a dreame, pleasing to the affection, gorgeous and full of ioy,
and so full of show and variety, that when I held down my

head as wearyed with looking so hie, me thoght it was a griefe to me to awaken so soone" (B3v). Dugdale gives both the Dutch and French credit for the arch and entertainment.

As the procession moves into Cheapside, Dugdale adds an episode not found in other reports. He also reveals something about the movement of spectators, apparently trying to keep up with the pageant — rather like Dugdale himself I suspect: "the strong streame of people violently running in ye midst toward Cheap-side, ther our Triumphant rides garnisht with troups of royalty, & gallant personages" (B3v). On top the great conduit in Cheapside "stood a prentise in a black coate, a flat cap seruant like." Dugdale reports the apprentice's speech with an accompanying disclaimer: "now whether he spake this or no, I heard not it, but ye manner of his speech was this, comming to me at the 3. or second hand." The speech follows:

> What lack yon gentleman? what wil you buy? *Silkes, Sattens,*
>   *Taffaties &c*
> But stay bold tonge, stand at a giddie gaze,
> Be dim mine eyes, what gallant traine are heare:
> That strikes mindes mute, and puts good wits in maze,
> O tis our King, Royall KING IAMES I say:
>   Passe on in peace, and happy be thy way,
>   Liue long on Earth, Englands great Crowne to sway.
> Thy Cittie gratious King, admires thy fame,
> And on their knees, prayes for thy happy state:
> Our women for thy Queene ANN whose rich name,
> Is their created blisse, and sprong of late;
>   If womens wishes, may preuaile thus being.
>   They wish you both long liues, and good agreeing.
> Children for Children, pray before they eate,
> At their vprising, and their lying downe:
> Thy sonnes and daughters, princely all compleat,
> Royall in bloud, children of high Renowne.
>   But generally, togither they incline,
>   Praying in one, great King for thee and thine.
>   (B3v–B4)

Dugdale does not know whether this person was a self-appointed participant or not, "but howsoeuer forward loue is acceptable, and I would the *King* had hard them" (B4). How Dugdale could get access to these additional speeches remains a bit of a mystery; but given his reportorial skills, one accepts the probable reliability of these events and speeches.

Dugdale's reports of the four remaining arches disappoint somewhat: either he wearies of describing them or he did not have a good view of them. James did not hear the apprentice figure because he pressed on to the next arch: "the sight of the Trophie at Soper-lane ende, made him the more forward" (B4) — the *Nova Faelix Arabia* arch, the first designed by Dekker. But Dugdale could not see the arch well: "the deuise of that a farre off I could not coniecture: but by report it was exceeding" (B4). He notes that the arch was not as high as the others, an impression not borne out by the details in Dekker's text. On the "stage" of the arch were, according to Dugdale, "enacted strange things, after which an Oration deliuered of great wisedome, both the sides of this Pageant were deckt gallantly" (B4). The "strange things" may be the action at the Fount of Virtue where the sound of Fame's trumpet rouses the Senses, Detraction and Oblivion seek to drink at the Fountain, but all changes with the arrival and presence of James. Circumspection, portrayed by a boy of St. Paul's choir, addresses the king and explains the arch (*Dekker*, 2:278–79).

At the Cross in Cheapside, "beautifully guarded and adorned," the Recorder and Aldermen "on a scaffold, deliuered him [James] a gallant Oration and withall a cup of beaten gold" (B4). (Dekker records the speech, 2:282). The next arch, at the Little Conduit in Cheap, Dugdale describes as "very artificial indeede, of no exceeding height, but prety & pleasing in ye manner of an arbor, wherein were placed all manner of wood inhabitants" (B4). Dugdale correctly describes the *Hortus Euporiae*, meant to be the Garden of Plenty, who reigns over it with Peace. The "wood inhabitants" appear in Harrison's drawing, and the words may also refer to Sylvanus who brought James to the arch. Capturing some sense of the decoration, Dugdale writes: the arch had "diuers shows of Admiration, as Pompions, Poungarnets, & all kinde of fruit, which ye Lords highly commended" (B4). The speaker at the arch draws the familiar metaphorical comparison of this garden to the kingdom itself (*Dekker*, 2:284). In this case Dugdale apparently came sufficiently near the arch to discern its basic design.

Dugdale notes one of the perils of the conduits running bountifully with wine, namely that "many were shipt to the Isle of sleepe, that had no leasure for snorting to behold ye days Triumph" (B4v). The New World arch in Fleetstreet, designed by Dekker with a speech of Zeal written by Thomas Middleton, gets dense and oblique treatment from Dugdale. He tries to say in a rather opaque passage that this arch reminded the royal party of some of the earlier arches: "it seemed to them to haue gone back againe, and where [were] but then at the crosse in Cheape" (B4v). The salutation to James reminds him of the greeting at the Little Conduit in Cheap, "& all else but y^e *Exchange* & gratious street." When Dugdale gets around to describing the arch itself, all he notes is that on top "was placed a *Globe*, of goodly preperation" (B4v). He does not note, for example, that the Four Elements turned the Globe, a point made clear in Harrison's text. Though his eye focuses on the most striking feature of the arch, the great globe itself, he omits the other equally interesting details. Again he does not recognize Justice, the principal figure, whom Dekker thinks pointless to describe: "I hope you will not put me to describe what properties she held in her hands, sithence euery painted cloath can informe you" (2:295).

Jonson designed the last two arches, but Dugdale treats them summarily. Of the Temple of Janus device, located at Temple Bar, Dugdale finds it "neither great nor smal but finely furnisht, some compared it to an Exchange shop, it shined so in ye dark place & was so pleasing to ye eie" (B4v). Dugdale does not make clear how the arch could remind one of an Exchange shop. Nothing in Jonson's text indicates why or how the arch could be shining. Dugdale does add something not in Jonson's text, namely information that "a yong man an Acter of the ye Cittie so deliuered his mind & the manner of all in an Oration" (B4v). Either Dugdale is correct, and we can add another professional actor to the list of those involved with the royal entry, in this case presumably giving the speech of Genius; or Dugdale confuses the actor here with William Bourne, of Prince Henry's company, who gave the speech of Zeal at the previous arch, the New World one in Fleetstreet. I incline toward giving Dugdale the benefit of doubt, especially in light of his kinship to Armin of the King's Men. Certainly there would be nothing unusual or surprising about a professional actor's giving the speech written by Jonson.

Of the last device, located in the Strand and also designed by Jonson, Dugdale reports briefly: "In yᵉ *Strand* was also an other of smal motion, a piramides fitly beseeming time & place" (B4v). Jonson's text confirms part of what Dugdale says: "The Inuention was a Rainebow, the Moone, Sunne, and those seuen starres, . . . aduanced betweene two magnificent Pyramid's, of 70. foot in height, on which were drawne his Maiesties seuerall pedigrees Eng. and Scot" (*Jonson*, 7:106). Such towering structures would easily catch the spectator's eye. The royal party did not tarry in the Strand: "I am sure wearied with ye shows as the stomack may glutton, the daintiest courts staid not long, but passed forward to ye place appointed" (B4v). A letter from John Geynkyn and others to the Privy Council reveals some of the difficulties of getting the financial cooperation of citizens, specifically in the Strand area. The "inhabitants between Temple Bar and Charing Cross" had been ordered by Privy Council "to arrange a pageant to receive the King joyfully and loyally as he passed through London to Westminster." But, complain the letter writers, the "Petitioner and many other poor people and artisans have contributed liberally towards the same, but some of the better sort have refused to do so. They should be commanded to donate money or be summoned before the Council for contempt."[15]

Dugdale's text ends with a benediction in behalf of James, Anne, Henry, "and all their princely progenie, yt no harm neuer come neere them, not touch them" (B4v). Historical retrospection sees poignant irony in Dugdale's wish, as the royal family will face serious threats ahead — for example, the Gunpowder plot, the untimely and unexpected death of Henry, and the marriage of Princess Elizabeth that took her away from England for decades. But for the moment Dugdale captures the spirit and hope of the people on the occasion of James's magnificent royal entry. Furthermore, he offers an illuminating perspective on the pageant; nothing here hints of the condescension seen in the texts of Jonson and Dekker. Instead, an unvarnished enthusiasm pervades the text. As I have demonstrated, Dugdale's account becomes particularly valuable for the additional information, speeches, and interpretations that he provides. Future studies of this incomparable civic pageant should, I think, come to terms with Dugdale's version. His text constitutes one more building block that shores up the pageant against its reputation for insubstantiality.

TEN

Pageants, Masques, and Scholarly Ideology

In his *Age of Shakespeare*, published in 1908, Algernon Swinburne characterized the 1604 civic pageant presented to King James as "huge, costly, wearisome, barbaric and pedantic."[1] In his chapter on Middleton, Swinburne refers to the "rational regret" that a modern reader experiences "at the reckless profusion of literary power which the great poets of the time were content to lavish on the decoration or exposition of an ephemeral pageant" (176). Ninety years later I'm not sure that our perspective has changed very much. I suppose that I am asking this question: why do so many critics even at the end of the twentieth century, typically cross to the other side of the street when they see a civic pageant approaching? Possibly because they share the assumptions implied or stated by a number of writers spanning several centuries who seem to have taken seriously Prospero's reference to "insubstantial pageants." J. B. Heath, in a history of the Grocers guild, who sponsored the 1613 Lord Mayor's Show, writes that pageants "seem to have afforded great delight to the rude and uncultivated understandings of those for whose entertainment they were intended."[2] Obviously, dramatic entertainment that appealed to the rude masses need not be taken seriously. Elitism rules the day.

I have been stimulated to think anew about this topic by John Peacock's recent book, *The Stage Designs of Inigo Jones: The European Context* (Cambridge, 1995). In this persuasively argued, handsomely produced, and expensive ($145) book, Peacock insists on the prominence of Inigo Jones as emissary of Continental art. Indeed, Peacock claims that Jones rather single-handedly ushered in Renaissance art to England. Peacock writes at one point: "As the first English artist to acquire a deep and inward knowledge of the whole Renaissance tradition, he [Jones] was able to grasp just how marginal to that tradition was the visual culture of his own country: in spite of the impact of Holbein and numerous lesser continental artists, English art was still in outer darkness."[3] I am intrigued and, I might add, annoyed by the concept of England's visual culture as being in "outer darkness." I do not have the time or talent to convince everyone that such was not the situation: suffice it that I offer a case for the contribution of the architect Stephen Harrison, who antedates Jones's work on the court masque and who reveals a keen understanding of visual representation in the construction of pageant triumphal arches.

We may rightly ask why Harrison's artistic contribution has received so little attention. The answer derives in part because we cannot document any other work done by him. Second, he chose the wrong medium to work in: that is, he chose marginal drama, a street civic pageant. This alone might be sufficient to doom him to obscurity. He settled for using his artistic talent in the service of the rude and uncultivated masses, who may have lived in darkness other than visual. In other words, search as we might on the internet, we will not find a website for Stephen Harrison.

He designed the triumphal arches for the royal entry
pageant presented to King James I on 15 March 1604 in London's streets. Although James had been proclaimed King of
England nearly a year earlier, the ravages of the plague kept
postponing his official entry into the City of London. Indeed,
his coronation on St. James Day (25 July) was a muted affair,
devoid of most of the pomp and circumstance associated with
such events. Harrison himself writes in his *Arches of Triumph*

The Londonium arch located at Fenchurch

(1604): "These five Triumphall Arches were first taken in hand in the beginning of Aprill 1603, presently after his Majesty was proclaimed. It being expected that his passage would have bene through his honourable City and Chamber to his Coronation upon Saint James his day following: But by reason of the sicknesse, it pleased his Majestie to be Solemnely Crowned at Westminster, without sight of these Triumphs."[4] Harrison adds: "The gladsome and long-desired Morning at length is come, In which the Streetes seeme to be paved with people, that in heapes flocke together, to behold their proud heads that were advanced in this manner." Delay seems only to have fanned the flames of expectation.

This pageant makes several claims on our attention.[5] Apparently Shakespeare and the fellow members of the King's Men were present along London's streets, dressed in their livery as servants of the royal household. We know that the well-established actors Edward Alleyn and William Bourne performed in the pageant. And for the first time in English history we can identify major dramatists who wrote for a royal entry pageant: Thomas Dekker, Ben Jonson, and Thomas Middleton (who contributed only the speech of Zeal). Dekker made the greatest contribution of the three. But surely the choice of these three prominent dramatists tells us something about the importance of this dramatic entertainment. City records document the considerable expense that London incurred in order to celebrate the somewhat new sovereign, who would move from the Tower on the east westward through the city for Westminster and the royal palaces. Along the way at various stations the king would be greeted with dramatic tableaux. Near the end of his text Dekker records something of the city's planning and preparation. Dekker writes: "The Citie elected sixteene Comitties, to whom the Mannaging of the whole busines was absolutely referred."[6] He cites the names of some of the workers and notes that 80 joiners and 60 carpenters worked on the project. Dekker adds: "Over whom, *Stephen Harrison* Joyner was appoynted chiefe; who was the sole Inventor of the Architecture, and from whom all directions, for so much as belonged to Carving, Joyning, Molding, and all other worke in those five Pageants of the Citie (Paynting excepted) were set downe" (303).

Not only did Harrison serve as architect for the triumphal arches (finally seven in number), but also he left behind a published text, his *Arches of Triumph* (1604), with engravings of these arches done by William Kip (reproduced throughout this chapter). Thereby Harrison provides the most extensive pictorial record of a street pageant in the Tudor-early Stuart era. Although Inigo Jones made extensive drawings for the court masques, they were not published in his lifetime; indeed, not until the twentieth century does such pictorial evidence become available.

Harrison's first arch (p. 166) located in Fenchurch and designed by Jonson, presents the City of London carved in miniature. A silk curtain covered the arch until King James's arrival. Jonson explains the meaning: "The Allegorie being, that those clouds were gathered upon the face of the Citie, through their long want of his most wished sight: but now, as at the rising of the Sunne, all mists were dispersed and fled."[7] The Genius of the City, portrayed by the actor Edward Alleyn, and Tamesis, played by a child actor, offered speeches of welcome to James. Divine Wisdom ruled over the arch. Gilbert Dugdale, who, as noted in the previous essay, saw the 1604 pageant and wrote about it, describes the Fenchurch arch: "The Citie of London very rarely and artificially made, where no church, house nor place of note, but your eye might easily find out, as the *Exchange, Coleharber, Powles, Bow Church, &c.*"[8] I suggest that the perspective from which we view the city on the arch corresponds to a position on the South Bank near the Globe Theatre.

The second arch (p. 169) that prepared by the Italian merchants living in London and described in Dekker's text, contained a large square amid four Corinithian columns. This

The Italian pageant at Gracechurch

represented "King *Henry* the seventh . . . royally seated in his Imperiall Robes, to whome King *James* (mounted on horsebacke) approches, and receyves a Scepter . . ." (*Dekker,* 2:262). This painting presents James's genealogy, underscoring his claim to the English throne. The founder of the Tudor line gives his blessing and kingdom to James, founder of the Stuart line. On the top of the arch "stood a person carved out to the life, (a woman) her left hand leaning on a sword, with the poynt downeward, and her right hand reaching foorth a Diadem, . . . to bestow upon his Majestie" (263). The Italian speaker offers wishes: "live, though mightiest of Princes, in all happinesse: Reigne, thou wisest of Monarchs, in all prosperity" (266).

At the Royal Exchange, the Dutch merchants of London had erected an arch (p. 171) that includes in its upper reaches a picture of King James in his royal robes. At the top stands Divine Providence, and on either side of James stand Justice with her sword and Fortitude with her pillar. In the middle, in a spacious square room 17 "yong *Damsels*, (all of them sumptuously adorned, after their countrey fashion,) sate as it were in so many Chaires of State, and figuring in their persons, the 17. *Provinces* of *Belgia*, of which every one caried . . . a Scutchion . . ." (*Dekker,* 2:268). The speaker hopes that the Belgian provinces may continue to have England's protection, as they did in Elizabeth's reign.

Tapping into iconographical traditions, Dekker, at the Nova Faelix Arabia arch at Soper-lane End (p. 172) presents Fame, describing her as a "Woman in a Watchet Roabe, thickly set with open Eyes, and Tongues, a payre of large golden Winges at her backe, a Trumpet in her hand" (2:276). All these symbols display "but the propertie of her swiftnesse, and aptnesse to disperse Rumors." Beneath Fame is the Fount of Virtue, surrounded by the Five Senses, and near them the malign figures of Detraction and Oblivion, who attempt to suck the fountain dry. But, Dekker adds, "a strange and heavenly musicke

The Dutch arch at the Royal Exchange

suddainly striking through their eares, which causing a wildnes
and quicke motion in their lookes, drew them to light upon
the glorious presence of the *King* . . ." (278). His presence

Nova Faelix Arabia arch at Soper-lane

defeated them. The figure Circumspection speaks, delivering "to his Majestie the interpretation of this dumbe Mysterie" (279). James, Circumspection explains, as the new Phoenix, rising from the ashes of the first, brings in his person a new spring.

The engraving makes clear that the arch at the Little Conduit in Cheapside (p. 175) appeared as a summer arbor, a garden presided over by the allegorical figures of Peace and Plenty, seated in the upper section. Sylvanus spoke to the king and led him to this arch. Dekker describes Peace as "richly attired, her upper garment of carnation, hanging loose, a Robe of White under it. . . . In one hand shee held a *Caducaeus* . . . In the other, ripe eares of corne gilded: on her lap sate a Dove" (2:285). Plenty sat on her left hand, a "rich mantle of Gold traversing her bodie. . . . on her head a crowne of Poppy and Mustard seede . . . In her right hand a *Cornucopia*" (286). Below Peace and Plenty sit Chruso, Argurion, Pomona, and Ceres. On one side sit the Nine Muses, and across, the Seven Liberal Arts. Vertumnus, the master Gardner and husband to Pomona, also addressed the king, exploring the garden metaphor.

A great globe, located in the middle section, dominated the arch at the Conduit in Fleet Street (p. 176). Justice presided over the arch, appropriately costumed, as Dekker notes: "I hope you will not put mee to describe what properties she held in her hands, sithence every painted cloath can informe you" (2:295). Under her stood Virtue, and under her, Fortune, whose foot helped turn the globe, assisted by the Four Elements. The Four Cardinal Virtues and the four kingdoms (England, Scotland, Ireland, France) stood on opposite sides of the globe. The speech of Zeal, written by Thomas Middleton, emphasizes how James has brought union to the kingdom, once by Brutus divided.

Harrison's last engraving shows the arch at Temple Bar (p. 178), the Temple of Janus, the dramatic action designed by Jonson. This arch mixes classical and allegorical subjects. Peace was "the first and principall person in the temple" (*Jonson*, 7:97) with Plutus standing nearby. Jonson carefully provides the symbolic details of all the figures. Each virtue, such as Quiet, Liberty, Safety, and Felicity, has an opposing vice underfoot. Jonson explains the "dumbe argument" of the arch: "those golden times were returned againe, wherein *Peace* was with us so advanced, *Rest* received, *Libertie* restored, *Safetie* assured, and all *Blessednesse* appearing in every of these vertues her particular triumph over her opposite evill" (100). The Genius of the City returns, having first been portrayed by Jonson in the Fenchurch arch; and he engages in extensive dialogue with a *Flamen*, offering "My cities heart; which shall for ever burne / Upon this altar . . ." (103).

Examining Harrison's arches, we can better appreciate John Peacock's assessment of them: "In fact the arches are teeming farragos of infelicitous detail, their chaos emphasised by a busy, rebarbative Flemish mannerist style" (63). By contrast, "Jones's inventions of this kind at once set higher standards, and really do measure up to Alberti's criterion." I call this special pleading, making the world safe for Inigo Jones, erecting a wall against Harrison. Even Peacock's smooth, direct rhetoric in the sentence about Jones contrasts mightily with the robust name-calling of the sentence about Harrison's arches. How can we take arches seriously that have been characterized as "teeming farragos," full of "infelicitous detail" and guilty of a chaotic, "rebarbative" style? Visual outer darkness prevails. I suppose that Peacock would have to rail against the infelicitous details of many a gothic cathedral. As one looks at all of Jones's drawings and sketches, might not one find an infelicitous detail or two? I think so. Other than these unflattering and prejudicial comments about Harrison, Peacock has nothing else to say about any civic pageant. Clearly he intends to privilege the work of Jones.

By contrast, I want to examine five areas of Harrison's contribution and achievement on the basis of his book, *Arches of Triumph.* I see Harrison as theorist, practitioner, historian, publisher, and cultural participant. I cannot argue that this accomplishment rivals Jones's because Jones enjoyed a 35-year career. But surely on the basis of this one pageant Stephen

Hortus Euporiae (The Garden of Plenty) arch in Cheapside

Harrison merits our serious attention. Harrison's text provides engravings of the arches, rendered by William Kip; the text of some of the speeches; a description of what happened at the

The New World arch in Fleet Street

arches; and, fourth, some additional information about the preparations and details of the procession on 15 March. Thirty years ago I noted discrepancies between Harrison's *Arches* and the literary texts provided by Dekker and Jonson.[9] Here I concentrate on Harrison's accomplishment in designing and constructing those teeming farragos of arches that nevertheless grip our attention.

In the Epistle Dedicatory, addressed to the Lord Mayor Sir Thomas Bennett, Harrison sketches a theoretical basis for what he has done. He focuses on his art as a means of countering the presumed ephemeral nature of the pageant itself, this insubstantial pageant faded. He praises the Mayor, Aldermen, and all those involved in the pageant for their "free . . . cleare, and verie bounteous disposition . . . with the sparing of no cost" that brought forth the magnificent entertainment "but upon one day" (sig. B1). That glorious event, Harrison writes, "is here newe wrought up againe, and shall endure forever." The art of Harrison's book of engravings thus recaptures the special occasion and grants it revival and permanence. Harrison puts the matter succinctly: "For albeit those Monuments of your *Loves* were erected up to the Cloudes, and were built never so strongly, yet now their lastingnes should live but in the tongues and memories of men: But that the hand of Arte gives them here a second more perfect beeing. . . ." The hand of art provides "lastingnes." Indeed, art gives the event a "second more perfect being." Harrison is somewhat disingenuous; after all, Dekker and Jonson's texts already exist, providing a kind of permanence for the day. But those texts did not include the drawings of the triumphal arches. We might read those texts and yet not know precisely what the arches looked like, therefore making a reconstruction of the event more difficult. Harrison's book solves the problem: through its printed text and engravings it fixes the event in a more perfect way — indeed in a way that few spectators actually standing in London's streets could have completely appreciated.

After apologizing for the delay in getting the book put together, Harrison makes a final point in the Epistle Dedicatory: he offers a unique contribution. Harrison writes: "I would

The Temple of Janus at Temple Bar

not care if these unpainted *Pictures* were more Costly to me, so that they might appeare curious enough to your Lordship and Worships; yet in regard, that this present Age can lay before you no President that ever any in this land performed the like, I presume these my endeavours shall receive the more worthie liking of you." Harrison speaks aptly: no artistic precedent exists for the book that he has produced. He knows that he leaves a unique legacy: a complete pictorial record of a pageant. He "performs" in his book a work of art the likes of which the country has not seen before. If not exactly a profound theorist about art, Harrison at least exhibits having thought about what he has done, how his art perpetuates the art of the event itself, helping confer lastingness on it. The hand of art gives the arches here a "more perfect being," an idealized representation of what stood in London's streets. Dekker writes in his prefatory Ode in Harrison's text: "where now stand, / (built by thy hand) / Her Arches in new state; so made, / That their fresh beauties n'ere shall fade: / Then of our English Triumphes rear'st the Fame, / Bove those of old, But above all, thy name" (sig. B1v).

I suppose that to see Harrison as a "practitioner" risks focusing on the obvious. He helped design and certainly construct the triumphal arches. As he writes: "In which time, the streetes for that purpose [the pageant] were diligently surveyed, heights, breadts, and distances taken, as it were to make Fortifications for the Solemnities: Seven peeces of ground (like so many fields for a battell) were plotted forth, upon which these Triumphes should be erected" (sig. C1). The technical problems include not only designing the arches but also figuring out how and where they will fit in London's narrow streets. Envisioning a Platonic arch constitutes only part of the task; Aristotelian reality must place that arch in the confined space of a street through which traffic must continue to move and around which spectators can gather on the festive day. In sometimes brilliant ways Harrison solved practical problems. For example, of the Garden of Plenty arch Harrison writes: "The first *Pegme* was a sommer Arbor, and seemed to growe close to the little *Conduit in Cheape*, which joyning to the backe of it, served (or might bee supposed to have bene) as a Fountain to water the fruits of this *Garden of Plenty*" (sig. G1). Symbol and reality meet in a real-world urban setting: art appropriates the setting that it occupies. Harrison demonstrates his technical skill in the New World arch, which contained a Globe, "seene to move being fild with all the estates that are in the land; And this Engine was turned about by foure persons, representing the foure *Elements*, (*Earth, Water, Aire*, and *Fire*) who were placed so queintly, that the Globe seemed to have his motion even on the Crownes of their heads" (sig. H1). These details, not available in Dekker's text, indicate a sophistication that we usually associate with Jones and the masques. We can add to Harrison's practical tasks the job of overseeing all the workers.

Harrison says of the first arch, the one that depicts the City of London, that it "was erected in *Fanchurch-streete*, the backe of it so leaning on the East ende of the Church, that it overspread the whole streete" (sig. C1). He adds technical details: "the *Perpendicular-line* of the whole *Frame*, (that is to say, the distance from the bottome to the top,) as the *Ground-line*, is (also in this, so in all the rest) to be found out and tried by the *Scale*, divided by 1.2.3.4. and 5. and set at the lower end of the Peece." The architect demonstrates his practical knowledge of the ancient orders of architecture when he describes the first arch: "This Gate of *Passage*, then . . . was derived from the *Tuscana* (beeing the principal pillar of those 5. upon which the *Noble Frame of Architecture* doth stand,) for the *Tuscane Columne* is the strongest & most worthy to support so famous a Worke, as this *Fabricke* was. . . ." Writers about architecture had recognized the Tuscan column as the simplest and strongest of the five orders of architecture.

Harrison also sprinkles throughout his text many terms that have their primary association with architecture. He includes, for example, postern, term (as in the Garden of Plenty arch), corbel, capital, cant, cornice, frieze, architrave, baluster, pilaster. Many of these words had only recently entered the English language, according to evidence in the OED. Therefore, Harrison stands in the near-front ranks of linguistic innovation, a means of assisting the establishment of these terms in the English language.

As we notice in the engravings, Harrison, in addition to the Tuscan column in the first arch, uses Corinthian columns in the second and third arches (the Italian and Dutch arches), pyramids in the New Arabia arch, four great French terms in the Garden of Plenty, and round towers and ballisters in the New World arch. In the last arch, the Temple of Janus, Harrison reveals his practical knowledge of the other orders of architecture, even as he self-consciously has moved from the simplest column (the Tuscan) in the first arch to the most famous (the Composita) in the last triumphal arch. Harrison writes: "The wals and gates of this Temple were brasse; . . . All the *Frontispice* . . . was beutified and supported by twelve rich *Columnes*, of which the foure lowermost, being great *Corinthian* pillers. . . . so did wee thinke it fit, that this our *Temple*, should end with the most famous *Columne*, whose beauty and goodlinesse is derived both from the *Tuscane, Doricke, Ionicke* and *Corinthian* . . . [with] the name of *Composita* or *Italica*" (sig. I1).

Where did Harrison get such knowledge? The answer leads me to talk about him as a "historian." Certainly artists have been historians — and vice versa. One need only recall Shakespeare's great contribution to an understanding of English history through his plays; indeed, as many recent commentators have suggested, Shakespeare functions as historiographer. Harrison probably got historical information from John Shute's

The First and Chief Groundes of Architecture (London, 1563).
Shute offers an abbreviated version of Vitruvius's great first
century book, *De Architectura*, often translated in the Renaissance. In addition, Shute provides insights from the work
of Sebastiano Serlio. Indeed, Shute's work may be the principal means by which Vitruvian ideas arrived in England. In his
learned and extensive chapter 3, "Architecture," John Peacock
writes about the architectural impact of Inigo Jones's trip to
Italy and his reading of Vitruvius. Peacock notes: "From the
start, a major point of reference was the text of Vitruvius,
which he [Jones] read and annotated in Daniele Barbaro's Italian edition" (55). Of course, Jones could have gleaned Vitruvian
ideas from Shute's 1563 English book, one that Peacock nowhere mentions.

Named in 1615 as Surveyor of the King's Works, Jones began in earnest his career as an architect of built structures.
But, as Peacock rightly argues, he had already been pursuing
architectural principles in the masques. Peacock writes: "But
long before this Jones the masque designer was representing
himself as an architect, and rightly so in the Vitruvian context which he was trying to transplant. One of the first things
he set about was to publicise the very concept of the 'architect', which was relatively new to England, the Renaissance
concept of an individual with overall responsibility for a
project, guaranteed by creative and intellectual authority" (58).
But we recall that Dekker, at the end of his pageant text, refers to Harrison as "The sole Inventor of the Architecture,"
having oversight of all the work for the pageant. John Shute
on the title page of his book refers to himself as "Paynter and
Architecte"; similarly, Harrison on the title page of *Arches*
designates himself "Joyner and Architect." Jones clearly had
English precursors who understood Vitruvius and who thought
of themselves as "architects." In a sense, Harrison functions
as a conduit through whom Vitruvian principles flowed, his-
torically connecting himself to Vitruvius by way of John Shute.

I cite some examples of Harrison's rather direct borrowing from Shute. Of the first arch, London carved in miniature, Harrison writes: "The cheekes or sides of the Gate, were . . . doubly guarded with the Portraitures of *Atlas* King of *Mauritania*, who (according to his owne shortnesse and thicknesse) from the *Symetry* of his foote, caused a pillar to be made, whose height with *Base* and *Capitall* was 6. times the thicknesse in height" (sig. C1). This echoes Shute, who writes of the Tuscan column: "This pillor is the strongest and most able to beare the greatest of burten of al the others. And that same strength cometh by his shortenes, therefore he is likned unto Atlas, kinge of Maurytania, and the piller is named Tuscana, whose heyth must be with the Basis and Capitall .6. times his thicknes in heigth."[10] Of the Composita column that forms the basis for Harrison's last arch, the Temple of Janus, Harrison says that the column's beauty and goodness derive from all the others "and received his [its] full perfection from *Titus Vespasian*, who advanced it to the highest place of dignitie in his *Arch Triumphall*" (sig. I1). Clearly Harrison follows Shute who writes: "This piller was first buylded to his perfection in the time of Titus, Vespasianus, who sette it at hys triumphe in the highest place of hys arche Triumphall, and called it Composita, or as some doo name her Italica" (sig. B2). Harrison perpetuates an architectural tradition that embraces Vitruvius, Serlio, and the homegrown John Shute — all this before Inigo Jones became an active architect supposedly, in John Peacock's view, bringing Continental art and tradition at long last to England and thereby chasing away outer darkness.

On his title page Harrison affirms: "Invented and published by Stephen Harrison Joyner and Architect." John Windet, who had in 1603 become printer to the City of London, printed the book, as the colophon makes clear. But the book is "to be sold at the Author's house in Lime-street, at the signe of the Snayle" (sig. K1). Therefore, part of Harrison's contribution comes from his serving as publisher and bookseller of this extraordinary book. In his text, Dekker signals such activity by Harrison: "But an excellent hand being at this instant curiously describing all the seven [arches], and bestowing on them their faire prospective limmes, your eye shall hereafter rather be delighted in beholding those Pictures, than now be wearied in looking upon mine" (2:260). Stephen Harrison: architect, theorist, practitioner, historian, and now publisher and seller of the book — I don't think that Inigo Jones on his best day could have surpassed such a variety of accomplishments.

As publisher, Harrison served in a sense as "architect" for the book. He arranged for odes to be written by Dekker and John Webster for inclusion in the book, odes that (not surprisingly) extol Harrison's accomplishment. He engaged William Kip to make the engravings. The book itself manifests a self-consciousness about the product as book. For example, Harrison includes the Epistle Dedicatory, addressed to the Mayor and other civic officials, where, as I have already commented, Harrison writes about his art and the generosity of the city. Dedicatory epistles increasingly became mainstays of books, most often used as a means of expressing gratitude for patronage or actively seeking patronage. Harrison thus places his book squarely in the age-old aristocratic patronage system, signing himself as "Most affectionately devoted to your Lordship and Worships." In that dedication Harrison also refers to the difficulty of making this book and apologizes for delay.

In the body of the book he occasionally offers readers guidance, as when he writes of the Italian arch: "I referre you to the Modell or Peece itselfe, for the *Front* of it, as the next leafe will shewe you, so likewise proportionall was the back side to the fore-*Front*" (sig. D1). The concern for the reader becomes most obvious and self-conscious in the "Lectori Candido" (sig. K1), placed at the end, as in Dekker's text. In this, Harrison addresses the reader directly. This document joins with the Epistle Dedicatory to constitute two common items found in the paratextual material of books of the late Tudor-early Stuart period. However much time Harrison has spent studying architecture, he has also cast a keen eye on the makeup of books.

Harrison begins the "Lectori Candido" simply and directly: "Reader, The limmes of these great *Triumphall* bodies (lately disjoynted and taken in sunder) I have thou seest (for thy sake) set in their apt and right places againe" (K1). I have done nothing but in care of thee, Harrison seems to be saying. He returns to the argument of the Epistle, that his art and work will help these arches now to stand as "perpetuall monuments." And he acknowledges again the support of the city: if his labors "yeeld thee either profit or pleasure, thou art . . . to pay many thankes to this honourable Citie, whose bounty towards me, not onely in making choise of me, to give directions for the intire workmanship of the . . . [arches] . . . but also (in publishing these *Peeces,*) I do here gladly acknowledge to have bene exceeding liberall" (K1).

The address to the reader becomes a means of offering additional information: "Nor shall it be amisse in this place to give thee intelligence of some matters (by way of notes) which were not fully observde, nor freely inough set downe in the Printed Booke of these *Triumphes.*" The inadequate book to which Harrison refers must be Dekker's published pageant text. Harrison then proceeds to provide details, such as: the King departed the Tower between 11 a.m. and noon and before 5 p.m. had completed his passage through the city; the Liveries of the Companies with all their banners and decorations reached from Mark lane to the arch at Temple Bar; the conduits at Cornhill, Cheapside, and Fleetstreet ran with claret wine "very plenteously," which "ran the faster and more merrily downe into some bodies bellies." But regarding the speech of Sir Henry Montague, Recorder of the city, and all the songs, Harrison writes: "I referre you to the Booke in print, where they are set downe at large." Harrison closes by observing: "The Citty elected 16. Committies to whom the managing of the whole businesse was absolutely referred: of which number 4. were Aldermen, the other 12. Commoners." Harrison has lifted this statement verbatim from Dekker's text. One book refers to another — the activity of a shrewd architect-publisher.

The cumulative effect of all of Harrison's accomplishments compels us to see him as a major participant in a major cultural event — in some ways *the* most important public event of King James's early English reign. The City of London offers this pageant to the king as a sign of its gratitude and hope for the king and his royal family. The pageant symbolically ratifies James's kingship, since this had not been possible in the plague-filled days of 1603. Indeed, the March pageant takes place just four days before James opened his first Parliament. While scholars have typically focused on the contributions of Dekker and Jonson, I underscore the accomplishment of the architect Harrison, without whose work the pageant would not have occurred and without whose book we would have an incomplete record of the event. In contrast to Harrison's overseeing this great public event, Inigo Jones captures our attention for his indoor, limited, private court masques. I thereby circle back to the fundamental question of why scholars and critics have elevated Jones and the masques and have largely ignored Harrison and the civic pageants.

Writing about Thomas Middleton's 1619 Lord Mayor's Show *The Triumphs of Love and Antiquity*, Gerard Langbaine, in one of the earliest works of English dramatic criticism (1691), says of the pageant: "I think [it] no ways deserv'd either the Title of a *Masque*, under which Species it has been hitherto rank'd, nor so pompous a Title, as the Author has prefix'd."[11] From the seventeenth century, then, the term *masque* seems reserved for elevated entertainment, to which a mere Lord Mayor's Show cannot aspire. Langbaine in fact lists the contents of Middleton's entertainment, but nowhere else in his treatise discusses any pageant. This early critic has established a hierarchy, a pecking order that remains in place 300 years later.

Twentieth century scholars and critics have been eager to explore the masque's connection to European traditions. This has helped lead, I believe, to a privileged position for the masque, in contrast to the pageant. It may at moments be difficult, however, to sort out cause from effect. Nevertheless, the concentration on Continental indebtedness has a way of ennobling the masque, making it worthy of our attention. This approach plays into the excessive aristocratic gaze of much criticism, an unspoken, unacknowledged ideology of privilege. Unwittingly, many critics have tacitly accepted J. B. Heath's assumption that street pageants served the "rude and uncultivated" desires of the masses; therefore, they need not concern us. If we concentrate sufficiently — even overwhelmingly — on the masque, perhaps pageants will go away. To put the matter another way: who needs Stephen Harrison if Inigo Jones is available?

In the four volumes of *The Elizabethan Stage*, E. K. Chambers devotes almost twice as much space to masques as he does to pageants. Jones merits considerable discussion; Harrison does not warrant mention. Similarly, in the seven volumes of *Jacobean and Caroline Stage*, G. E. Bentley includes exactly five entries on the subject of pageants while having over 200 references to masques.[12] Chambers enunciates the idea of the masque's connection to Italian entertainments.[13] This concept Enid Welsford vigorously pursues in her 1927 study *The Court Masque*, where she writes: "From the time of Henry VIII to the outbreak of the Civil War, the history of our English masque is the history of the absorption (and modification) of influences coming from Italy, either directly or by way of France."[14] The French *ballet de Cour* and the Italian intermezzo and masquerade all happily converge in the English masque. Specifically, Jonson's *Masque of Queens* (1609) "is the first work to show unmistakable traces of the influence of those Florentine revels of 1608, which were to have such a very great effect on the history of the English court masque" (183); meanwhile, *The Vision of Delight* "shows the influence of France as well as of Italy" (202). In her 1929 book, *The Origin of the Masque*, Cornelia Baehrens picks up this idea, insisting that "there is no denying the fact that the masque was shaped under foreign influence, the tracing of which will be our endeavour in the subsequent chapters."[15] She therefore concentrates on Italian, Burgundian, and French influences on the English masque. Baehrens does manage to pay passing attention to some progress pageants but generally finds them inferior, arguing that neither the Kenilworth pageant of 1575 nor the Norwich shows in 1578 "could boast of anything so refined as the French *spectacles*" (107). She also mentions that writing such pageants could not have been difficult, requiring no great literary talent or dramatic power (108).

Allardyce Nicoll in 1938 argues that "basically the means employed in the presentation of the masques at the English court were the same as those employed during the same period in the production of Italian *intermezzi* and operas."[16] Because of Jones's debt to Continental examples, a focus on Italian procedure seems amply justified, Nicoll writes. Stephen Orgel sees Jones's visual illusion of reality in the masques as "something remarkable and largely unfamiliar, contrived out of Italianate devices."[17] During the reign of Charles I, Roy Strong writes, England "suddenly became a focal point for everything of any importance that was happening within Europe in the arts."[18] Together with Jonson, Jones "created that most distinctive manifestation of the art of the festival at the Stuart court, the masque." Therefore, we cannot be the least bit surprised to encounter this statement in John Peacock's 1995 book: "The generic affinities of the masque were European rather than domestic, less with contemporary English drama than with courtly continental forms like the Italian *intermedio* or the French *ballet de court*" (4). The ideas of Chambers, Welsford, and Baehrens are alive and well at the end of the twentieth century.

In the midst of such Continental plenitude, we need only choose whether we want to focus on Italian, French, or possibly Burgundian traditions in order to understand the English court masque. At the least we know that the English masque rests securely within a foreign and approved tradition. It has nothing to do with "contemporary English drama," according to Peacock, an idea implicitly accepted by other critics. No one can sensibly deny the masque's connection to various European dramatic traditions, but to look only in that direction risks myopia. Why not look in the direction of Stephen Harrison and the street pageants? The critical gaze should be refocused to look not only across the waters to the Continent but also to glance around the scruffy streets of London.

In an ambitious undertaking, Graham Parry seeks to encompass "Stuart culture" in his 1981 book. He writes compellingly of the 1604 royal entry pageant: "Combining architecture with emblem, tableau, drama and music, the event demonstrates compactly how the arts served the monarchy by projecting a state mythology, and also offers a view of the iconography prevailing at the beginning of James's reign."[19] Parry takes us through this pageant skillfully, and he acknowledges the contribution of Stephen Harrison. But he concludes about this pageant: "As such, this complex of music, morality and spectacle in its flamboyant architectural setting, aided by mechanical devices and celestial speaking figures, was well on the way to the Court masque" (20). Perversely, the pageant becomes part of the evolution of the masque, which implies that we should remember this pageant solely because it points the way for the court masque. It was "well on the way"; a few nudges here, a few tucks there, and the pageant could be a masque! This stands the cultural project on its head. Parry discusses no other civic pageant; he does include the obligatory chapters on the court masques and a chapter on Inigo Jones. Parry insists: Jones "was England's universal man — architect, mechanic, mathematician, artist, designer of sets and costumes, antiquary and connoisseur" (146); he had "become the complete expositor of Jacobean taste" (153). "Unique in his range of skills and knowledge, he [Jones] alone in England was capable of proposing an architecture that was the accepted measure of civility throughout Europe" (162–63). We cannot seem to get very far from the Continental measure of things, one that defines "civility." Surely we might want to quarrel with the notion of Jones as the "complete expositor of Jacobean taste."

In the 1990 *Cambridge Companion to English Renaissance Drama*, Martin Butler writes on private and occasional drama.[20] While this piece includes material about Inns of Court drama and mentions some progress entertainments, it says nothing about Lord Mayor's Shows or other kinds of civic pageants. It focuses mainly on court masques as the quintessential occasional drama, noted for their "unprecedented density of classical learning and symbolic meaning" (138). Most recently, a new anthology of essays has appeared, *A New History of Early English Drama* (1997). The editors, John Cox and David Scott Kastan, announce that the book's "primary aim is to provide the most comprehensive account yet available of early English drama."[21] They add that "readers can consult individual essays on specific topics in the confidence that what they are reading is reliable and authoritative." Expectations rise. It turns out that this "new" history has some old problems, at least on the subject of civic pageants. We find an excellent essay by Gordon Kipling on royal entry pageants, but his discussion ends with Elizabeth's pageant of 1559.[22] It contains no mention of Lord Mayor's Shows or of progress pageants: "civic culture" seems quite limited. No other essay fills the gap. According to this new history, civic pageants end with Elizabeth's 1559 entertainment. We pick up a thread in Graham Parry's essay, "Entertainments at Court" (195–211), which focuses almost exclusively on the court masque. We find a by now very familiar point: "Florence and the Medici court lay behind the Stuart masque," the "result of Continental influence infiltrating England" (201). Nothing new here. Parry says of the *Masque of Blackness* (1605): "Here for the first time was a full integration of text and spectacle . . ." (200). No history here. Did not the 1604 civic pageant under the guidance of Dekker, Jonson, Middleton, and Harrison offer a striking example of the integration of text and spectacle? So, in 1997 "comprehensive" means total disregard for Lord Mayor's Shows and scant attention to other civic pageants. The ideology of privilege survives intact.

It need not be so. Several decades ago Glynne Wickham observed: "The Lord Mayor's Show, engaging as it did the attention of the leading dramatists, actors, musicians and artificers of the day is a neglected source of theatrical history, and as a peripheral influence upon stage spectacle it is at least as important as that of Mask, Ballet and Italian opera."[23] Wickham argues further that in the Jacobean and Caroline periods the Lord Mayor's Show can be seen "as deliberately rivalling the opulent masks of the Court at Westminster" (2:237). For the most part Wickham's arguments have been ignored.[24] We have to wonder why. In a recent classroom edition of court masques — none of civic pageants exists — David Lindley, the editor, observes that despite a "thin trickle of major studies over the years, the court masque remains marginal to the study of the great age of English drama."[25] If the position of the court masque remains "marginal," then words fail us to define the scholarly place of civic pageants.

In trying to recuperate Stephen Harrison's contribution to dramatic art, I have intended to call renewed attention to such civic pageants in an attempt to redress what I see as an imbalance, brought about by scholarly neglect and prejudice. I could just as easily have focused on Gerard Christmas and his sons John and Matthias who, for over 20 years, served as architects and artificers for Lord Mayor's Shows, and whose work dramatists regularly praised in pageant texts.[26] We do not lack material: a multitude of printed texts prepared by the major dramatists of the period, archival city records of expenditures, eyewitness accounts, and other manuscript records. We seem only to lack will. And yet, civic pageants, in contrast to masques, captured the attention of thousands of spectators in London's streets or wherever they took place. Standing in Cheapside, for example, seeing the dramatic performance, observing the colorful costume, hearing the music, feasting on symbolic and iconographical display, spectators could have had an experience not unlike that which they could have found across the river in public theaters. As scholars and critics we must offer a new comprehensive history that includes and elevates civic pageants. Fortunately, we do not have to choose between Inigo Jones and Stephen Harrison; we only have to choose to examine both of them in the plenitude that constitutes theatrical activity in this, its richest moment.

NOTES

Notes to Introduction

1. Gerald Graff, "The Scholar in Society," in *Introduction to Scholarship in Modern Languages and Literatures*, ed. Joseph Gibaldi (New York: MLA, 1992), 349.

2. *The Future of Doctoral Studies in English*, ed. Andrea Lunsford, Helene Moglen, and James F. Slevin (New York: MLA, 1980), v and vi.

3. J. Isaacs, "Shakespearian Scholarship," *A Companion to Shakespeare Studies*, ed. Harley Granville-Barker and G. B. Harrison (Cambridge: Cambridge University Press, 1934), 305.

4. Wayne Booth, "The Scholar in Society," in *Introduction to Scholarship in Modern Languages and Literatures*, ed. Joseph Gibaldi (New York: MLA, 1981), p. 120.

5. Willa Cather, *The Professor's House* (1925; New York: Random House, 1990), 16.

6. Stephen Orgel, "Making Greatness Familiar," in *Pageantry in the Shakespearean Theater*, ed. David M. Bergeron (Athens: University of Georgia Press, 1985), 23.

7. Leeds Barroll, "A New History for Shakespeare and His Time," *Shakespeare Quarterly* 39 (1988): 441–64.

8. R. Malcolm Smuts, *Court Culture and the Origins of a Royalist Tradition in Early Stuart England* (Philadelphia: University of Pennsylvania Press, 1987).

Notes to Chapter One

1. S. Schoenbaum, *Internal Evidence and Elizabethan Dramatic Authorship: An Essay in Literary History and Method* (Evanston: Northwestern University Press, 1966), 150.

2. (Oxford: Clarendon Press, 1923), 2:194n.

3. In the *Calendar of Salisbury MSS. at Hatfield House* (London, 1894), 5:487.

4. *RES* 1 (1925): 76–76; *William Shakespeare: A Study of Facts and Problems* (Oxford: Clarendon Press, 1930), 2:320–21.

5. "*Richard II* or *Richard III* or . . .?," *Shakespeare Quarterly* 9 (1958): 204–06.

6. *The Heritage Shakespeare: The Histories* (New York: Heritage 1958), 86.

7. *King Richard II* (London: Methuen, 1961), xxx.

8. Louis B. Wright and Virginia LaMar, eds., *Richard the Second* (New York: Washington Square Press, 1962), viii.

9. *A Shakespeare Companion 1664–1964* (London: Duckworth, 1964), 412 and 229.

10. O. J. Campbell, ed., *The Reader's Encyclopedia of Shakespeare* (New York: Thomas Crowell, 1966), 690.

11. In his edition of *Richard II*, *The Complete Pelican Shakespeare*, gen. ed., Alfred Harbage (Baltimore: Penguin, 1969), 633.

12. Irving Ribner and G. L. Kittredge, eds., *The Complete Works of Shakespeare* (Waltham, Mass.: Xerox, 1971), 717. Note below how Ribner alters Kittredge's original position.

13. In his edition of *Richard II*, *The Complete Signet Classic Shakespeare*, gen. ed. Sylvan Barnet (New York: Harcourt Brace Jovanovich, 1972), 437.

14. *The Complete Works of Shakespeare* (Glenview, Ill.: Scott, Foresman, 1973), 1314; *The Complete Works of Shakespeare*, 4th edition (New York: Longman, 1997), A–10.

15. *The Riverside Shakespeare*, gen. ed. G. Blakemore Evans (Boston: Houghton Mifflin, 1974), 800. The 1997 edition of the Riverside restates Baker's point, although an Appendix raises doubts about the meaning of the evidence, see 845 and 1963.

16. *King Richard II*, ed. Andrew Gurr (Cambridge: Cambridge University Press, 1984), 1.

17. Stanley Wells, Gary Taylor, John Jowett, and William Montgomery, *William Shakespeare: A Textual Companion* (Oxford: Clarendon, 1987), 117.

18. *The Norton Shakespeare*, eds. Stephen Greenblatt, Walter Cohen, Jean E. Howard, and Katharine Eisaman Maus (New York: W. W. Norton, 1997).

19. "The Date of 'Richard II,'" *Notes & Queries* 195 (1950): 402–04.

20. Matthew Black, ed., *A New Variorum Edition of Richard the Second* (Philadelphia & London: J. B. Lippincott, 1955), 393–95.

21. *The Complete Works of Shakespeare* (Chicago: Scott, Foresman, 1951), 643. One might question Craig's use of the word "recently" to describe Chambers's find, especially when the same statement is repeated in the 1961 reissue of Craig's edition.

22. G. B. Harrison, ed., *The Complete Works* (New York: Harcourt Brace, 1952).

23. Charles J. Sisson, ed., *The Complete Works* (London: Oldhams Press, 1954), 449.

24. Robert T. Petersson, ed., *Richard the Second* (New Haven: Yale Univ. Press, 1957), 155.

25. *The Complete Works of Shakespeare* (Boston: Ginn, 1936), 505. Greer cites Kittredge in a footnote but gives him no credit for arguing against the Hoby letter.

26. *Richard II* (Cambridge: Cambridge Univ. Press, 1939), viii, ix. This view is accepted also in Wilson's revised edition of 1951.

27. William A. Neilson and Charles J. Hill, eds., *The Complete Plays and Poems of William Shakespeare* (New York: Houghton Mifflin, 1942), 598.

28. O. J. Campbell, ed., *The Living Shakespeare* (New York: Macmillan, 1949), 182.

29. Evelyn May Albright, "Shakespeare's *Richard II* and the Essex Conspiracy," *PMLA* 42 (1927): 688.

30. For a discussion of textual matters see the survey by Matthew Black, ed., in the Variorum edition, *Richard the Second* (Philadelphia: J. B. Lippincott, 1955), 355–92.

31. Black, 370–71; Peter Ure, ed., *King Richard II*, the Arden Shakespeare (London: Methuen, 1961), xiv–xv. Except for quotations from Q1, I quote from Ure's edition.

32. Ure, xiv.

33. "The Play Performed at the Globe on 7 February, 1601," *Notes & Queries* 197 (1952): 270–71. Other essays by Greer on the subject of the deposition scene are: "The Deposition Scene of 'Richard II'," *N&Q* 197 (1952): 492–93; "More about the Deposition Scene of 'Richard II'," *N&Q* 198 (1953): 49–50.

34. *Calendar of State Papers Domestic, Elizabeth 1598–1601* (London, 1869), 575.

35. Ibid., 578.

36. W. W. Greg, *Richard the Second*, Shakespeare Quarto Facsimile no. 13 (Oxford: Clarendon, 1966), viii. Quotations from Q1 will be from this facsimile.

37. Margaret Shewring, *King Richard II* (Manchester: Manchester University Press, 1996), 23. In a similar vein Malcolm Page, *Richard II* (Atlantic Highlands, NJ: Humanities Press, 1987), had written that "although *Richard II* was printed in 1597, the deposition scene was omitted; the content was too subversive at that date" (37).

38. Russ McDonald, *The Bedford Companion to Shakespeare* (New York: St. Martin's, 1996), 55.

39. Leeds Barroll, "A New History for Shakespeare and His Time," *Shakespeare Quarterly* 39 (1988): 448; 441–64.

40. Janet Clare, "The Censorship of the Deposition Scene in *Richard II*," *Review of English Studies* 41 (1990): 92–93; 89–94.

41. Cyndia Susan Clegg, "'By the choise and inuitation of al the realme': *Richard II* and Elizabethan Press Censorship," *Shakespeare Quarterly* 48 (1997): 433; 432–48. Clegg calls attention to my essay, "*Richard II* and Carnival Politics," *Shakespeare Quarterly* 42 (1991): 33–43, in which I place the deposition scene in the midst of an instable text that corresponds to a carnivalesque attitude in the play.

Notes to Chapter Two

1. Such as Sydney Anglo, *Spectacle Pageantry, and Early Tudor Policy* (Oxford, 1969), 344–59; Ernest W. Talbert, *The Problem of Order* (Chapel Hill, N.C., 1962), 79–88; Robert Withington, *English Pageantry: An Historical Outline*, 2 vols. (Cambridge, Mass., 1918), 1:199–203; John Nichols, *The Progresses and Public Processions of Queen Elizabeth*, new ed., 3 vols. (London, 1823), 1:38–60; Richard DeMolen, "Richard Mulcaster and Elizabethan Pageantry," *Studies in English Literature* 14 (1974): 209–21; David M. Bergeron, *English Civic Pageantry 1558–1642* (London and Columbia, S. C., 1971), 12–23; and Bergeron, "Medieval Drama and Tudor-Stuart Civic Pageantry," *Journal of Medieval and Renaissance Studies*, 2 (1972): 279–93.

2. Bergeron, *English Civic Pageantry*, 12–13.

3. Bergeron, *English Civic Pageantry*, 13; for further discussion see the DeMolen essay cited in n. 1.

4. I will cite the facsimile edition, *The Quenes Maiesties Passage*, ed. James M. Osborn (New Haven, Conn., 1960). For additional information about the editions of this entertainment see my *English Civic Pageantry*, 13n. The most recent edition is that by Arthur F. Kinney in *Elizabethan Backgrounds* (Hamden, Conn., 1975), 7–39. Kinney discusses in detail the textual relationships of the three editions (9–11). He credits George Ferrers as author, citing Neville Williams (9), but I know of no evidence for this claim, while

the information about Mulcaster is unmistakable. Kinney quotes the colophons of the two editions as "1558" rather than 1559 because they follow old-style, rather than new-style, chronology. More puzzling is his statement that this pageant for Elizabeth "had little or no precedent. . . . Only Mary Tudor had had pageants . . ." (7). But beginning in the sixteenth century with Catherine of Aragon's royal entry in 1501, there were a number of such pageant entertainments — see Anglo (n. 1 above).

5. I am especially indebted to Laetitia Yeandle of the Folger staff who kindly and expertly checked my transcriptions.

6. *Historical Manuscripts Commission, Seventh Report*, Part I (London: HMS Office, 1879), 614.

7. Folger Library MS.L.b.108.

8. Quoted in Bergeron, *English Civic Pageantry*, 14.

9. Albert Feuillerat, *Documents Relating to the Office of the Revels in the Time of Queen Elizabeth* (Louvain, 1908), 82. Folger MS.L.b.517 provides a different list of material purchased by the Revels from the same Henry Becher, beginning with January 1. The bottom of the MS is signed: "by mr henry Becher / the coppie of his byll."

10. Feuillerat, 88.

11. I am indebted to the American Philosophical Society for a grant that made this research possible.

Notes to Chapter Three

1. Werner Gundersheimer, "Patronage in the Renaissance: An Exploratory Approach," in *Patronage in the Renaissance*, ed. Stephen Orgel and Guy Lytle (Princeton: Princeton University Press, 1981), 23; 3–23.

2. Glynne Wickham, *Early English Stages 1300 to 1660* (New York: Columbia University Press, 1963), 2:94. Thomas Middleton's *A Game Of Chess* (1624) shows how one dramatist, writing on topical matters, did not suffer prior censorship. Indeed, this highly controversial play about the proposed Spanish marriage of Prince Charles was licensed by Sir Henry Herbert. Only after several performances and protest from the Spanish Ambassador did James shut down the play. The King's Men under James's patronage successfully performed this play without government censorship; the forbidding of production came only after controversy and political pressure.

3. E. K. Chambers, *The Elizabethan Stage* (Oxford: Clarendon Press, 1923) vol. 4. Appendix B, 168ff.

4. Chambers, *Elizabethan Stage*, 4:176.

5. *A Calendar of Dramatic Records in the Books of the Livery Companies of London 1485–1640*, ed. D. J. Gordon and Jean Robertson (Oxford: Malone Society, 1954), 63. All quotations of guild records will come from this Malone Society *Collections III*.

6. *Henslowe's Diary*, ed. R. A. Foakes and R. T. Rickert (Cambridge: Cambridge University Press, 1968), 126–28.

7. "Women as Patrons of English Renaissance Drama," in *Patronage in the Renaissance*, ed. Orgel and Lytle, 274–90; and included in this volume.

8. See Virgil B. Hetzel, "The Dedication of Tudor and Stuart Plays," *Wiener Beiträge zur Englischen Philologie* 65 (1957): 74–86. Although as I make clear in my study of women patrons, Heltzel's view needs to be modified slightly, his study remains a good place to begin investigation of the topic.

9. For further information see my Introduction in *Thomas Heywood's Pageants: A Critical Edition* (New York: Garland, 1986). Quotations will be from my edition.

10. Heywood quotes Juvenal. See *Fair Maid of the West*, ed. Robert K. Turner, Jr. (Lincoln: University of Nebraska Press, 1967), 93.

11. *The Jew of Malta* (1633), sig. A3v.

12. *The Iron Age* (1632), sig. A3v.

13. *The Dramatic Works of Thomas Heywood*, ed. R. H. Shepherd (1874; rpt., New York: Russell & Russell, 1964), 4:3.

14. Heywood, *Englands Elizabeth* (1631), sig. A5v–A6.

15. Heywood, *Pleasant Dialogues and Dramma's*, ed. W. Bang, *Materialien zur Kunde des älteren Englischen Dramas* (Lovain, 1903). All quotations will be from this edition of Heywood's 1637 work.

Notes to Chapter Four

1. See the argument of Jean Gagen in *The New Woman: Her Emergence in English Drama 1600–1730* (New York, 1954), 16 and in Pearl Hogrefe, *Tudor Woman: Commoners and Queens* (Ames, Iowa, 1975), 142.

2. Catherine M. Dunn, "The Changing Image of Woman in Renaissance Society and Literature," in *What Manner of Woman: Essays on English and American Life and Literature*, ed. Marlene Springer (New York, 1971), 15–38; David J. Latt, "Praising Virtuous Ladies: The Literary Image and Historical Reality of Women in Seventeenth-Century England," in *What Manner of Woman*, ed. Springer, 39–64. Apparently neither writer had a chance to consult Hogrefe's book.

3. *Shakespeare and the Nature of Women* (London, 1975), 5.

4. Other studies that are of some interest: Gamaliel Bradford, *Elizabethan Women* (Cambridge, Mass., 1936); Carroll Camden, *The Elizabethan Woman* (Houston, 1952); Ruth Kelso, *Doctrine for the Lady of the Renaissance* (Urbana, Ill., 1956); Mary R. Mahl and Helene Koon, eds., *The Female Spectator: English Women Writers before 1800* (Bloomington, Ind., and London, 1977); M. Philips and W. S. Tomkinson, *English Women in Life and Letters* (Oxford, 1926); Roger Thompson, *Women in Stuart England and America: A Comparative Study* (London and Boston, 1974).

5. V. Sackville-West, *The Diary of the Lady Anne Clifford* (London, 1923). G. E. Bentley in *Jacobean and Caroline Stage* (Oxford, 1956) has cited most, but not all, of Lady Anne's theatrical references. See also George C. Williamson, *Lady Anne Clifford . . . Her Life, Letters, and Work* (Kendal, 1922).

6. For brief discussion see David M. Bergeron, *English Civic Pageantry 1558–1642* (London and Columbia, S.C., 1971), 62. For the text of the entertainment see John Nichols, *Progresses of Elizabeth* (London, 1823), 3:130–36.

7. J. H. Wiffen, *Historical Memoirs of the House of Russell* (London, 1833), 2:14.

8. Hogrefe, *Tudor Women*, 133–34.

9. For a list see Herford and Simpson, *Ben Jonson* (Oxford, 1950), 10:440–45.

10. Herford and Simpson, *Ben Jonson* (Oxford, 1925), 1:143. The speculation that the play was *The Sad Shepherd* is inconclusive.

11. Bentley, *Jacobean and Caroline Stage*, 3:453.

12. Bentley, *Jacobean and Caroline Stage*, 4:549.

13. Bentley, *Jacobean and Caroline Stage*, 4:917–20.

14. "The Dedication of Early English Plays," *Life and Letters* 3 (1929): 31.

15. In *Studies in English Language and Literarure Presented to Professor Dr. Karl Brunner*, ed. Siegfried Korninger, *Wiener Beiträge zur Englischen Philologie* 65 (1957): 74–86.

16. In a brief note Franklin B. Williams calls attention to the prominence of women as patronesses of all forms of writing. He finds that 733 women had books dedicated to them in the STC period ("The Literary Patronesses of Renaissance England," *Notes and Queries* 207 [1962]: 365).

17. Robert Wilmot, *Tancred and Gismund* (London, 1591), sig. *2^{v}.

18. *The Works of Thomas Middleton*, ed. A. H. Bullen (London, 1886), 7: 141.

19. *The Lady's Trial* (London, 1639), sig. A3^{v}.

20. Kyd, *Cornelia* in *The Works of Thomas Kyd*, ed. F. S. Boas (Oxford, 1955), 102.

21. References come from Franklin B. Williams, *Index of Dedications and Commendatory Verses in English Books before 1641* (London, 1962). Arthur Freeman explores Kyd's relationship to the Radcliffe family, suggesting that Henry, fourth Earl of Sussex might have been a patron of Kyd; see *Thomas Kyd: Facts and Problems* (Oxford, 1967), 34–37.

22. *The Duke of Milan* (London, 1623), sig. A3. As the recent editors of Massinger point out, Katherine Stanhope was the "sister of Fletcher's patron, the earl of Huntingdon, and this relationship is surely the reason for Massinger's approaching her" (*The Plays and Poems of Philip Massinger*, ed. Philip Edwards and Colin Gibson (Oxford, 1976], 1:xxxiii).

23. Brandon, *The Virtuous Octavia* (London, 1598), sig. A2.

24. Herford and Simpson, *Jonson*, 10: 50.

25. *The Alchemist* (London, 1612), sig. A2^v.

26. *2 The Cid* (London, 1640), sig. A4.

27. *The Vow Breaker* (London, 1636), sig. A3.

28. *The Dramatic Works and Poems of James Shirley*, ed. Alexander Dyce (1833; rpt. New York, 1966), 2:272.

29. *The Workes of Mr. Iohn Marston* (London, 1633), sig. A3. Elizabeth's husband, Henry Cary, was the subject of Jonson's *Epigramme* lxvi.

30. See Patricia Thomson, "The Patronage of Letters under Elizabeth and James I," *English* 7 (1949): 278–82. Also see her essay, "The Literature of Patronage, 1580–1630," *Essays in Criticism* 2 (1952): 267–84.

31. Herford and Simpson, *Jonson*, 10: 440.

32. Herford and Simpson, *Jonson*, 10: 197.

33. Joan Rees, *Samuel Daniel: A Critical and Biographical Study* (Liverpool, 1964), 90.

34. John Buxton, *Sir Philip Sidney and the English Renaissance* (London, 1954), 229.

35. *The Vision of the Twelve Goddesses*, ed. Joan Rees, in *A Book of Masques in Honour of Allardyce Nicoll* (Cambridge, 1967), 26.

36. Hogrefe, *Tudor Women*, 124. In her dissertation Mary Ellen Lamb suggests that the importance and extent of the countess's patronage has been exaggerated: "her husband's wealth, her brother's fame, and her own reputation for generosity were probably responsible for the many single works dedicated to her by authors who do not seem to have been acquainted with her" ("The Countess of Pembroke's Patronage," Ph.D. Dissertation, Columbia University, 1976, 255). But some 30 texts were dedicated to her, the second highest number of books dedicated to a woman other than royalty (the first being the Countess of Bedford with 38) — see Williams, "The Literary Patronesses of Renaissance England," 366. Lamb further

claims that "A patron's influence cannot be assumed for every author who dedicated a work; it must be indicated in some other way besides a dedication or the possible use of a literary model" (241). Such a view creates more problems than it solves. The simple act of dedicating a text does indicate influence, whatever it may prove precisely about an act of patronage.

37. *Countess of Pembrokes Ivychurch* (London, 1591), sig. A2.

38. *The Countess of Pembrokes Arcadia* (London, 1598), sig. ¶3.

39. Gager, *Ulysses Redux* (Oxford, 1592), sig. A2.

40. One might also include Christopher Marlowe in the list of dramatists who wrote dedications to the countess, though Marlowe's statement is prefixed to *Amintae Gaudia Authore Thoma Watsono* (1592). The dedication, signed by "C. M." and in Latin, sounds several familiar themes. Marlowe promises that "in the foremost page of every poem" he will "invoke thee as Mistress of the Muses to my aid" (Mark Eccles's translation in *The Complete Works of Christopher Marlowe*, ed. Fredson Bowers [Cambridge, 1973, 2:539]. Marlowe's exact relationship to the countess is indeterminate.

41. See, for example, Alexander M. Witherspoon, *The Influence of Robert Garnier on Elizabethan Drama*, Yale Studies in English 65 (New Haven, 1924), 67, and *passim*.

42. Rees, *Samuel Daniel*, 43.

43. Rees, *Samuel Daniel*, 48.

44. Daniel, *Cleopatra* (London, 1594), sig. H5, lines 1–8.

45. Rees, *Samuel Daniel*, 149.

46. Daniel, *Certaine Small Workes* (London, 1611), sig. E4.

Notes to Chapter Five

1. *The Works of Francis Bacon*, ed. James Spedding, Robert Ellis, and Douglas Heath, 14 vols. (London, 1868–90), 6:11.

2. *The History of the Reign of King Henry the Seventh*, ed. F. J. Levy (Indianapolis: Merrill, 1972), 65.

3. *The Political Works of James I*, ed. Charles H. McIlwain (Cambridge: Harvard University Press, 1918), 272.

4. Ibid., 271.

5. *The Dramatic Works of Thomas Dekker*, ed. Fredson Bowers, 4 vols. (Cambridge: Cambridge University Press, 1953–1961), 2:262. For a discussion of this pageant, see my *English Civic Pageantry 1558–1642* (London: Arnold; Columbia: University of South Carolina Press, 1971), 71–89.

6. *Pageants and Entertainments of Anthony Munday: A Critical Edition*, ed. David M. Bergeron (New York: Garland, 1985), 9.

7. Martin Elsky, *Authorizing Words: Speech, Writing, and Print*

in the English Renaissance (Ithaca: Cornell University Press, 1989), 195. The chapter on Bacon (184–208) is an excellent study of Bacon as a writer who sought court favor and became also something of a champion of the printed text.

8. *The Letters and the Life of Francis Bacon*, ed. James Spedding (London, 1874), 7:303.

9. Bacon, *Henry the Seventh*, ed. Levy, 79.

10. S. B. Chrimes, *Henry VII* (Berkeley: University of California Press, 1972), 302.

11. Judith H. Anderson, *Biographical Truth: The Representation of Historical Persons in Tudor-Stuart Writing* (New Haven: Yale University Press, 1984), 185.

12. For detailed discussion of the relationship of James and Anne, as well as other members of the Stuart royal family, see my book, *Royal Family, Royal Lovers: King James of England and Scotland* (Columbia: University of Missouri Press, 1991).

13. Francis Osborne, *Traditional Memoirs* (1658), in *Secret History of the Court of James the First*, ed. Sir Walter Scott, 2 vols. (Edinburgh, 1811), 1:196.

14. William Sanderson, *A Compleat History of the Lives and Reigns of Mary Queen of Scotland and of Her Son and Successor, James* (London, 1656), 474.

15. Godfrey Goodman, *The Court of King James the First*, ed. John S. Brewer, 2 vols. (London, 1839), 1:168.

16. *Calendar of the Manuscripts of the Marquis of Salisbury* (London: HMC, 1965), pt. xix:308.

17. Arthur Wilson, *The History of Great Britain* (London, 1653), 79.

18. *Calendar of State Papers Venetian, 1603–1625*, vols. 10–18 (London: HMSO, 1900–1912), 15:307.

19. *Letters of King James VI & I*, ed. G. P. V. Akrigg (Berkeley: University of California Press, 1984), 369.

20. Ibid., 370n.

21. *Calendar of State Papers Venetian*, 15:495.

22. *The Letters of John Chamberlain*, ed. Norman E. McClure, 2 vols. (Philadephia: American Philosophial Society, 1939), 2:242.

23. *The Works of Francis Bacon*, 4:302.

Notes to Chapter Six

1. David Harris Willson, *King James VI & I* (London: Jonathan Cape, 1956), 95. Marina Warner in her *Joan of Arc: The Image of Female Heroism* (New York: Alfred Knopf, 1981) has ably demonstrated how a feminist reinterpretation of a historical figure alters

the received view. She writes of her purpose: "I am trying to see how Joan fitted into an intellectual and emotional tradition of thought concerning women" (9–10). Such a perspective has largely been missing in interpretations of Queen Anne. Feminist historians have on the whole paid more attention to the way in which women's condition has been socially constructed. On this point one can look at the work of Nancy F. Cott, among others, especially her book *The Grounding of Modern Feminism* (New Haven: Yale University Press, 1987). Focusing on the women's suffrage movement in the United States, Cott skillfully shows how different historians have responded to this historical event in her essay, "Feminist Theory and Feminist Movements: The Past Before Us," in *What is Feminism?*, ed. Juliet Mitchell and Ann Oakley (Oxford: Basil Blackwell, 1986), 49–62.

2. William Harris, *An Historical and Critical Account of the Life and Writings of James the First, King of Great Britain* (London, 1753), 35.

3. Samuel R. Gardiner, *History of England from the Accession of James I to the Outbreak of the Civil War 1603–1642*, 10 vols. (1883–84; rpt. New York: AMS Press, 1965), 3:294.

4. Charles Williams, *James I* (1934; rpt. London: Arthur Barker, 1951), 104.

5. Godfrey Davies, "The Character of James VI and I,"*Huntington Library Quarterly* 5 (1941–42): 41.

6. For discussion of this matter and others pertinent to Anne, see my book *Royal Family, Royal Lovers: King James of England and Scotland* (Columbia: University of Missouri Press, 1991).

7. William McElwee, *The Wisest Fool in Christendom: The Reign of James I and VI* (New York: Harcourt, Brace, 1958), 67.

8. G. P. V. Akrigg, *Jacobean Pageant or the Court of King James I* (London: Hamish Hamilton, 1962), 21.

9. Otto J. Scott, *James I* (New York: Mason/ Charter, 1976), 218.

10. Roy Strong, *Henry, Prince of Wales and England's Lost Renaissance* (London: Thames & Hudson, 1986), 16.

11. Maurice Lee, Jr., *Great Britain's Solomon: James VI and I in His Three Kingdoms* (Urbana: University of Illinois Press, 1990), 74.

12. Catherine Macaulay, *The History of England from the Accession of James I to the Elevation of the House of Hanover* (London, 1766), 1:153–54. One notes with interest that Horace Walpole praised the "manly" qualities of Macaulay's history.

13. Ethel Carleton Williams, *Anne of Denmark: Wife of James VI of Scotland: James I of England* (London: Longman, 1970), 67.

14. *The Letters of John Chamberlain*, ed. Norman Egbert McClure (Philadelphia: American Philosophical Society, 1939), 1:187.

15. Antonia Fraser, *King James VI of Scotland I of England* (New York: Knopf, 1975), 53.

16. Caroline Bingham, *James I of England* (London: Weidenfeld and Nicolson, 1981), 78.

17. Caroline Bingham, *James VI of Scotland* (London: Weidenfeld and Nicolson, 1979), 121.

18. Barbara Kiefer Lewalski, *Writing Women in Jacobean England* (Cambridge: Harvard University Press, 1993).

19. Leeds Barroll, "The Court of the First Stuart Queen," in *The Mental World of the Jacobean Court*, ed. Linda Levy Peck (Cambridge: Cambridge University Press, 1991), 191–208; 325–32.

20. *Memoirs of Maximilian de Bethune, Duke of Sully*, trans. Charlotte Lennox (London, 1756), 2:181.

21. Arthur Wilson, *The History of Great Britain, Being the Life and Reign of King James the First* (London, 1653), 79.

22. *Calendar of State Papers Venetian 1603–1607* (London, 1900), 10:513.

Notes to Chapter Seven

1. All quotations from Middleton will be from my edition of his civic pageants to be included in *The Complete Works of Thomas Middleton*, gen. ed. Gary Taylor (Oxford: Oxford University Press, 2000). I cite the line numbers from this edition.

2. William Gifford, ed. *The Works of Ben Jonson*, 9 vols. (London, 1816), 6:325n.

3. John Nichols, *The Progresses, Processions, and Magnificent Festivities of King James the First*, 4 vols. (London, 1828), 2:681n.

4. J. Payne Collier, ed. *The Downfall of Robert Earl of Huntington* (London, 1828), 5.

5. *The Works of Thomas Middleton*, ed. Alexander Dyce, 5 vols. (London, 1840), 5:220n.

6. Frederick W. Fairholt, *Lord Mayors' Pageants*, Percy Society (London, 1843), pt. 1, 32.

7. *The Works of Thomas Middleton*, ed. A. H. Bullen, 7 vols. (London, 1886), 7:234n.

8. Josiah H. Penniman, *The War of the Theatres* (Philadelphia: University of Pennsylvania Press, 1897); and Roscoe Addison Small, *The Stage-Quarrel between Ben Jonson and the So-Called Poetasters* (Breslau: Marcus, 1899).

9. Frederick Gard Fleay, *A Biographical Chronicle of the English Drama 1559–1642*, 2 vols. (London: Reeves & Turner, 1891), 2:97.

10. George Unwin, *The Gilds and Companies of London* (London: Methuen, 1908), 279, 280.

11. Robert Withington, *English Pageantry: An Historical Outline*, 2 vols. (Cambridge: Harvard University Press, 1918–20), 2:33n.

12. Celeste Turner [Wright], *Anthony Mundy: An Elizabethan Man of Letters* (Berkeley: University of California Press, 1928), 159.

13. R. C. Bald, "Middleton's Civic Employments," *Modern Philology* 31 (1933–34), 72.

14. *Collections III: A Calendar of Dramatic Records in the Books of the Livery Companies of London 1485–1640*, ed. D. J. Gordon and Jean Robertson (Oxford: Malone Society, 1954), xxxv.

15. Jean Robertson, "*Rapports du Poète et de l'artiste dans la préparation des cortèges du Lord Maire (Londres 1553–1640),*" in *Les Fêtes de la Renaissance*, ed. Jean Jacquot (Paris: Éditions du Centre National de la Recherche Scientifique, 1956), 272.

16. Peter G. Phialas, "Middleton and Mundy," letter to *TLS*, 23 November 1956, 697.

17. Richard Hindry Barker, *Thomas Middleton* (New York: Columbia University Press, 1958), 15.

18. David M. Holmes, *The Art of Thomas Middleton: A Critical Study* (Oxford: Clarendon, 1970), 216.

19. M. C. Bradbrook, "The Politics of Pageantry: Social Implications in Jacobean London," in *Poetry and Drama 1570–1700: Essays in Honour of Harold F. Brooks*, ed. Antony Coleman and Antony Hammond (London: Metheun, 1981), 70.

20. Gail Kern Paster, *The Idea of the City in the Age of Shakespeare* (Athens: University of Georgia Press, 1985), 149.

21. David M. Bergeron, *English Civic Pageantry 1558–1642* (London: Arnold; Columbia: University of South Carolina Press 1971), 179.

22. *Pageants and Entertainments of Anthony Munday: A Critical Edition*, ed. David M. Bergeron (New York: Garland, 1985), 142.

23. Philip J. Ayres, "Anthony Munday," *Elizabethan Dramatists*, vol. 62 of *Dictionary of Literary Biography* (Detroit: Gale, 1987), 241.

24. T. H. Howard-Hill, "Thomas Middleton," in *Jacobean and Caroline Dramatists*, vol. 58 of *Dictionary of Literary Biography* (Detroit: Gale, 1987), 211.

25. *Henslowe's Diary*, ed. R. A. Foakes and R. T. Rickert (Cambridge: Cambridge University Press, 1968), 201.

26. *Dictionary of Literary Biography*, 62:236.

27. Malone Society, *Collections III*, 86.

28. Corporation of London, Repertory, XXXII, fol. 372.

29. John Stow, *Survey of London* (London, 1618), sig. *1.

30. Jeffrey A. Masten, "Beaumont and Fletcher: Collaboration and the Interpretation of Renaissance Drama," *ELH* 59 (1992): 337–56.

31. Stephen Orgel, "What Is a Text?" *Research Opportunities in Renaissance Drama* 24 (1981): 6. Orgel depends in part on G. E. Bentley's *The Profession of Dramatist in Shakespeare's Time, 1590–1642* (Princeton: Princeton University Press, 1971). See especially Bentley's chapter 8, "Collaboration," 197–234.

32. Margreta de Grazia and Peter Stallybrass, "The Materiality of the Shakespearean Text," *Shakespeare Quarterly* 44 (1993): 279. This important essay appears on pages 255–83.

33. James Shapiro, *Rival Playwrights: Marlowe, Jonson, Shakespeare* (New York: Columbia University Press, 1991).

Notes to Chapter Eight

1. Norbert H. Platz, "Ben Jonson's *Ars Poetica*: An Interpretation of *Poetaster* in Its Historical Context," in *Salzburg Studies in English Literature* 12, ed. James Hogg (1973), 1.

2. Two twentieth century scholars redefined the "War": Alfred Harbage, *Shakespeare and the Rival Traditions* (New York: Macmillan, 1952); Robert Sharpe, *The Real War of the Theatres* (Boston: D. C. Heath, 1935). Harbage sees the war in terms of the struggle between public and coterie theaters, and Sharpe sees it as a contest between opposing acting companies. Obviously, I focus on the nineteenth century's understanding of the war.

3. Isaac Disraeli, *Quarrels of Authors; or, Some Memoirs of Our Literary History*, 3 vols. (London: J. Murray, 1814). The Jonson material appears in volume 3, 123–67.

4. Algernon Swinburne, *A Study of Ben Jonson*, ed. Howard B. Norland (Lincoln: University of Nebraska Press, 1969), 22.

5. Quoted in *Poetaster*, ed. Tom Cain (Manchester: Manchester University Press, 1995), 30. All quotations from *Poetaster* will be from this edition.

6. James P. Bednarz, "Representing Jonson: *Histriomastix* and the Origin of the Poets' War," *Huntington Library Quarterly* 54 (1991): 23.

7. In fact, at the end of *Conversations*, Drummond portrays Jonson as a self-centered braggart.

8. C. H. Herford, Introduction, *Ben Jonson*, ed. Brinsley Nicholson (London: T. Fisher Unwin, 1894), 1:xxix.

9. C. H. Herford and Percy Simpson, eds. *Ben Jonson* (Oxford: Clarendon, 1925), 1:29.

10. Timothy Murray, *Theatrical Legitimation: Allegories of Genius in Seventeenth-Century England and France* (New York: Oxford University Press, 1987), 73. See also the essays in *Ben Jonson's 1616*

Folio, ed. Jennifer Brady and W. H. Herendeen (Newark: University of Delaware Press, 1991).

11. Joseph Loewenstein, "Printing and 'The Multitudinous Presse': The Contentious Texts of Jonson's Masques," in *Ben Jonson's 1616 Folio* (1991), 183; the essay appears pp. 168–91. See also Loewenstein's earlier essay, "The Script in the Marketplace," *Representations* 12 (1985): 101–14.

12. *The Dramatic Works of Thomas Dekker*, ed. Fredson Bowers (Cambridge: Cambridge University Press, 1955), 1:309. All quotations from Dekker will be from this edition.

13. Gerard Langbaine, *An Account of the English Dramatic Poets* (Oxford, 1691), 123.

14. Cyrus Hoy, *Introductions, Notes, and Commentaries to Texts in "The Dramatic Works of Thomas Dekker"* (Cambridge: Cambridge University Press, 1980), 1:180. Hoy offers a helpful summary of the plays reputedly involved in the war.

15. William Gifford, *The Works of Ben Jonson*, 9 vols. (London, 1816). All quotations from Gifford will be from this edition.

16. See Peter Martin, *Edmond Malone Shakespearean Scholar: A Literary Biography* (Cambridge: Cambridge University Press, 1995). See especially chapter 2 for Malone's battle with Steevens and chapter 5, "Scholarship and Strife."

17. Frederick Gard Fleay, *A Biographical Chronicle of the English Drama 1559–1642*, 2 vols. (London, 1891), 2:69.

18. Edmond Malone, ed., *The Plays and Poems of William Shakespeare*, 21 vols., ed. James Boswell (London, 1821), 1:xxx–xlvii.

19. Alexander B. Grosart, ed., *The Poems of John Marston* (Privately printed, 1879), 2:xlviii,

20. Robert Cartwright, *Shakespere and Jonson: Dramatic versus Wit-Combats* (London: John Russell Smith, 1864), 73.

21. *The Works of Thomas Dekker*, ed. Richard Herne Shepherd (London, 1873), xiv–xv.

22. A. H. Bullen, ed., *The Works of John Marston* (London, 1887), 1:xxx.

23. Josiah H. Penniman, *The War of the Theatres* (Philadelphia, 1897), 13.

24. Roscoe Addison Small, *The Stage-Quarrel between Ben Jonson and the So-Called Poetasters* (Breslau, 1899), 7.

25. Herbert S. Mallory, ed., *Poetaster by Ben Jonson* (New York: Henry Holt, 1905), xxvii. Mallory makes a similar statement on xxix.

26. Felix E. Schelling, *Elizabethan Drama 1558–1642* (1908; rpt. New York: Russell & Russell, 1959), 485.

27. Anne Barton, *Ben Jonson, Dramatist* (Cambridge: Cambridge University Press, 1984), 80.

28. David Riggs, *Ben Jonson: A Life* (Cambridge: Harvard University Press, 1989), 74.

29. W. David Kay, *Ben Jonson: A Literary Life* (New York: St. Martin's, 1995), 56.

30. *Ben Jonson: Three Comedies*, ed. Michael Jamieson (Baltimore: Penguin, 1966), 335.

31. Richard Simpson, *The School of Shakespeare*, 2 vols. (New York: J. W. Bouton, 1878), 1:5.

32. For further exploration of the matter of collaboration as a replacement scenario, see my "Thomas Middleton and Anthony Munday: Artistic Rivalry?" *SEL* 36 (1996): 461–79, included in this collection of essays.

33. John Marston, *The Malcontent*, ed. M. L. Wine (Lincoln: University of Nebraska Press, 1964), 3. This is Wine's translation of the original Latin.

34. Herford and Simpson, *Ben Jonson*, write: "Jonson and Dekker were hostile collaborators in the speeches for this entertainment" (10:386). I know of no evidence that suggests hostility. David Riggs repeats this idea in his biography of Jonson, 111.

35. I wish to thank Roslyn Knutson for sharing her work in progress: *Hot Anger Soon Cold: Commerce among the Elizabethan Playing Companies, 1598–1603*. We share a skepticism about how the nineteenth century understood the War of the Theaters. Knutson focuses on commercial relationships among the acting companies.

36. Jeffrey Masten, *Textual Intercourse: Collaboration, Authorship, and Sexualities in Renaissance Drama* (Cambridge: Cambridge University Press, 1997), 4.

Notes to Chapter Nine

1. Gilbert Dugdale, *The Time Triumphant, Declaring in briefe, the ariual of our Soueraigne* (London: printed by R. B., 1604), STC 7292. All quotations are from this original text.

2. Glynne Wickham, *Early English Stages* (London, 1959), 1: 51–111 *passim*. Wickham does not cite Dugdale at all, nor does he mention him in his essay, "Contribution de Ben Jonson et de Dekker aux Fêtes du couronnement de Jacques 1er," in *Les Fêtes de la Renaissance*, ed. Jean Jacquot (Paris, 1956), 279–83. David M. Bergeron, *English Civic Pageantry 1558–1642* (London and Columbia, S.C., 1971), 71–89. On 88, I cite Dugdale in a footnote, acknowledging that his text may be an eyewitness account, "though somewhat inaccurate." The latter phrase is misleading. Robert Withington, *English Pageantry: An Historical Outline* (Cambridge, Mass., 1918),

1:222–26, cites Dugdale in a footnote but does not discuss his contribution. In the commentary on the entertainment in *Ben Jonson,* ed. C. H. Herford, Percy and Evelyn Simpson (Oxford, 1950), 10:386–92, there is no mention of Dugdale. A more recent discussion of the royal entry is in Cyrus Hoy's *Introduction, Notes, and Commentaries to Texts in "The Dramatic Works of Thomas Dekker"* (Cambridge, 1980), 2:128–58. Hoy makes no reference to Dugdale in his excellent commentary on Dekker's part of the entertainment.

    3. *The Progresses of King James the First* (London, 1828), 1:419. Dugdale's text is also printed in Edward Arber's *An English Garner* (Birmingham, 1882), 5:639–56. Arber freely changes spelling, punctuation, and syntax. Nichols is more faithful to Dugdale.

    4. *A True Discourse* (London, 1604), sig. D4. E. K. Chambers had noted in passing the kinship of Dugdale and Armin in his section on Armin in *The Elizabethan Stage* (Oxford, 1923), 2:299–300.

    5. See my "Venetian State Papers and English Civic Pageantry, 1558–1642," *Renaissance Quarterly* 23 (1970): 37–47.

    6. *The Dramatic Works of Thomas Dekker* (Cambridge, 1955), 2: 231–52. All quotations from Dekker will be from this edition. Two sources list Dugdale as a dramatic text for this entertainment: Chambers, *The Elizabethan Stage,* 3:70, and Alfred Harbage and S. Schoenbaum, *Annals of English Drama 975–1700,* (Philadelphia, 1964), 88–89. It is a little misleading to think of Dugdale's description as a dramatic text in any conventional sense.

    7. Nichols prints *ills* instead of *evils.*

    8. Chambers, *The Elizabethan Stage,* 2:208–09.

    9. *Arches of Triumph* (London, 1604), sig. K1. The text, without the drawings, is in Nichols, 1:329–30, *331–*334. I cite the original edition.

    10. Herford and Simpson, *Jonson* (Oxford, 1941), 7:90.

    11. "Harrison, Jonson, and Dekker: The Magnificent Entertainment for King James (1604)," *Journal of the Warburg and Courtauld Institutes* 31 (1968): 445–48. Additional discrepancies are noted in *English Civic Pageantry,* 71–89.

    12. In the commentary volume (vol. 10) on Jonson the editors write: "Dekker in his unacted device made the Genius of the City a Woman" (388).

    13. Arthur Wilson, *The History of Great Britain, being the Life and Reign of King James the First* (London, 1653), 12–13.

    14. Nichols rather garbles this passage because he apparently misunderstands the punctuation mark after "King." Arber has it right.

    15. *Calendar of the Manuscripts of the Marquess of Salisbury* (London, 1973), 23:128.

Notes to Chapter Ten

1. Algernon Swinburne, *The Age of Shakespeare* (London: Chatto & Windus, 1908), 70.

2. J. B. Heath, *Some Account of the Worshipful Company of Grocers of the City of London*, 3rd ed. (London, 1869), 85n.

3. John Peacock, *The Stage Designs of Inigo Jones: The European Context* (Cambridge: Cambridge University Press, 1995), 7. In some ways Peacock echoes the much earlier work of Reginald Blomfield, *A History of Renaissance Architecture in England, 1500–1800,* 2 vols. (London: George Bell, 1897). Blomfield writes: "The years which Inigo Jones spent in Italy were not in vain. He returned to England filled with the very spirit of the great Italian artists of the Renaissance, and lifted the art of his country on to an altogether different plane" (1:103).

4. Stephen Harrison, *Arches of Triumph* (London, 1604), sig. C1. For a discussion of the engravings, see Arthur M. Hind, *Engraving in England in the Sixteenth & Seventeenth Centuries*, 2 vols. (Cambridge: Cambridge University Press, 1955), 2:17–29.

5. For an extended discussion of this pageant, see my *English Civic Pageantry 1558–1642* (London: Arnold; Columbia: University of South Carolina Press, 1971), 71–89.

6. *The Dramatic Works of Thomas Dekker*, ed. Fredson Bowers (Cambridge: Cambridge University Press, 1955), 2:302.

7. *Ben Jonson*, ed. C. H. Herford and Percy Simpson (Oxford: Clarendon Press, 1941), 7:90. All quotations from Jonson are from this edition.

8. Gilbert Dugdale, *The Time Triumphant* (London, 1604), sig. B2v. See the previous essay in this volume for a discussion of Dugdale's contribution.

9. See my, "Harrison, Jonson and Dekker: The Magnificient Entertainment for King James (1604)," *Journal of the Warburg and Courtauld Institutes* 31 (1968): 445–48.

10. John Shute, *The First and Chief Groundes of Architecture* (London, 1563), fol. 4v. All quotations from Shute are from this edition. Two years before the publication of this book Shute designed the devices for the Lord Mayor's Show of 1561, according to records in the Merchant Taylors's Books. Thus, he had a connection to civic pageantry, which may heighten the possibility that Harrison looked to his work for information.

11. Gerard Langbaine, *An Account of the English Dramatic Poets* (Oxford, 1691), 374.

12. G. E. Bentley, *The Jacobean and Caroline Stage*, 7 volumes (Oxford: Clarendon Press, 1941–68).

13. E. K. Chambers, *The Elizabethan Stage*, 4 vols. (Oxford: Clarendon Press, 1923), 1:152.

14. Enid Welsford, *The Court Masque: A Study in the Relationship between Poetry and the Revels* (Cambridge: Cambridge University Press, 1927), 81.

15. Cornelia Emilia Baehrens, *The Origin of the Masque* (Groningen: Dijkhuizen and Van Zanten, 1929), 49.

16. Allardyce Nicoll, *Stuart Masques and the Renaissance Stage* (rpt. New York: Benjamin Blom, 1963), 26.

17. Stephen Orgel, *The Jonsonian Masque* (Cambridge: Harvard University Press, 1965), 3.

18. Roy Strong, *Art and Power: Renaissance Festivals, 1450–1650* (Woodbridge: Boydell, 1984), 153.

19. Graham Parry, *The Golden Age Restor'd: The Culture of the Stuart Court, 1603–42* (Manchester: Manchester University Press, 1981), 1.

20. Martin Butler, "Private and Occasional Drama," in *The Cambridge Companion to English Renaissance Drama*, eds. A. R. Braunmuller and Michael Hattaway (Cambridge: Cambridge University Press, 1990), 127–59.

21. *A New History of Early English Drama*, eds. John Cox and David Scott Kastan (New York: Columbia University Press, 1997), 1.

22. Gordon Kipling, "Wonderfull Spectacles: Theater and Civic Culture," 153–71.

23. Glynne Wickham, *Early English Stages, 1300 to 1660* (New York: Columbia University Press, 1963), 2:200.

24. Of course pageants have not been ignored everywhere. For example, I call attention to the fine discussion in Daryl W. Palmer's *Hospitable Performances: Dramatic Genre and Cultural Practices in Early Modern England* (West Lafayette: Purdue University Press, 1992), chapter 4, 119–55.

25. David Lindley, ed., *Court Masques: Jacobean and Caroline Entertaiments, 1605–1640* (New York: Oxford University Press, 1995), x.

26. See my article "The Christmas Family: Artificers in English Civic Pageantry," *ELH* 35 (1968): 354–64.

INDEX

Henry VII, 15
Henry VII, 15, 39, 170
Henry VIII, 187
Henry, Prince, 89–92, 97, 150–51,
  155, 162
Henslowe, Philip, 3, 47, 115–16
Herbert, Mary, 58, 68–72, 200n36
Herbert, Philip, 48
Herbert, Sir Henry, 197
Herbert, William, 48, 60
Herford, C. H., 66, 127, 130, 138, 141,
  208n34, 208–09n2
Hermann, E., 144
Hertford, Earl of, 48
Hetzel, Virgil B., 198
Heywood, Thomas, 13–14, 43–55:
  Carey's patronage of, 52–55;
  citizens, noblemen patrons of, 51–
  52; guilds and, 50–51
Hieronimo (fictional character), 134
*History of England from the
  Accession of James I. . . , The*, 93
*History of Renaissance Architecture
  in England*, 210n3
*History of the Reign of King Henry
  the Seventh, The*, 74–86
Histriomastix, 59, 129, 139
Hoby, Sir Edward, 7, 13–14, 21–25, 35
Hogrefe, Pearl, 68
Holland, Earl of, 48
Holmes, David, 114
Holofernes (fictional character), 18
Holte, John, 41
Honourable Entertainments, 112–13
Horace, 128, 129
Hortus Euporiae, 160–61, 175
Hospitality (fictional character), 54
Howard, Charles, 61
Howard, Mary, 61
Howard-Hill, T. H., 115, 119
Hoy, Cyrus, 129, 209n2
Hunsdon, Baron of (Henry Carey), 52
Hymenaei, 66

Ibsen, 4
Iliad, 63
Intermezzo, Italian, 187, 188, 189
Iron Age, The, 51
Isaacs, J., 3
Italy, 62, 187, 188, 189

Jacobean and Caroline Stage, 187
Jacobean court, 7, 9, 46–47, 74, 75, 96,
  115, 190–91
James (king), 57, 59, 93, 166: address
  to Parliament, 76; and Anne, 81–
  87, 93; Bacon's commentary on,
  74–86; as editor, 78–79; evidence
  about, 7, 9, 14–15, 17, 28; patronage
  of, 45, 49, 145; royal entry of, 147–
  63, 186; Williams on, 93–94;
  Willson biography of, 89
James, Saint, 167
Janus, 6
Jew of Malta, 51
Joan of Arc, 202–03
John Drum's Entertainment, 129
Jones, Inigo: Anne and, 96; artistic
  rivalry and, 101; evidence about,
  18; masques, pageants and, 165,
  168, 174–76, 180, 182–84; notes
  on, 186–88, 190, 192, 210n3
Jonson, Ben: artistic rivalry and, 101,
  105–07, 109–10, 122; Folio (1616)
  of, 126, 127–31; King James I and,
  76, 149, 154, 161–63; metonymy
  and, 4, 6, 9–10, 16–17; notes on,
  186, 188, 206n7, 208n34; pageants,
  masques and, 167–68, 173–74, 177;
  patronage of, 48, 58, 60, 63, 65–67;
  war of the theaters and, 123, 125–
  30, 132–36, 139–42, 144–45
Justice, 161, 170, 173

Kastan, David Scott, 190
Kay, David, 142
King's Men, 43, 45, 46, 148, 162, 167,
  197n2
Kip, William, 168, 176, 184
Kipling, Gordon, 190
Kittredge, G. L., 22, 24–25
Knutson, Roslyn, 208n35
Kyd, Thomas, 62, 69, 200n21

Lady of May, The, 68
Lady's Trial, The, 61
Lamb, Mary Ellen, 200–01n36
Lancaster House, 39, 76
Langbaine, Gerard, 129, 131, 186–87
Law, Matthew, 28
Lawrence, W. J., 59–60
"Lectori Candido," 185
Lee, Maurice, 92
Leicester, Earl of, 48, 59
Leicester's Men, 44
Levy, F. J., 80